Housing Finance in Emerging Markets

Doris Köhn • J.D. von Pischke
Editors

Housing Finance in Emerging Markets

Connecting Low-Income Groups to Markets

Springer

Editors
Doris Köhn
Senior Vice President Africa
and Middle East
Palmengartenstr. 5
KfW Entwicklungsbank
60325 Frankfurt am Main
Germany
info@kfw-entwicklungsbank.de

Dr. J.D. von Pischke
2529 Trophy Lane
Reston, VA 20191-2126
USA
vonpischke@frontierfinance.com

ISBN 978-3-642-42263-8 ISBN 978-3-540-77857-8 (eBook)
DOI 10.1007/978-3-540-77857-8
Springer Heidelberg Dordrecht London New York

Cover design: WMXDesign GmbH, Heidelberg, Germany

Printed on acid-free paper

Springer is part of Springer Science+Business Media (www.springer.com)

Preface

Over the last two decades KfW Entwicklungsbank has established financial sector development as a pillar of its business in developing and emerging markets. It is widely recognized that a prospering economy that creates income and jobs for the poor requires a vibrant private sector and a dynamic, disciplined financial sector. KfW Entwicklungsbank support of the financial sector is illustrated by a portfolio of approximately EUR 4.5 billion managed by more than 50 dedicated professional staff. For a development bank that is using public funds, and to an increasing extent market funds for its business, periodic reality checks on our clients' needs are important to ensure that we address relevant development challenges in our effort to contribute to the Millennium Development Goals.

To enhance the content of our operations we seek open feed-back from and dialogue with our international development partners, which include policy makers and experts from the financial sector. Since nearly a decade, KfW is organizing, with the support of the German Government and other development financiers, an annual international financial sector symposium.

The Importance of Housing Finance for the Poor

The past decades have witnessed growing urbanization in middle and low income countries. In 2005 about 42% of the people in the 10 largest middle and low income countries lived in urban areas. Urbanization in low and middle income countries will continue to grow because of migration to cities. Better income opportunities are found in urban areas with continued overall population growth. Currently more than 5.6 billion people live in middle and low income countries, and that number will grow at more than 70 million per year.

The trend of urbanization and population growth is both a source of development opportunities and of challenges for the housing sector. While middle and low income countries witnessed an encouraging per capita GDP growth over the past decade through 2009, the depth of financial systems, especially in the mortgage finance area, trails far behind those in more advanced economies. In middle and low income countries mortgage loans amount to less than 15% of GDP, while those well exceed 35% in the US and the EU.

Worker remittances and the rising incomes of many households create an increasing demand for housing. However, access to funding remains a major constraint, especially for low income households.

Hernando de Soto has perhaps pointed to one of the biggest obstacles for housing finance, i. e. the absence of registered land titles and the difficulty of legal land and property acquisition in low income countries. This and unstable macroeconomic conditions driven by high inflation and frequent, erratic exchange rate movements preclude many households in low income countries from having access to funding for housing investments at reasonable cost from banks.

The development benefits of housing are enormous. The Monterrey Consensus emphasizes adequate housing and shelter as a prerequisite for "enabling people living in poverty to better adapt to and benefit from changing economic conditions and opportunities." Furthermore, housing investments may contribute significantly to reaching the Millennium Development Goals by improving the living conditions of the poor. Important additional benefits include raising the energy efficiency of households and providing basic needs in the context of post-conflict reconstruction.

For these compelling reasons, governments, development finance institutions (DFIs) including KfW, and the market have recognized the urgency of addressing these issues and enhancing access to housing finance for the poor. In recent years KfW has undertaken housing finance projects in Armenia, Russia, Serbia, South Africa, Ukraine, India, Pakistan, and Sri Lanka.

The Focus of This Book

The sub-prime mortgage crisis in the US that triggered the continuing global financial crisis mirrors the severe flaws of incentives, inadequate supervision and the abuse of instruments in advanced economies. The origins and consequences are by now well known and widely publicized. The impact of the current crisis on development finance was the topic of the KfW International Financial Sector Symposium held in December 2009, the results of which are published on http://www.kfw-entwicklungsbank.de/EN_Home/Sectors/Financial_system_development/Events/Symposium_2009/index.jsp. While the book discusses relevant experiences of the recent crises, prudence and the more conservative approaches taken in low and middle income countries have largely shielded these countries (except for some in Eastern Europe) from the adverse impact of the financial crisis.

We have also deliberately excluded public policy debate on land use and mortgage legislation. This area has been extensively discussed in a number of international fora organized by the World Bank and UN Habitat. This level of interest has produced numerous publications by well renowned scholars such as Hernando de Soto.

This book focuses on how to develop and integrate housing finance into a sustainable financial system in a developing country. It explores solutions that enable low-income families to obtain better access to housing finance.

Despite the severe damage that some structured finance products had on the public reputation of the market in the context of the crisis, KfW Entwicklungsbank experience in housing finance underscores that structured finance remains a valid instrument if appropriately used in collaboration with reputable partners. For us this essentially means transactions with four basic characteristics: a) maturities of funding and assets are adequately aligned, b) transactions and motives are easy to understand, c) the assignment of risks are sound and transparent and d) not least which are fair to the customer.

We believe that responsible finance policies on the part of lenders are essential for ensuring the transmission of benefits of financial services to customers, and thus they form an essential part of our due diligence process.

I would like to thank the authors, the German Ministry of Economic Cooperation and Development and the Swedish International Development Cooperation Agency for sponsoring the Financial Sector Symposium. I would also like to thank Roland Siller and Monika Beck for their consistent support within KfW, and not least Klaus Glaubitt. The team that organized the Symposium and made this publication possible included Mark Schwiete, Jana Hoessel, Silvia Popp, Barbara von Toll, Tina Knoch, Rainer Hartel and Giuseppe Violante.

November 2010

Doris Köhn
Senior Vice President,
KfW Entwicklungsbank

Table of Contents

Chapter 1

Introduction: The Challenges of Housing Finance

J. D. von Pischke

Former President, Frontier Finance International, Inc.

Housing finance involves challenging policy issues. Welfare, political and economic interests overlap and collide. The consequences of bad government policies and dysfunctional market behaviour can be immense, as demonstrated by the subprime mortgage debacle that originated in the United States and spread to other financial markets in 2008 and 2009. On a broader scale ineffective public housing, land and housing finance policies are demonstrated by the poor living conditions in massive slums in many developing countries.

This book focuses on the integration of housing finance in financial system development in ways that will create greater access to more and better housing. From this perspective housing policy can emerge as a positive sum game, making housing finance and housing finance policy both efficient and equitable.

This introduction provides summaries of the subsequent chapters. Five core chapters are contributed by David Porteous, Marja C. Hoek-Smit, Hans-Joachim Dübel, and Michael J. Lea. These provide the framework for measures to strengthen housing finance and its development and reform. Supplementary chapters offer case studies that have made a difference from financial and welfare perspectives, offering comparisons of different approaches to housing market development.

Housing finance issues appear to be among the most challenging topics in development finance. Large paradigm shifts would be required to improve housing and housing conditions in many countries. Given the basic parameters of land, land use, land rights, location and public sector incentives, and not least high population pressure associated with rapid urbanisation. An enormous amount of work remains to be done. However, progress is being made in a number of countries and more could follow from proposals explored in this collection.

David Porteous notes that the volume of housing finance has risen sharply in many developing countries as a result of the liberalisation and development of mortgage markets. Simultaneously, microfinance has pioneered approaches to clients who were previously regarded as "un-bankable." Money is fungible and hence each of these types of loans are, in practice, used for diverse purposes. While the loans may be similar, the institutional arrangements for generating them and assessing their soundness have been quite separate. Measuring access and hence

D. Köhn and J.D. von Pischke (eds.), *Housing Finance in Emerging Markets: Connecting Low-Income Groups to Markets*, DOI 10.1007/978-3-540-77857-8_1,

repayment capacity rather than loan use offers a new approach, an innovation in housing finance.

Porteous estimates that this refinement in the valuation processes currently used in housing finance could revolutionise middle-income housing finance. It could open the way for standard 20-year mortgages for a third or more of the households in middle-income countries. However, the conditions in poor countries are usually quite different and considerably more challenging.

This author provides empirical evidence from research in eight quite diverse countries. The research explored how poor households actually finance their housing, what entities currently provide housing finance, and how poor households could be connected with retail financial services. In other words, what are the limits in housing finance markets and how can they be overcome? In this task, the volume of lending is less important than how access expands: structural issues abound.

Marja C. Hoek-Smit explores the *roles of the private and public sectors in the expansion of housing finance markets*. Households below the 65th percentile of the income distribution in emerging and developing countries rarely have access to formal housing markets. A number of legal and structural issues hinder expansion and make these markets vulnerable. Important issues include the inappropriate involvement of state institutions, nontransparent subsidies and regulatory barriers.

Problems that make housing markets difficult include: a) the lack of formal property rights, b) poorly functioning land markets, c) weak regulatory regimes, d) low incomes and limited access to finance, e) lack of housing products, and f) difficulties in obtaining credit for home improvements. Private lenders may not wish to enter the market because of risks and the lack of tools to manage them. Erratic enforcement of property rights is also a barrier.

Public policy reform is tremendously important in these circumstances. However, housing policy reform is usually difficult to achieve because of the role of government-owned housing finance institutions. Subsidies and regulations should be designed to increase housing supply and demand, and to improve the efficiency, stability and equity of housing systems. Reforms could include the reduction of implicit subsidies and the use of regulation to promote competition. Other measures could include liquidity guarantees and tax incentives, and mitigating construction lending risk where contractors face long and large contingent liabilities. Credit information systems and other measures to reduce transaction costs are helpful. These reforms may also improve land market efficiency.

Hans-Joachim Dübel deals with regulation, specifically the *impact that financial regulation and state intervention has on access to housing*. His major focus is on low-income households. His thesis is that the structure of the financial sector in general, and commercial banking specifically, is not able to play an optimum role in making housing more accessible towards the bottom end of the market. In fact, when the focus is on housing costs and standards, the bottom end reaches well above the 50th percentile of the population of most countries. In some ex-colonial nations, or in some of those relying on expatriate advisors, mortgage market structures may retain the footprint of the former coloniser, barely modifying the business model and consequently serving only the elite.

As with financial markets generally, liberalisation of mortgage markets leads to increases in housing finance in the form of new instruments and new players. An integrated, seamless financial sector is required for optimum results. This would require more competition and less regulation in retail lending, mortgage market activities that convey more information to consumers, and a willingness to use microfinance techniques. Consumer credit risk assessment tools should increasingly be used as criteria for access to housing finance: the role of collateral should be minimised. Financial education for consumers should therefore also be strongly promoted. Mexico and Thailand are leaders in adopting such procedures.

Dr. Michael J. Lea presents the case for the *wholesale funding of retail housing finance*. The liberalisation and globalisation of financial markets makes wholesale or second-tier funds widely available through capital markets and through lender-to-investors sources. These new channels also help lenders manage the risks of housing lending. Funding sources include private equity, long-term private debt, deposits and government or government–directed credit. Expected returns, operating costs and the ability to manage risk determine the funding sources.

Creating a wholesale funding channel requires good quality assets, characteristics understandable to investors, standardised documents and procedures, high quality servicing and collection, and workable appraisal standards. Against these, the challenges are the lack of performance histories, presumed high default rates, weak or lacking valuation data, enforcement problems and the transaction costs of small retail loans.

These problems can to some extent be overcome by credit enhancement. Internal credit enhancement uses waterfall techniques such as excess spread, over-collateralisation, subordination, reserve funds and cash collateral accounts, and early amortisation if negative events occur. External credit enhancement consists of guarantees. Public sector guarantees include issuer, agency and development agency guarantees, and political risk insurance. Private sources include monoline financial guarantees and liquidity facilities offered by banks.

Housing and its finance changed relatively rapidly into market-oriented systems in formerly planned economies in Central and Eastern Europe (CEE). Friedemann Roy explores this experience and its applicability elsewhere in areas that are stable and growing. Parts of Sub-Saharan Africa (SSA) may fit this description with growth rates of 5 to 6 percent. Political conditions remain fragile, but lenders are becoming active. Some are entering nascent mortgage markets.

In the affected parts of Europe, an enabling environment became possible with the demise of planned economies. As markets emerged with decreasing inflation and lower interest rates, household incomes rose and primary mortgage markets grew. In some cases subsidies were offered. Funding instruments evolved, patterned on institutional forms in the wealthier, traditionally liberal parts of Europe.

Inadequate legal and regulatory frameworks make economic growth difficult for SSA. For example, property registries, credit bureaus and foreclosure rights are usually insufficient to provide confidence. Physical infrastructure is often costly to build and maintain. Term credit is hard to obtain. Existing housing finance institutions are generally quite limited relative to the size of populations or of the national economy. South Africa is a frequent exception; Ghana and Kenya appear promising.

Given present institutional arrangements in SSA, efforts that could help to develop housing finance generally include creative microfinance and housing microfinance, mobile banking, and remittance-based products. Improved risk management and better access to long-term funds may promote savings and liquidity. Flourishing primary mortgage markets require access to long-term funding, which is a priority. Mortgage lending is emerging in urban areas, incremental increases in loan terms are offered, and more sophisticated products are available, but long-term funding remains a challenge.

Wars in Bosnia and Kosovo in the former Yugoslavia displaced many people, destroyed livelihoods, and ruined infrastructure. Much of the housing stock was affected. The demand for post-war reconstruction and rehabilitation was large.

The role and impact of funds established by KfW and other European development agencies between 1998 and 2004 for *rebuilding and improving the housing stock* is documented by Nico van der Windt, Rolf Dauskardt, Martin Heimes and Jana Hoessel. These funds provided wholesale resources to partner lending institutions (PLIs) – commercial banks and microfinance institutions – in the countries affected. The use of funds and the terms and conditions applied were determined in ways that moved closer and closer to appropriate market conditions as reconstruction was phased out. The partner retail financial institutions assumed default risk and used their own lending criteria.

Analysis undertaken in 2006 in Kosovo and Bosnia reported continued progress: housing continued to improve and housing finance was well integrated into retail commercial finance. Borrowers tended to be better educated and with higher than average incomes. However, lower-income households were included. About 50 percent of borrowing households had monthly incomes of less than EUR 500 (USD 750). One-third of borrowers from MFIs (microfinance institutions) had household incomes of less than EUR 300 (USD 450). The corresponding fraction for bank clients was less than EUR 400 (USD 600) per month. Home improvements, mostly for bathrooms and kitchens, were the most common loan purpose. Using various criteria, research demonstrated that borrowers' conditions improved and that the funds' influence was broadly positive.

In 2005 various Balkan funds were consolidated into the European Fund for Southeast Europe (EFSE) with the objective of providing sustainable housing finance, agricultural credit, and micro and small enterprise finance. EFSE was tiered into three risk tranches, permitting a permanent funding flow on commercial terms.

Mark Schwiete, Stefan W. Hirche and Jana Hoessel summarise *KfW's efforts to advance financial sector development in the housing sector*, focused primarily on the poor. This activity is part of KfW's use of Financial Cooperation as an essential element in German Development Cooperation. Housing is an important element in promoting poverty alleviation, and KfW Entwicklungsbank has been active in housing finance for more than 15 years.

KfW Entwicklungsbank's housing finance initiatives are based on an holistic effort to develop partner countries' financial systems. These have been most active in Southern and Eastern Europe, in part as reconstruction after armed conflicts in the region. Residential mortgage bond securitisations have been issued in Russia and Ukraine; in the latter country energy efficient housing loan products are being promoted. Further afield, KfW has participated in housing finance in South Africa, where more than 150,000 home loans have been disbursed. Housing finance for disaster relief include activities in India, Pakistan and Sri Lanka.

KfW's strategic focus for the housing sector is based on selecting receptive financial institutions as business partners, assisting regulatory authorities to protect consumer interests, and engaging donors and investors who have long-term interests and promote good governance.

CHAPTER 2

Housing Finance and Financial Inclusion

David Porteous

Director, Bankable Frontier Associates

Abstract

This chapter locates international housing finance within the emerging focus on financial inclusion in developing countries.

It does this by collecting and analyzing indicators of the extent of access to housing finance in a sample of developing countries, with a special focus on low-income borrowers. A top down view of the reach of the traditional mortgage instrument is complemented by a bottom-up view of the use of financial instruments for housing purposes by low-income households.

Using measures of depth, affordability and completeness, the chapter shows that, while mortgage finance has been growing rapidly in many developing countries over the past decade, its reach is limited in developing countries: at most, a third of households in typical middle-income countries has access to mortgages. This proportion is much lower in low-income countries.

While housing microfinance is increasingly hailed as a vital solution for those whom mortgages cannot reach, its scale remains limited in most places, although it is growing along with microfinance in general. In practice, poor people mainly finance their housing using savings.

Despite increased availability of datasets which enable the measurement of access in developing countries, there is still a shortage of consistent, reliable indicators about housing finance markets and about the performance of housing finance portfolios over time.

Using the lens of access, the chapter demonstrates that it is possible to segment the population into different groups with different potential to be reached by different instruments. At very least, this analysis should clarify that the housing finance system alone cannot solve problems of lack of income or of affordability. However, in the future, the success of a housing finance system should be measured not only by the volumes of lending alone but also by the extent that access expands to appropriate forms of housing finance.

D. Köhn and J.D. von Pischke (eds.), *Housing Finance in Emerging Markets: Connecting Low-Income Groups to Markets*, DOI 10.1007/978-3-540-77857-8_2,

Introduction[1]

> *"In fact, because many of the countries where housing finance has developed in recent years are so populous ... a majority of people in developing countries, if not a majority of the countries, now have access to market-based mortgage credit."*
>
> Buckley and Kalarickal 2005:247

Providing housing finance on a large scale to borrowers in the USA who could not afford to repay was one of the main causes of the global financial crisis which started in 2007. In the widespread disruptions in financial markets which have followed, the contagion has not, however, spread so far as to dismiss the proposition that better access to formal financial services, including housing finance, is a positive force for economic development. In fact, it is noteworthy that the approach adopted by the G20 group at the heart of coordinating the international response to the crisis prominently includes a renewed commitment to financial inclusion: "We commit to improving access to financial services for the poor. We have agreed to support the safe and sound spread of new modes of financial service delivery capable of reaching the poor and, building on the example of micro finance, will scale up the successful models of small and medium-sized enterprise (SME) financing."[2]

The goal of greater financial inclusion has in fact grown in prominence in developed and developing countries over the past decade. Supporting international initiatives have also gathered momentum. In 2009, the Alliance for Financial Inclusion was started as a network promoting south-south learning exchange among financial policy makers on what those 'safe and sound new modes of delivery' might be. The concept of financial inclusion is defined differently in different places, and in most places remains somewhat vague: 'providing access to financial

---

1 My thanks to those who provided assistance, especially at country level: Jim Hokans (Ghana), Kecia Rust (South Africa), Alan Elizondo (Mexico), Mehmood Bughio (Pakistan), Mher Yedigaryan (Armenia), Noah Sawyer (Honduras), Ljubica Gelev (Serbia), and Dev Goel (India). KfW officers, especially Cerstin Sander, helpfully commented on earlier versions. Other helpful contacts include Bertrand Renaud, Bob Buckley, Daryl Collins, Asif Dowla, Tim Eliott, Friedemann Royand Stuart Rutherford. Those who provided valuable information on their portfolios and experience included Christy Stickney (Habitat for Humanity, LAC), BethRhyne and Nino Mesarina (ACCION International), Harish Khare (HDFC), Mariana Balestrini (BCEI), Smbat Nasibyan (Conversebank, Armenia), Frieder Wöhrmann (ProCredit Holding) and Mirjana Zakanji (ProCredit, Serbia). Anne-Marie Chidzero and Andrea van der Westhuizen of FinMark Trust helpfully provided FinScope data for Zambia.

2 Clause 41 in the communique issued after the Pittsburg Summit, September 2009, available via http://www.g20.org/Documents/pittsburgh_summit_leaders_statement_250909.pdf.

services tailored to the needs of the population' or similar. However, broader access to credit, including loans for housing, is an important component of greater financial inclusion.

While the volume of housing finance grew rapidly in many developing countries in the decade up to 2008 (and already, post-crisis, the growth has resumed in some), the majority of people in these countries do not yet have access to formal housing finance, whether through mortgages or housing microloans. Understanding the reach and application of these two different instruments is vital, if housing finance is to be regarded as a core enabler and component of the broader goal of financial inclusion, alongside other components which are in vogue post crisis, such as retail savings and SME finance.

Using the lens of financial access, this chapter bridges these two strong currents of international housing finance of the past decade: the growth of mortgage lending in many developing countries, and the expansion of microfinance, including for housing purposes. On the surface, these two instruments appear very different. The mortgage differs from the microloan in term, collateral and interest rate. Furthermore, the development of the mortgage market requires a relatively high degree of legal certainty and longer term funding capacity, while microfinance has often thrived in countries with low legal certainty and rudimentary financial markets.

But in practice, the distinctions between the two are increasingly blurred: traditional mortgage lenders have started in some places to 'downscale' into unsecured loan products, while microfinance institutions have become regulated and offer longer term, larger home improvement loans, and in some cases, even mortgages. Even the purpose of the two types of loans may not be that different in practice: even though secured by a house, mortgages are used for a variety of purposes, including providing working capital for small businesses. Similarly, while ostensibly for business funding, in some countries 20–30% of traditional microenterprise loans have been used for home improvement.[3]

The blurring of traditional instrument distinctions is recognized in recent research underpinning the emerging policy emphasis on broad financial inclusion. A multi-country study of the financial lives of poor people recounted in *Portfolios of the Poor*[4] (Collins et al. 2009) based on carefully assembled individual 'financial diaries' has shown that people in developing countries already typically use a range of different financial instruments and varied providers — sometimes formal, often informal — in order to help accumulate 'usefully large lump sums' in the words of Stuart Rutherford, one of the pioneers of the approach. Financial instruments — whether savings, credit or insurance — help the lives of poor people to the extent that they make it easy to overcome these cash flow problems. Seen

---

3 This range has been consistently found in various household level surveys; for example see Hokans (2008).

4 See Collins, D et al (2009) *Portfolios of the Poor: How the World's Poor Live on $2 a Day*, Princeton: Princeton University Press.

through this lens, buying a house, or even improving an existing house, requires a usefully large lump sum of money.

Having access to a financial product is not the same as using it: some people may choose for example not to borrow, though they are able to, and therefore self-exclude from certain credit markets. Distinguishing between different types of exclusion is important for targeting policy. This requires that access be defined and measured, using data sets which ask appropriate questions relevant to usage and non-usage. FinScope surveys, pioneered by FinMark Trust and now available for more than fifteen mainly African countries[5], have sought to do this. Using this data, it is possible to apply the access frontier approach[6] to housing finance markets.

By applying these tools and using this data, this chapter therefore seeks to locate housing finance in the mainstream of the financial inclusion agenda. To do so, the chapter frames key access-related questions from the perspective of each traditional instrument — mortgage and microloan. Taking a 'top down' view, the first section compiles and analyses some dimensions of the reach and completeness of mortgage market across a diverse sample of eight developing countries (see Box 1). As the volume of mortgage finance expands in these countries, the key questions are: *how does mortgage finance contribute to reducing the lump sums required to buy a house; and how broadly does access to mortgage finance extend among different segments within developing countries*? These questions are addressed in sections 2 and 3.

Then, a 'bottom up' view reveals that, whether or not they actually have formal title to the land, home owners generally invest to improve their houses over time, financed by formal and informal savings. For the purposes of understanding access to formal housing finance other than mortgage finance, the questions here are: *how do poor households finance their housing needs? Who do current providers serve?* These questions are answered in section 4, drawing on data from the financial diaries of the poor in three developing countries and on the client profiles and experiences of several leading housing microlenders in different countries.

These two perspectives – top down and bottom up – are then brought together to sketch a generic profile of the reach of formal housing finance in a developing country. Using this profile in a particular context, policy makers can aim to advance the access frontier for housing finance in a way that the overall goals of financial inclusion and financial sector development can be achieved.

---

5 For a list of country surveys completed, see www.finscope.co.za.

6 See Porteous, D J (2008) "Applying the Access Frontier", *Enterprise Development and Microfinance,* Volume 19, Number 2, June, pp. 137-153.

Box 1: Developing Country Sample Frame

Given the difficulties of assembling relevant data across developing countries and the resource limitations of this chapter, we collected data on a sufficiently large set of developing countries to achieve the following objectives: to cover

- middle- and low-income countries,
- varied geographic regions, and in the process
- most types of developing country housing finance systems as identified by Renaud (1999).

The objectives must be balanced against the constraint that in each case, a local contact was necessary in order to obtain and/or validate country-level data, which was obtained from or verified by local correspondents.

The result was a sample of eight countries: Armenia, Ghana, Honduras, India, Mexico, Pakistan, Serbia and South Africa.

Basic background indicators for each country are given in Table 1, together with a comparison to an average for OECD high income countries (far right column).

Table 1. Country background profile

Country		Armenia	Serbia	Mexico	India	Honduras	South Africa	Pakistan	Ghana	OECD High
Region		Central Asia	Eastern Europe	LAC	South Asia	LAC	SSA	South Asia	SSA	na
2008 GDP per capita–current US$	$	3,873	6,811	10,232	1,017	1,823	5,277	991	713	42,100
Population 2008	Mill.	3	7	106	1,139	7	49	176	23	872
Homeownership	%	93	89	78	87	80	72	78	57	43–80
% Urban	%	64	52	77	30	48	61	36	50	77
M2/GDP	%	19	34	26	73	50	64	83	46,5	98
World Bank country income classification		Lower middle	Upper middle	Upper middle	Lower middle; blend	Lower middle	Upper middle	Lower middle	Low	na

Sources: GDP, population, % urban, M2/GDP: World Development Indicators, mainly 2008, for M2/GDP (OECD): IMF: International Financial Statistics, mainly 2008

Country classification: World Bank, http://data.worldbank.org/about/country-classifications/country-and-lending-groups#Low_income. Groups are based on 2008 GNI per capita via the World Bank Atlas Method, a switch from the publication's earlier use of gross national product per capita.

Homeownership: various years from official sources, accessed via list compiled by Andrew Gall available via http://www.housingfinance.org/Content/ContentPage.php?interest=100370; except for South Africa: Porteous & Hazelhurst 2004

OECD High: high income countries which are members of OECD only

The Changing Frontier of Mortgage Markets

> *"Only a quarter to a third of households in most emerging markets can afford a mortgage to purchase the least expensive developer built unit."*
>
> Ferguson 2004

Bruce Ferguson expresses above a commonly held view in housing finance: that mortgages reach a minority of the population in developing countries. Is this statement still true, after the rapid growth in mortgage markets in many developing countries up until 2008 at least? How can the level of mortgage market development be compared across countries, and what can be learned, especially about access to housing finance? This section reports on empirical measures of the size, depth and completeness of mortgage markets across the chosen sample of eight developing countries. Then the following section expands the analysis of access in two developing countries – South Africa and Zambia.

Empirical Measures

There are three main categories of empirical measures of mortgage markets: depth and growth, affordability, and completeness. These are applied as consistently as data allows across the developing country sample to provide a comparative perspective.

Depth and Growth

The conventional measures of the depth of mortgage markets are:

- Value of residential mortgages outstanding per capita; and
- Value of residential mortgages outstanding to GDP.

In our sample, mortgage balances outstanding per capita vary considerably: from US$5 in Ghana in 2005 to US$1300 in South Africa.[7] Similarly, the household penetration varied from less than 0.03% in Ghana to 10.9% in South Africa. This contrasts with almost half (47.9%) of all US households in 2004, which had a mortgage secured by their primary residence. Among US homeowners only, the percentage rises to over two-thirds (69.3%).[8]

---

7 In most of the countries, neither the number of mortgages nor the number of households is known with any certainty.

8 Federal Reserve Bulletin 2006, p. A26.

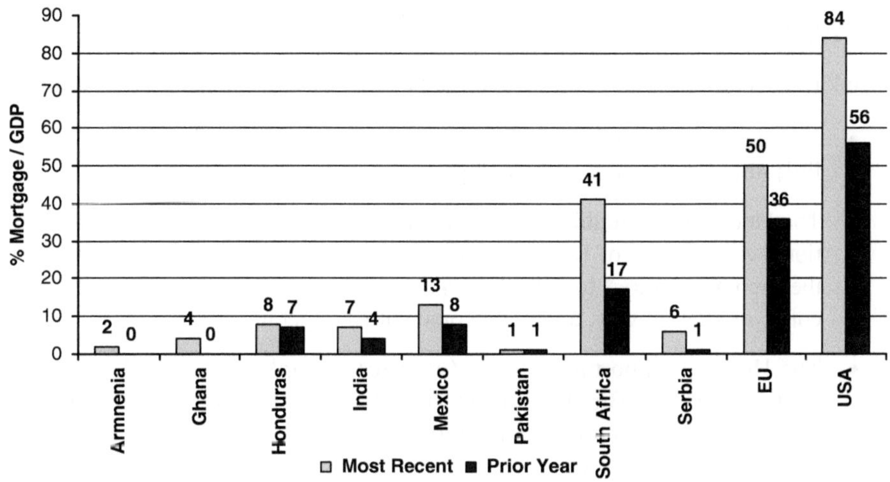

Fig. 1. Residential mortgages have increased relative to GDP

Note: Years used in each case: Armenia: 2007/2002, Ghana: 2006/2003, Honduras: 2006/2000, India: 2009/2002, Mexico: 2007/2000, Pakistan: 2007/2004, South Africa: 2009/2000, Serbia: 2008/2004, EU: 2008/2000; US: 2008/ 2000

Sources: developing country sample: see country references; EU; USA: EMF, M. Lea (2006)

Figure 1 shows the ratio of residential mortgages outstanding to GDP for the most recent available year (2006–2008 in most cases) and a previous year (mostly 2000–2002), which varies by country depending on data availability since these numbers are not systematically collected or reported. The numbers from the developing country sample are benchmarked against numbers for the US and EU. The sample spans a considerable range: from South Africa, where the ratio approaches the levels of some Eastern European countries, to Ghana and Armenia where mortgage markets surpassed the threshold of 1% of GDP only in recent years.

However, underlying some of the smallest numbers are rapid increases: in India, for example, the ratio has increased very fast, and new housing lending continues to increase rapidly in the aftermath of the financial crisis. Other middle income countries have been more affected: mortgages outstanding to GDP declined slightly in 2009 in South Africa; and in Mexico, where the total number of new residential mortgages granted in 2009 fell by some 10%; but by much more (60%) among the specialized construction lenders, Sofoles, which have been badly affected by constrained liquidity and rising defaults.

Mortgage Affordability

Struyk (2005) outlines three typical measures used to assess housing affordability:

- Average house price/average income – a commonly used ratio, but it says little about the means of financing;
- The Housing Affordability Index (HAI), as used in Australia and by the National Association of Realtors in the US, considers the relationship between the income required to afford a representative house and representative income, or alternatively, a target income with a target house price;
- The Housing Opportunity Index (used for example by the National Association of Home Builders in the US) measures the proportion of homes within a specific market that a typical household earning the median income could afford to buy.

Struyk demonstrates the sensitivity of results based on using only one indicator and cautions that too much focus on mortgage affordability may eclipse consideration of the other costs of home ownership.

To assess affordability from an access-based perspective, the lump-sum costs are calculated in each case for:

- closing the purchase of a mortgage-financed dwelling, including the deposit required by the mortgage lender as well as any additional taxes and fees paid on transfer; and
- paying the monthly mortgage instalment thereafter, which is a function of the percentage of the house price to be financed, the term and rate.

This study collected data available in the eight countries in 2006 on the value of (a) an average mortgage-financed house; (b) the smallest formally constructed house widely available; and (c) the smallest mortgage loan generally available (which may not be for home purchase).

For cross-country comparison of the resulting nominal values of lump sums in each case, the lump-sum numbers, expressed in current US dollars, are normalized by *monthly-equivalent* GDP per capita in US dollars.[9] This measure provides an indication of the relative lump-sum financing burden across countries: a higher number implies that relative to GDP per capita, the lump-sum cost threshold is higher (and therefore less affordable) for more people. The results are shown in Table 2.

Clearly, rows 1 and 2 of Table 2 are very sensitive to the average price of housing assumed in each category, as well as to the financing features – in particular, the maximum term of the loan and the maximum available loan-to-value (LTV) ratio.

---

9 Mean household income would be a preferable measure but is not available for all countries.

Table 2. Mortgage affordability measures

Mortgage installment on:		Armenia	Ghana	Honduras	India	Mexico	Pakistan	South Africa	Serbia
1. Average mortgaged house/ GDP pc (monthly)	%	371	1,079	217	778	58	1,608	420	220
2. Smallest formal new house/ GDP pc (monthly)	%	na	634	na	na	22	1,891	160	87
3. Smallest available mortgage/ GDP pc (monthly)	%	74	507	109	72	12	197	12	24
4. Upfront lump sum required (incl deposit)/GDP pc monthly)	%	1,912	1,184	na	1,636	27	2,335	237	815

Sources: Calculated using data obtained from country references

na: Not available

pc: per capita

Not surprisingly, relative affordability was highest in those markets – such as Mexico, Honduras, South Africa – which were relatively more developed; especially in those like Mexico where a large subsidised mortgage system for formal sector employees extends the reach of housing finance to lower-income groups. Serbia is an interesting exception, since mortgage finance is relatively new, but appears to be relatively affordable. By contrast, the less-developed mortgage systems in Ghana and Pakistan are accessible only to borrowers with incomes much higher than national averages.

Seen in this way, the eight countries provide an interesting cross-sectional view of different stages in mortgage market development. Figure 2 below traces this development from an early stage, where term and LTV (loan-to-value ratio) are low, represented best by Armenia where mortgage markets are very new; moving to a second stage in which loan terms are longer (between 10 and 20 years) and LTVs rise to 80%, such as in Pakistan; to a third position in which the loan term is stretched to the conventional maximum of 20 years (Serbia, Ghana, Honduras). From this third position, some markets have stretched the boundaries further: for example, in Mexico, low-income loans are available with terms of 25 years; and in South Africa, where terms are limited to 20 years, but where LTVs on certain properties could exceed 100% due to the ability of borrowers to capitalize closing costs.

The interest rate on a mortgage is also a key dimension of financing. The absolute level critically affects affordability, and whether rates are fixed or variable allocates the interest rate risk between lender and borrower in different ways.

The progression observed in Figure 2 is summarized in Table 3, which shows the four basic clusters of mortgage market features in stylized form as the basis for the lump sum calculation in Figure 3. Figure 3 calculates the lump sum required to buy a house costing US$42,600 (the simple average of mortgaged housing stock across these countries) with a mortgage loan based on the average features in the cluster indicated by the number in the figure. Lump-sum costs here include the one-off sum required at closing (deposit plus any costs and taxes) and the first month's installment, which is expressed relative to a monthly income level ($1983) at which the installment at stage 1 is considered affordable (assuming a maximum installment of 25% of income).

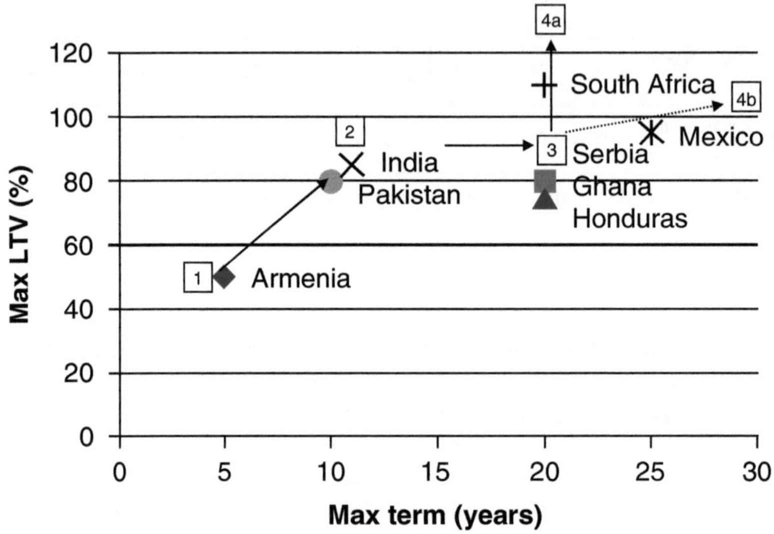

Fig. 2. The progression of key mortgage market features

Source: General loan characteristics: country respondents; terms refer in general to low-income mortgages which are differentiated from general mortgages.

Table 3. The progression of mortgage markets: assumptions

Stage →	0	1	2	3	4a	4b	4c
Description	No mortgage market	Undevel-oped	Lengthen term; raise LTV	Lengthen term	Maximise LTV	Maximise term	More com-petitive (4%–2.5% margin)
Other costs/house price	5%	5%	5%	5%	5%	5%	5%
Interest rate	na	14%	14%	14%	14%	14%	12.5%
Max LTV	na	50%	80%	80%	100%	95%	100%
Max term (mos)	na	60	120	240	240	300	240
Country example		Armenia	Pakistan	Ghana, Honduras	South Africa	Mexico	USA

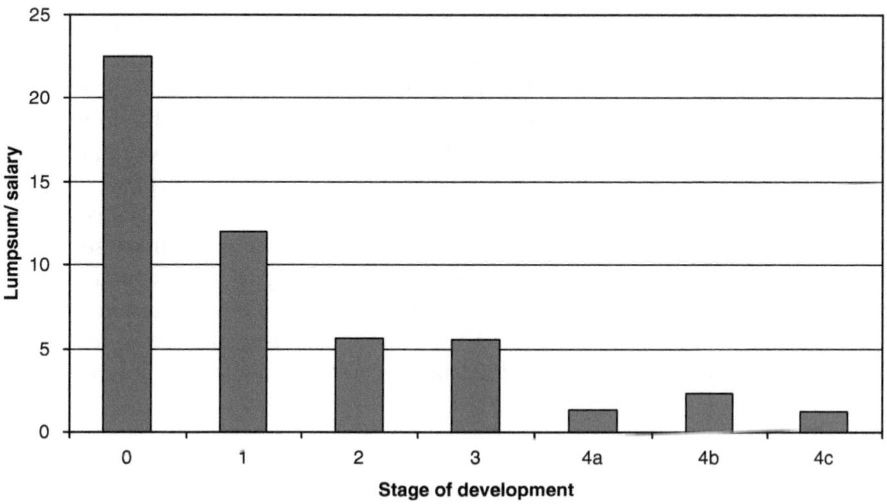

Fig. 3. Housing finance reduces initial lump sums for house purchase

Source: Lump sum/salary is the multiple of upfront costs (deposit plus assumed extra costs) plus the monthly installment due on a $42,600 house under the various product assumptions in Table 3 above, relative to the monthly salary level at which the instalment at stage 1 is affordable at a typical 25% instalment-to-income level.

Figure 3 clearly shows that the biggest gains from smoothing the lump-sum costs of acquiring a house occur in the early stages of market development. Moving from having no mortgage (stage 0) to stage 1 reduces the financing burden by 50%; the financing burden is halved again between stages 1 and 2. Beyond this, the progression reflects trade-offs: rising LTVs reduce the initial deposit required but increase the monthly installment. Beyond the point at which loans have LTVs of 95% or more, with terms of 20 years or more, further changes produce relatively little impact on affordability: 4a, 4b, and 4c are quite similar.[10] Even if competition squeezes lender margins from 4% to 2.5% (a level common for larger loans in middle income markets), that is, to position 4c, it has relatively little additional effect on lump-sum affordability.

Market Completeness

The preceding analysis shows that mortgage markets in developing countries have been converging toward a mortgage product with similar basic features but many variations. The availability of a range of product features is one indicator of the completeness of mortgage markets. In a landmark 2003 study of various European

[10] Note that the change across stages 4a, 4b or 4c is not expected to be linear, since these represent different vectors of movement from stage 3, based on a single loan characteristic that is different in each case.

mortgage markets,[11] Low, Dübel and Sebag-Montefiore developed the completeness approach to incorporate access dimensions that determine which groups can afford mortgages while also considering the distribution channels available. Their methodology is summarized in Box 2 and is available in detail in Annex 3 of their report at www.hypo.org. This methodology was substantially applied to the developing country sample with some minor changes described in Annex A of this chapter.

In each case, the completeness characteristics were assessed by a country expert, usually located in the respective country or, if not, at least with in-country support.[12] The underlying characteristics which generated the scoring for each country are reported in Table 1 of Annex A. Figure 4 below compares the overall scores for the developing country sample, using two EU countries as a benchmark with the caveat that their scores were calculated for 2003 and are therefore not strictly comparable.

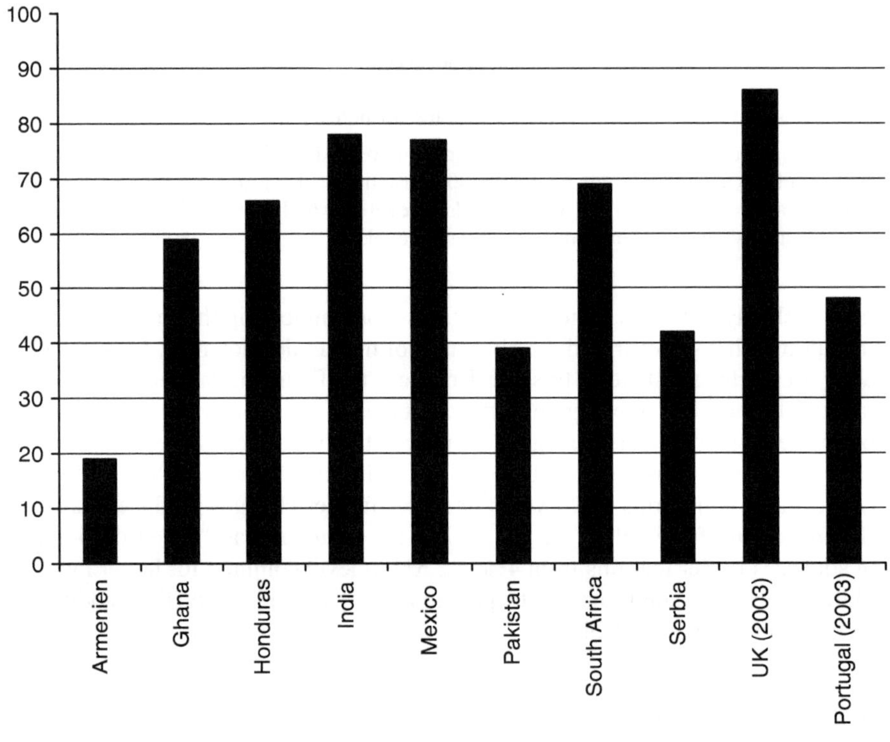

Fig. 4. MOW completeness measures across country (max=100)

Source: UK, Portugal: MOW (2003)

Others: calculated from data obtained from country sources for 2006.

[11] Conducted by Mercer Oliver Wyman (MOW), a consulting firm.

[12] This assessment was originally done in 2006 and individual country measures may have changed since then; but the direction of change is believed to be in line with the progression described in the text.

Box 2: MOW Measure of Mortgage Market Completeness

In 2003, authors Low, Dübel and Sebag-Montefiore, working for consulting firm Mercer Oliver Wyman (MOW), published a study of mortgage markets in EU countries. Their study was commissioned by the European Mortgage Federation to assess the potential benefits, costs and obstacles associated with integrating European mortgage markets. The project involved the collection of extensive comparative data on prices, costs, product range and profitability of mortgage markets across eight EU countries.

MOW developed a measure of mortgage market completeness. This measure involves scoring the product and channel attributes of a national mortgage market against a hypothetical full list of desired attributes in categories such as:

- Risk tolerance (weighted 35%) – which borrower groups can access a mortgage;
- Product range (weighted 50%) – what range of products is available;
- Distribution (weighted 10%) – how easy it is to access the mortgage product; and
- Availability (weighted 5%) – how easy it is to obtain information and advice on mortgage products.

The index has a maximum value of 100. European markets surveyed in 2003 had scores ranging from 86% (UK) to 47% (Portugal). Annex 3 of the MOW report provides an in-depth breakdown of the completeness methodology. The MOW report notes (p.23), "... the completeness index identifies the extent to which there are gaps in an individual market's product range, distribution or range of borrowers served relative to those available in other countries. We do not assess here whether there is a specific need for each product in the country or whether the need is provided outside the mortgage market."

Although the product list arguably reflects European experience, with scores obtained for example for mortgages on overseas holiday homes, the completeness measure nevertheless provides a starting point for consistent cross-country analysis. We have applied the same methodology, with minor exceptions, to calculate the equivalent scores for the developing country sample. Since the score represents the current (2006) position in these countries, it cannot be directly compared with 2003 European measures, which are likely to have increased in the intervening three years. Nonetheless, the EU measures provide rough developed market benchmarks, and the 2006 results are at least comparable across the sample of eight developing countries.

After the preceding analysis of sequential development, it is hardly surprising that Figure 4 shows a wide variation in completeness scores, from 20% in Armenia, where mortgage lending is relatively new, to over 80% in India, where a large number of lenders offer a wide range of products. What is more surprising is that even small mortgage markets score comparatively highly, as in Ghana which had few providers. While there may be some subjectivity in assessing the availability sub-score in each country, these overall scores suggest that mortgage markets in some of these countries are already relatively complete. However, while a useful indicator of relative market sophistication, completeness alone provides little guide to the depth or affordability of a system: other indicators such as the depth and affordability measures introduced earlier are necessary to provide a multi-dimensional perspective on the reach of a national mortgage finance system.

Going Deeper: Access Frontiers

The preceding section analyzed standard cross-country measures of mortgage depth, affordability and completeness. But these numbers alone give little sense of the extent to which mortgages are accessible across a population and in which segments. The access frontier approach, described in Box 3, seeks to separate out the underlying components of demand and supply in order to ask the questions: *what are the limits of access in the current market situation, and correspondingly, how might the frontier or current outer limit of access be expanded over time?*

This approach is applied here to explore the question: "how low can mortgage markets go?"

Box 3: The Access Frontier Approach

Two papers seek to provide a tool for the analysis of how markets provide access to goods and services over time. Beck and de la Torre (2006) provide rigorous microeconomic foundations to develop an "access possibilities frontier" for financial services. The frontier is shaped by the identification of different demand and supply constraints for a set of state variables. This enables differentiation among outcomes below a constrained optimum, and outcomes where the constrained optimum is too low, and where the outcome is too high. Using a similar approach without the microeconometric foundations, Porteous (2005, 2008) describes the access frontier as the maximum proportion of a population that can access a particular good or service using available products and technology. He uses a "market map" to indicate the trajectory of usage in a market over time, as well as to capture the different zones of provision. The key insight of the tool makes it possible to distinguish different possible categories of access to a good or service. Both papers use similar nomenclature to categorize a current and potential market into several zones:

- **Current market zone** – which includes current users;
- **A market enablement zone** – which includes those who do not currently use the product but are potentially eligible to obtain the product, and those who do not obviously self-select not to use it;
- **A market development zone** – which includes those who cannot access the product now because of structural features (such as location or characteristics);
- **A supra-market zone** – which comprises those who are denied access by virtue of their income alone, and may require non-market interventions such as subsidies in order to participate in the market.

To map a market into these zones, it is necessary to have supply-side information about product criteria (such as eligibility) and demand side information about users and potential users, including information about why they do not currently use a product. The FinScope™ surveys developed by FinMark Trust in South Africa are examples of surveys that provide demand side information for access frontier analysis. FinScope surveys use comprehensive face-to-face interviews on the financial service aspirations, usage and attitudes of a statistically representative sample of adults in a country. Note that, as a survey based on respondent knowledge, answers to questions like "Do you have a title deed?" could be inaccurate or unknown (an allowed category). To date, FinScope surveys have been completed in South Africa each year since 2003 and at least once in fourteen other countries including Zambia (2006) (see www.finscope.co.sa).

Meanwhile, the access frontier concept has been applied empirically to the market for bank accounts in South Africa (Porteous 2005), insurance in Ukraine and Georgia (Matul 2005) and mortgages in South Africa (Meltzer 2006).

Determinants of Access

Access to a mortgage is a function of:

- **borrower criteria** which define the risk of default and commonly include source and proof of income, age, level of income (to define affordability) and previous credit record; and
- **property criteria** which define the loss given default and commonly relate to the valuation of the property, which is in turn linked to its physical condition and how easily the value can be realized. The latter is a function of the tenure and court system, as well as the depth of the housing market.

To measure access requires the use of a nationally representative database in which various borrower characteristics can be cross tabulated with financial product usage and reasons for non-usage. FinScope databases provide this for certain countries.

Application of the property criteria ideally requires an inventory of housing stock with details of the tenure and condition, together with the ease and certainty of valuation. Such databases are typically not available on a national level, at least in the sample countries. Nonetheless, household surveys in which current occupants report on their housing situation may serve as a proxy. Access to a mortgage is limited to property owners, and among them, to those owners who have 'mortgage-able' tenure. Those with informal tenure do not have access to a mortgage, even if they claim to own the property; nor do renters, although they could become owners. Within the group with mortgage-able tenure, the property must meet further physical criteria to assure the lender that the structure will survive the term of the loan, and more importantly, at least preserve its value as collateral for the loan.

Using the tenure perspective as the first level of segmentation, the national market may be divided into four main categories:

1. Current mortgagors, who are assumed *de facto* to meet all criteria for borrower and property;
2. Owners with formal title to their property but no current mortgage;
3. Claimed owners without formal title; and
4. Renters.

Using FinScope data, Figure 5 shows the relative size of these categories for South Africa and Zambia as a percentage of all adults. The table that follows compares various characteristics of each category.

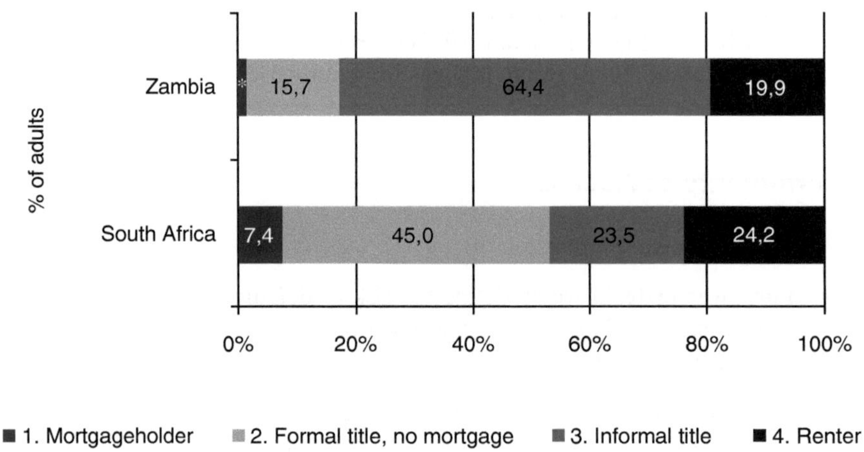

Fig. 5. Mortgage market access lens (% of adults)

Source and definitions: SA: FinScope 2004. Q refers to relevant question number in SA database; Current mortgage holder: Q49; Ownership status: Q48a,b,c

Zambia: FinScope Zambia 2006, data extracted by Christian Keulder of FinScope; *: Zambia: 1.4%

Not surprisingly, the percentage of people with mortgages and the percentage with formal property title are much higher in South Africa than in Zambia, reflecting higher average incomes and urbanization. More surprisingly, the level of renting is similar in both, although much of this is informal rental from small landlords.[13] Table 4 deconstructs the four groups further by other characteristics. ("Bond" is synonymous with "mortgage").

Table 4. Characteristics of tenure lens groups: South Africa and Zambia

% of total in each column group	1. Bond & formal title	2. No bond, formal title	3. No bond, informal	4. Renters
Of each column category:				
1. Location: % urban				
South Africa	98.5	57.1	53.4	87.3
Zambia	·····64.1·····		20.8	73.6
2a. Housing situation: living in a formal (South Africa)/brick (Zambia) house				
South Africa	99.8	74.7	62.5	89.2
Zambia	100	80.1	46.8	79.3
2b. % with water, sewage in house and cook with electricity (South Africa); use electric stove with oven (Zambia)				
South Africa	95.4	40.8	25.9	71.8
Zambia	·····46.5·····		4.8	28
% of total in each column group	**1. Bond & formal title**	**2. No bond, formal title**	**3. No bond, informal**	**4. Renters**
3. Attitudes				
3a. % who would invest in home improvement				
South Africa	25.1	25.4	19.5	24.6
Zambia	·····28·····		29	26
3b. % who see their home as tradable asset				
South Africa	78.2	34.4	13.1	0.0
Zambia	·····83.1·····		39	0.0

Source: as for Figure 5 calculated from FinScope SA (2004); FinScope Zambia (2006), in addition: 2a and 2b. House quality: Type of house Q46; services in house Q35: 3a. Home improvement: answer to question 14a, 1 21: "would consider investing in improving own house" 3b. Tradable asset: Answer to Q48d

[13] For a useful profile of small landlords and of informal (backyard) rental, see http://www.finmarktrust.org.za/documents/2006/JUNE/SSL_brochure.pdf.

Table 4 invites several observations:

- The desire to improve one's house (line 3a) is consistent across the groups in both countries at around 1-in-4 persons – i. e., it is not correlated with tenure – even extending to renters.
- Believing that one's house is a tradable asset is unsurprisingly correlated with tenure but particularly correlated with having a mortgage.
- While current bondholders (Group 1) are the smallest of the four groups in both countries, they are also not surprisingly the wealthiest and most urban.
- Group 2 – with formal tenure, but no bond – is the largest single group in South Africa, and is relatively large even in Zambia (15% of the population). Within this group, only 70–80% actually live in a formal house; fewer than half have a house with basic facilities such as indoor running water and sewage, which conventionally define the limits of mortgage-ability.
- Group 3 – owners without formal tenure – are more rural than other groups, as expected, and are the largest single group in Zambia today. Titling is therefore a bigger issue there.

Defining Access to Mortgages

Defining the limits of access to mortgages in these countries requires further analysis of the characteristics of borrowers in Group 2 since the mortgage access frontier lies inside this group. Those who own without formal tenure (Group 3) are clearly beyond the reach of the mortgage instrument, as are renters by definition (unless and until they purchase a house). In fact, renters in both countries are relatively better off on average than Group 3 members, as some may be able to obtain a mortgage when and if they choose to buy.

In fact, the minimum household income necessary to support the smallest available mortgage can be calculated as the income at which an instalment and other housing-related costs can be paid, leaving sufficient income to cover expenditure above a nationally defined expenditure line. The South African government and banks deemed the income threshold to be the local equivalent of around US$220 per month in 2006. This is the lower limit of the market targeted by banks to fulfil their social commitments to government in terms of the voluntary Financial Services Charter.[14] A similar exercise to define minimum thresholds has yet to be performed in Zambia. This income threshold alone reduces the eligible number in Group 2 in South Africa from 11.2 to 4.9 million adults. Of this number, 1.6 million are

[14] Under the Charter, South African banks entered a voluntary commitment in 2003 to issue about US$ 6 billion in relatively low-income mortgage loans over ten years, on a total current mortgage book of around $60 billion. For full Charter wording, see www.banking.org.za. The Charter essentially became defunct in 2009.

over 55 years old and would be unlikely to qualify for a mortgage because of their age. If one applies the minimum income and maximum age eligibility criteria together with the requirement that the house be formally built and have basic services such as water and sanitation, presently only 2.1 million people, or 17% of Group 2, have access to mortgage finance, but do not use it. This is equivalent to almost 8% of the adult South African population.

In access frontier language some 7% of adults in SA are current mortgageholders. A further 8% from Group 2 and potentially 11.5% from the renter group (that is, a total of 26.5% of adults) may be deemed to lie within the current access frontier. Others among the renter group are likely to have access: note, however, that because FinScope data are weighted primarily to the individual adult level, these are not household numbers. For mortgages in particular, household numbers are more relevant.

This is only a preliminary indication of how levels of access to the mortgage market may be assessed. Meltzer[15] has applied the access frontier approach in greater depth, using all available household survey data on households and housing types to analyse the "Charter target market" for mortgages in South Africa: households with monthly income above US$220 but below US$1100.[16] A third of all South African households, about four million, fall into this income range which lies between:

- Upper income households: some 20% of households which earn more than $1100 per month, for whom mortgage finance is generally accessible based on income and place and quality of residence; and
- Poor households: the balance of almost half of households earning less than $220 per month, who are considered by agreement between banks and government to be too poor to afford formal housing finance offered by formal institutions and to whom government subsidies are targeted.

Separating the various access criteria for this middle group, Meltzer portrays the various access zones in Figure 6.

Meltzer's analysis suggests that at most, 25% of the Charter target group (the first three bands from the left in Figure 6) can potentially obtain a mortgage, although only 5%, or one-fifth of those with access, currently have a mortgage. Eight percent, or close to a third of the group, are judged not to want a mortgage on the basis of factors such as age, leaving just 12%, or 480,000 households which comprise the prime target group. Of the rest of households in this range, just over half (54%) do not qualify for mortgages based on current lender criteria, although they may have access if these criteria change. Fully, a fifth of households are con-

---

15 See Melzer, I (2006) "The access frontier for housing finance in South Africa: how low can you go?", report prepared for Finmark Trust, available via http://www.finmarktrust.org.za/documents/2006/July/AccessFrontierTool.pdf.

16 Exchange rate: USD 1 = ZAR 6.8.

sidered too poor, in that even if their income falls within the range, household-level indicators of poverty (such as regularity of going without food) suggest that the additional burden of a mortgage would not be sustainable. Loosening financial eligibility criteria cannot solve what is fundamentally an affordability problem– indeed, this may exacerbate the problem as the sub-prime mortgage lending crisis in the USA has shown. This type of analysis makes it possible to draw this distinction more clearly.

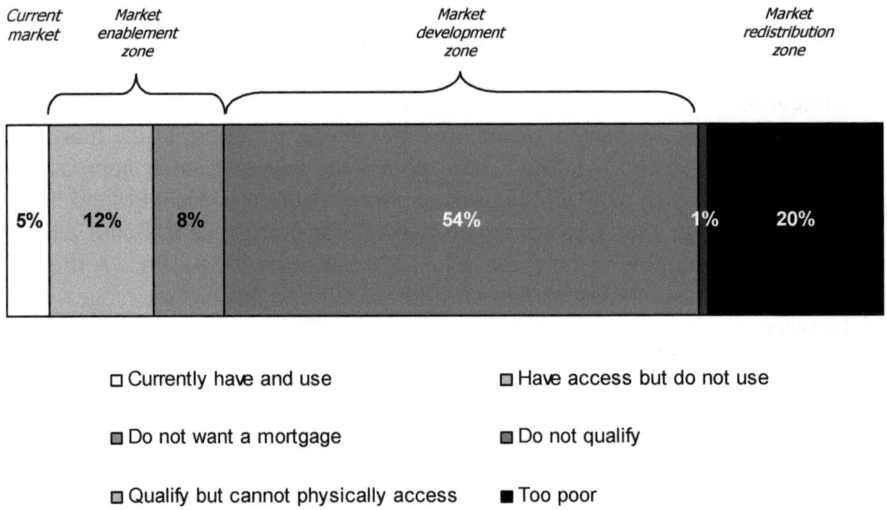

Fig. 6. Access frontier groups in the charter target market: South Africa 2005
Source: Meltzer (2006:3)

In Meltzer's assessment, there are around 1 million households (close to 10% of the national total) in the Charter target group within the current mortgage access frontier. Combined with the 20% of households which are upper income and currently have or have access to mortgages, just under a third of South African households have access to mortgages today.

Mexico, another middle income country with a relatively developed mortgage market, provides a counterpoint to the South African example: the national mortgage bank SHF has calculated that only those households then earning above $550 per month could afford a mortgage (Babatz 2005:16). This is 40% of the total number of households in Mexico. However, this proportion is based on borrower income alone and would also have to be assessed against property characteristics to be comparable to the number above for South Africa.

Therefore, Ferguson's norm that mortgages reach only a quarter to a third of households appears to hold even in these middle-income countries; certainly it is well below a majority of households. In low-income countries, the percentage is far lower. In Zambia, the maximum percentage with access to mortgages based on having formal tenure alone would be around 8%, possibly lower if borrower characteristics were also considered.[17]

The major instrument of housing finance therefore still has limited reach in developing countries. This empirical observation underlines the importance of careful analysis of the art of the possibility for mortgage finance. The access frontier can be pushed outwards over time through measures that improve tenure for those without formal tenure and improve risk assessment and management among the growing group in urban areas who may have formal tenure but no mortgage (Group 2). Even where mortgages are legally possible, they may have limited value as collateral where house prices are uncertain or cannot be realized. In such circumstances, mortgage lending assumes characteristics of unsecured lending or micro lending, where the lender has to manage its relationship with borrowers more intensively.

The Poor and Their Housing Finance: A Bottom-Up View

> *"As understanding of the need for ... housing microfinance grows, however, it is becoming clear that knowledge of its use at the household level is lacking. There are almost no studies of how poor households 'turn money into house.' This is problematic in two ways. On one hand, those who favor conventional mortgage models for the poor tend to assume that households are incapable of utilizing loan funds effectively, leading to a bias in favor of 'developer-driven' construction systems in which households are passive 'beneficiaries' of housing, even though they are expected to repay the loans that finance it. On the other hand, proponents of microcredit for incremental housing development often assume that poor households have the skills and opportunities to use such loans effectively – 'turning money into house.' In both cases, the focus is on finance rather than the end use of that finance."*
>
> Baumann in Kuyasa 2005:7

If mortgage finance at best reaches a third of the population in developing countries, how do most people finance their housing needs? This section compiles evidence from the demand and supply side of housing finance specifically for poor households in developing countries in order to help create a platform for topics that follow in this book. Microfinance is understood here as the full range of financial services offered to and used by low- and moderate-income households.

---

[17] Calculated as the 1% with mortgages plus the proportion of households with formal tenure who have mortgage-able houses as measured by basic services (i. e., 15% of 46%).

This client-based definition reflects the growing understanding, expressed for example in a CGAP publication *Access for All*[18] that, first, microfinance is about more than just microcredit: it includes inter alia microsavings and microinsurance. Second, microcredit is a broader category than loans to microentrepreneurs: while traditional microcredit has focused on this specific group, borrowers have often used their loans for purposes other than their businesses. Microfinance institutions provide an increasingly wide range of loan instruments, unsecured and secured, to serve their clients – including mortgages. Housing microfinance is therefore not only about unsecured home improvement loans, although this more restrictive definition is common and will be used here.

As microfinance blends into the mainstream of low-end retail financial services, it becomes harder to define. This integration is welcome, although it implies that microfinance has begun to lose its 'halo' effect as a special poverty alleviation tool. Some see microcredit as the developing world equivalent of 'sub-prime' lending in developed countries, since both focus on providing credit to those who previously were not considered creditworthy. However, an important difference is that most microfinance borrowers have been denied access to credit simply because the domestic financial sector was not able to cater cost effectively to their demand for small loans, not because of an impaired credit record. Exactly because microloans are unsecured, microlenders have in general had to pay much more attention to prudent lending and to recovery procedures than mortgage lenders who look mainly to the value of the collateral.

However, sub-prime lenders and investors in the USA and elsewhere are finding that the apparent security of mortgage collateral may be illusory if associated with lax lending standards and procedures and an economic downturn. Indeed, the average loan loss rate reported by the MIX Market (typically below 0.7% prior to 2009 when it rose to 1.1%) is still far closer to the standard loss rates experienced on prime mortgage loans in the USA (historically measured in single basis points for 1–4 family mortgage but rising to 0.4% in 2009 according to FDIC) than to the loss rate reported by US credit card lending banks (which was as high as 6% prior the financial crisis and has risen considerably since then).[19]

Which Housing Finance Instruments Do Poor People Use?

While *"housing microfinance is growing (among the urban poor) and looking very promising"*,[20] there is little firm published evidence of, in Baumann's words

[18] See Helms, B (2006) *Access for All: Building Inclusive Financial Systems*, Washington: World Bank.

[19] For MFIs: see MFI Trends Benchmark Series 2003-2005, available from http://www. themix.org/publication_detail.aspx?publicationID=214, US bank performance figures for 2005, available via html http://www.fdic.gov/bank/statistical/stats/2005dec/industry.html.

[20] See Fay, M & A Wellenstein (2005) "Keeping a Roof Over One's Head", Ch 3 in Fay, M (Ed) *The Urban Poor In Latin America,* World Bank.

above, *"how poor people turn money into house."* Fortunately, the Financial Diaries of the Poor methodology provides a finer grained understanding of poor households' use of financial instruments. The diaries methodology was developed by Stuart Rutherford in Bangladesh and has subsequently been refined. It is not based on one-off surveys, where respondents are likely to under-report certain categories (such as credit) and/or misunderstand survey questions, but rather on repeated interaction with the survey households over a prolonged period, usually a year. Diary-type exercises have been completed in Bangladesh, India and South Africa, as detailed in Box 4.

Box 4: Financial Diaries of the Poor

The financial lives of the poor are complex. Household membership and sharing arrangements are ever changing and often ambiguous, incomes originate from a variety of sources and livelihoods and cash flows are tiny and irregular. The first step to address the challenge of providing appropriate financial products to the poor is understanding the financial arrangements in which a household is already engaged.

The Financial Diaries studies aim to fill that gap by continuously tracking a small number of households across an extended time period. The first Financial Diaries study took place in Bangladesh in 1999. Forty-two households were interviewed across two research sites – one in the slums of Dhaka and the other in a rural village. Households were visited every fortnight for one year and asked about their financial transactions over this time.

The next study, in India, took the lessons learned from the Bangladesh Diaries and applied a more rigorous framework, particularly in the area of livelihoods. This study used 48 households across rural and urban sites and took place from September 2000 to September 2001.

Most recently, the South African Financial Diaries took a leap in rigour, using a specially built relational database to track daily cash flows across 152 households from November 2003 to December 2004. This study took place in three different areas: Langa, an urban township; Lugangeni, a rural village; and Diepsloot, a peri-urban township. This report draws largely on the larger and more quantitative dataset resulting from the South African Financial Diaries, using supplementary information from the Indian and Bangladesh Diaries.

In all three countries, the sample was drawn by means of a participatory wealth ranking. This methodology has been shown to be robust in identifying poor households in many countries. This method of sample selection provided for a broad selection of households across different housing, wealth levels and neighborhoods in an area.

The richness of the Financial Diaries allows us to delve deeply into the financial decision-making of the poor, to understand a bit more about what drives their economic behaviour. In all three countries, the quest to own a home or a piece of land was a key factor in their financial aspirations. The respondents we interviewed in the three countries spanned a number of different types of homes. In the rural areas, most respondents owned their homes (which varied in terms of strength and comfort of construction) and the parcel of land on which they stood. The luckiest would have a large piece of land to farm (in the case of India and Bangladesh) and a larger compound (in the case of South Africa). In the urban areas, a household might live in a mud hut, or a shack, or even (in some cases in South Africa) a permanent brick home. In the urban areas, there were also more households who rented a home. We learned, however, that respondents with shaky tenure in the urban areas could simultaneously be building a home in the rural areas.

Source: Daryl Collins, from a background paper "Housing and the finances of the poor" commissioned for this chapter using data from the three Financial Diaries projects available via http://www.finmarktrust.org.za/documents/2006/NOVEMBER/FDFN_housing.pdf

In their analysis of the financial diaries of poor households in the three countries, Collins et al. (2009) show that, of the large[21] lump sums raised by these households, 21% were used for land and buildings. Housing was in fact the second largest usage category: in India and Bangladesh investment in livestock came first, reflecting the mainly rural profile of the diary households there. In South Africa almost half of households had built their houses incrementally financed by savings. In rural areas, inheritance was a relatively common route to ownership. Very rarely did households in the diaries sample acquire a home using credit from formal sources such as a bank or retailer, or informal ones such a family or money lender.

The Financial Diaries survey in South Africa found that half of the very poor group spent 4–6% of their monthly income on housing. This percentage was similar for the relatively wealthier group surveyed. However, it is far below the overall average percentage of consumer expenditure on housing in India (11%) and South Africa (12%), which in turn is below developed country norms: these ranged from 18% as in the US and UK to 28% in Sweden and Denmark[22] in 2005. The lower proportion of housing expenditure in developing countries is both a cause and an effect of undeveloped housing finance: on the one hand, the figure is low because few households have to meet the expense of bond repayments; on the other hand, few people have bond repayments, in part because any additional housing investment above these low levels would displace necessities from the household budget.

21 Where large is defined relative to average monthly income in each country.

22 Euromonitor, World Consumer Lifestyles DataBook 2005, Table 3.122. for 2004: housing expenditure as % of total consumer expenditure.

The Financial Diaries also found evidence that a number of urban households make their main housing investment, or at least a significant investment, in rural areas. In Bangladesh, for example, 15% of households squatted or rented in the city but owned land in their home (rural) village. Twenty-four percent of Indian households in the urban Diaries sample raised lump sums for home construction, mainly in their home villages. The desire of urban workers to improve their rural houses is the basis of the business model of most of the lenders supported by the Rural Housing Loan Fund in South Africa.[23] Financial security was not the strongest motivation for this pattern of investment, but rather a sense of place and belonging close to relatives. As links to rural areas become more remote among later generations of urban migrants, it will be interesting to see how this investment pattern changes.

One would expect that households with secure tenure would be more willing to invest in their housing because they expect to capture the benefits. The Diaries found that poor people with formal tenure do indeed spend more of their income on housing. However, even shack dwellers with insecure tenure among Diaries respondents in South Africa spent a similar proportion of their income on housing as those in rural areas who may de facto have more security of tenure.

While there is clear evidence of considerable housing-related expenditure and activity among the poor, is this always, or even usually, a good thing for them? Fay and Wellenstein[24] have raised an important question about the underlying rationality of promoting home ownership among the urban poor given illiquid housing markets. Liquid assets are vital to the urban poor as a means of dealing with frequent income shocks; but because much urban housing of the poor is not readily saleable, housing may have poor investment characteristics relative to household priorities and objectives. In this sense, poor urban households may be over-investing in housing, whether or not they have tenure. Fay and Wellenstein did not have sufficient evidence to answer their question about over-investment; but clearly, housing resale markets in poor urban areas are highly desirable and necessary for improved economic welfare. Greater housing market liquidity would also reduce the risk to mortgage lenders since collateral becomes easier to value and realise.

A major research project entitled "The Workings of Township Property Markets" (TRPM 2004) assessed the state of resale markets in poorer urban areas in South Africa in some detail. The project identified four distinct types of urban property markets in township areas. Over the last 20 years in these locations low- and moderate-income black South Africans became empowered to hold title to houses in urban areas. The turnover of houses in these areas was considerably below the level in older areas with similar income profiles, although there were signs of an upward trend in more formal categories. This pattern suggested that it may be simply a matter of time for first-time homeowners to enter the resale market as sellers and for a

---

[23] For more information, see www.rhlf.co.za.

[24] See op. cit. Fay, M & A Wellenstein (2005).

market to emerge in the new housing developments in which first time buyers are concentrated. The recent residential property boom in South African suburban areas has also started to trickle into township areas, as buyers have sought to locate more affordable existing housing and as lenders have become more willing to finance houses in these areas as the value and potential liquidity has improved.

Interestingly, the TRPM household survey found evidence of an informal resale market more active than that in certain formally tenured places. Almost a quarter of households located in informal (shack) areas where no formal tenure was available reported 'purchasing' their dwelling during the preceding five year period – and they perceived that they had high levels of security of tenure, regardless of their legal status.

These informal transactions at the low end of the market confirm an observation underlying the 'dead capital' hypothesis of Hernando de Soto[25]. They also support the key conclusion of his thesis in *The Mystery of Capital* that, although informal markets are often vigorous and may replicate formal markets, their lack of formality bars homeowners from participating in wealth accumulation. The proposition that secure land titles are a necessary condition for sound mortgage finance is self-evident, but it is becoming clearer that titling alone is far from sufficient to create a working housing market.

In a large econometric study of homeowners in Peru who benefited from the large scale titling process that started in the 1990s, Field and Torero[26] find little evidence that commercial banks increased their lending to households who obtained their title through the titling program, controlling for other borrower characteristics.

However, there is evidence that households with tenure borrowed more in the form of mortgages from the state owned retail housing bank, Materials Bank. Field and Torero suggest that one reason why titling does not seem to improve access to private credit may in fact be a perverse incentive effect: newly entitled households showed less fear of losing their property in case of default because their title was conferred through a politically significant process. This attitude could cause private lenders to place less reliance on the title as realizable collateral. It is clear therefore that a title in itself has no magic effect on access to credit – rather, it is necessary insofar as it allows and encourages the development of an orderly resale market in which homeowners and their secured creditors have sufficient security to realize value when they need or choose to.

---

[25] See De Soto, H (2001) *The Mystery of Capital*, New York: Basic Books.

[26] See Field, E & M Torero (2006) "Do Property Titles increase credit access among the Urban Poor? Evidence from a Nationwide Titling Program", mimeo available from www.tinyurl.xx.

Who Connects Low-Income Households to Formal Housing Finance?

The Diaries surveys confirm that poor households seldom interact with formal sector financial institutions as compared to informal and semi-formal institutions. Still, the complexion of the market for financial services for the poor differed significantly in each of the three countries. While households across the board accumulated a majority of all lump sums through informal sources, a significant share (39%) of the lump sums of Bangladeshi households stemmed from microfinance institutions whereas, in South Africa, a far greater share of households relied upon formal sector institutions owing to the lack of a developed microfinance sector in this country. In India by contrast, just under three-quarters of lump sums came from informal sources.

The relatively limited presence of microfinance organizations in 'portfolios of the poor' has been corroborated by other data sources: Honohan[27] notes that even in countries like Bangladesh or Indonesia with highly active microfinance sectors, the penetration of microcredit is limited: clients as a percentage of population do not exceed 15%, and the ratio is usually much lower. As a percentage of total domestic credit, microloans are rarely above 3%.

Although the reach of formal microfinance may be low in absolute terms, it has grown fast in many places. This is in part due to widespread commercialization in which leading NGO microfinance institutions have become regulated entities, able to raise funding more easily and offer a wider range of products than just small working capital loans. Although microfinance institutions such as Grameen Bank have had housing loan programs since the 1980's, housing microfinance began to attract significant attention and to raise significant expectations only in the past decade. This section identifies the clients of housing microfinance providers, using borrower profiles. These profiles are available only at the level of individual institutions, and are not measured consistently. Hence, the full picture must be tentatively pieced together through the lens of representative institutions.

Housing microcredit is typically provided by three categories of lenders:

- **Traditional microfinance providers** (MFIs) that started making loans to microbusinesses and have more recently added housing microfinance. To this category belong Grameen Bank, which started lending for housing as early as 1984, ACCION affiliates such as MiBanco in Peru, and ProCredit subsidiaries such as ProCredit Serbia which started generally in the late 1990s.
- **Traditional mortgage banks or commercial banks** that serve the mainstream retail market but have downscaled by introducing low-end housing finance products. These institutions may or may not have any interest in or

[27] See Honahan, P (2004) *Financial Sector Policy and the Poor*, World Bank Working Paper No 42.

control over the use of loans by clients.[28] HDFC in India is an example of a successful mortgage lender which introduced a housing microfinance program in 1987, providing wholesale loans to NGOs to onlend to their members.

- **Specialist housing microfinance providers** (HMFIs) that focus solely or primarily on housing microloans. These may be divided into several subcategories:
  - *Commercial housing microlenders* such as the clients of the Rural Housing Loan Fund in South Africa. This group is usually treated as being separate from consumer lenders only when they have tapped a special source of funding, such as a state apex fund or institution that has encouraged or even subsidized a housing-focused approach and placed restrictions on its clients;
  - *NGO housing microlenders or housing providers* such as Habitat for Humanity, which have traditionally provided mortgages on houses built under its program, often at preferential terms. These may include no or low interest rates, although some recovery of the real cost of construction is often factored into the repayment terms;
  - *Building material suppliers* who sell on credit. While the highly structured savings to credit program Patrimonio Hoy of Cemex in Mexico was formerly seen as a leading model of this type of low-income lending for housing,[29] the company has recently decided to freeze its loan portfolio by establishing a moratorium on new loans.

Table 5 below summarizes the known profile of clients of a leading institution in each category.

Even though some of the lenders and programs named above are well-known and considered as leading examples, the second column of the table makes clear that even the cumulative number of microfinance clients served explicitly by housing microfinance to date remains relatively small. The actual number of microloans used for housing purposes is likely to be much higher, given findings cited earlier that 20% or more of general microloan portfolios are in fact used for home improvement purposes. Although relatively small, the housing microfinance portfolios of most (but not all) lenders above are growing – in some cases faster than the rest of their loan portfolios. In addition to unsecured home improvement loans, several of the lenders cited above offer low-end mortgages, although usually on

[28] For example, among large commercial microlenders, targeting moderate- to low-income salaried clients but with no restrictions on use of small, short term unsecured loans. Borrower surveys have consistently shown that around a third of the borrowers used loans for home improvements (ECI 2004).

[29] See Prahalad, C K (2004) *The Fortune at the Bottom of the Pyramid*, Philadelphia: Wharton Press and Segel, A & N Meghji (2005) "Patrimonio Hoy: A Groundbreaking corporate program to alleviate Mexico's housing crisis", mimeo Harvard Business School.

Table 5. Client profile of borrowers

Category	No. of HMF* clients & portfolio	Product(s)	Borrower income classification	Source
1. MFIs				
ACCION affiliates (Peru, Bolivia, Haiti, Dominican Republic, Ecuador, Paraguay, Mexico, Guatemala, Honduras, Nicaragua)	$230m outstanding; 108,000 borrowers in Dec. 2008	Unsecured micro-loans for home improvement; also mortgages in some cases	Mainly upper poor, near poor	www.Acción.org ACCION Insights 5,8,13
2. Traditional mortgage lenders				
HDFC (India)	$10m outstanding; 140,000 clients cumulatively	Microloans through NGOs for shelter and home improvement	Economically weaker sector; income <$80 per month	HDFC Innovation Case Study; Correspondence
3. Specialized housing lenders				
3a. Commercial HMFIs*: RHLF** clients (South Africa)	135,000 loans cumulatively (2006–2009) Net loan books around $19m (2009)	On-lending by RHLF clients for Unsecured micro loans; 1–4 years terms	Near poor; and non-poor. Just under half of borrowers' earn <$300 monthly; 80% <$800 per month	Pearson & Greef (2006) RHLF 2009 annual report
Category	**No. of HMF* clients & portfolio**	**Product(s)**	**Borrower income classification**	**Source**
3b. Housing NGOs_ Habitat for Humanity (LAC)	$70 million in 2006 portfolio; average 6800 new loans p. a.	7–15 year mortgages on houses built through assisted community building process	Minimum wages (MW) 2–5; poor to near poor	Interview with Christy Stickney, Director LAC
3c. Building materials suppliers: Patrimonio Hoy, Cemex (Mexico)[30]	145,000 cumulative customers through 2006	Savings to unsecured loans through supervised construction project cycle	MW 2–5 (household income $280–$900 per month); poor to near poor	Segel & Meghji (2005); Meeting with Israel Moreno, Director General

* HMF(I) = Housing Microfinance (Institution)

** RHLF = Rural Housing Loan Fund

[30] As of 2009, Patrimonio Hoy is no longer seeking to grow its credit portfolio in Mexico.

newly constructed houses. There is little evidence yet of flexible construction standards that, over time, would permit incremental improvements that could make a house mortgage-able if sold to a new buyer. Encouraging such standards could be an important part of building a link between housing microfinance and conventional mortgages.

Table 5 also shows that housing microfinance in most cases reaches only borrowers who may be described as the upper poor (income above 50% of national poverty lines) and near poor (household income up to 120% or 150% of the national poverty line). This group is already being targeted by consumer lenders in some developing countries.

Community-Based Approaches

An increasingly popular approach to reach lower levels of the income spectrum for housing finance is to promote community-based shelter funds and lending organizations. These are not shown above because the lending institutions are often semi-formal or even informal community-based organizations. Many are member-based with mutual forms of governance structures. UN Habitat's 2005 report on *Financing Urban Shelter* (Chapter 7) highlights the growth of community-based shelter funds as a significant trend in housing finance for the poor. This approach is relatively new and, as UN Habitat points out, there are few evaluations of its performance.

There are a number of working examples from the member organisations of the Shack Dwellers International Network (SDI) in various countries including India and SA among our sample. Most community funds follow group-based savings procedures to unlock loans for members. Loans are often group-based, as in traditional microfinance, and the proceeds may facilitate construction of infrastructure as well as individual houses. While both the community mobilization and the discipline of forced savings have many benefits, such as improved social capital in poor urban communities, some of these initiatives have not managed credit risk in a sustainable manner.

For example, Ballesteros and Vertido[31] report on the fifteen-year experience of the flagship Community Mortgage Program (DCMP) in the Philippines. Under this program, legally organized associations of up to 300 poor families obtain mortgage loans from the state-owned National Home Mortgage Finance Corporation to purchase land and develop infrastructure and housing on it. By 2003, the programme had reached only 138,871 households. More importantly, the repayment performance on the DCMP portfolio was poor, averaging under 80% – far below a sustainable level – although with considerable variation among group types. A key problem was 'recalcitrants' – households who benefit from the project but refuse to become members, with corresponding obligations, in the community association. The authors find that requiring members to save first in order to participate was correlated with better subsequent credit performance.

---

[31] See Ballasteros, M & D C Vertido (2004) "Can group credit work for housing loans? Some evidence from the CMP", PIDS Policy Notes No 2004-05.

Within the microfinance community, the performance and the role of community-managed loan funds (whether for housing or not) is a controversial issue. Murray and Rosenberg of CGAP (2006) reviewed the experience of dozens of community-managed loan funds supported by donors over the last 15 years. Asking which worked, they concluded that only two of the types considered appear viable. The first is savings-based groups not supported by external loan funding. The second is self-help groups that start with savings and then leverage bank funding (such as HDFC, CBO or NGO clients do). However, "where loans are financed by early injection of external funds from donors or governments, community-managed loan funds (CMLF) projects appear to fail so consistently that this model of microfinance support is never a prudent gamble" (p. 1).

Rapid scaling up of community shelter loan funds through external funding is not an easy answer to the challenge of extending the reach of housing finance.

Connecting the Pieces

Preceding sections have shown that national mortgage and microfinance markets can differ considerably in their reach and depth within ranges which vary for middle and low income countries. The top-down and bottom-up views may be combined to produce a generic income-based profile of the current range of housing finance instruments, shown in Figure 7.

The Figure portrays the finding that the conventional reach of mortgage finance in a typical middle-income country is found in the top 20–30% of households by income. Housing microfinance generally touches borrowers only in the next category down – the broad middle of the income distribution in which up to half of all households may be found. It is in this emergent group that unsecured consumer credit for employed workers and microfinance for self-employed people is growing fast. This access to consumer loans creates a credit record for the first time for some borrowers, enabling them to start to access larger, longer term credit; but for others, it also raises the risk of over-indebtedness which may crowd out the capacity to absorb finance for housing.

Housing microfinance in most places hardly touches the bottom 25–40% of the population,[32] who are very poor and often dispersed in rural areas which are costly to serve with credit or with physical infrastructure. While some specialized microfinance programs have managed to reach the very poor and destitute, they have usually done so as part of a structured, subsidized program such as BRAC's IGVGD Program[33].

32 As in so many aspects related to microfinance, Bangladesh may be an exception in that the reach of housing lending programs tied to other microfinance products appears to extend deeper.

33 Income Generation for Vulnerable Groups Development. For more information on the limited linkages between microfinance and transfers to the destitute and very poor, see Hashemi and Rosenberg (2006) CGAP Focus Note No. 34: "Graduating the Poorest into

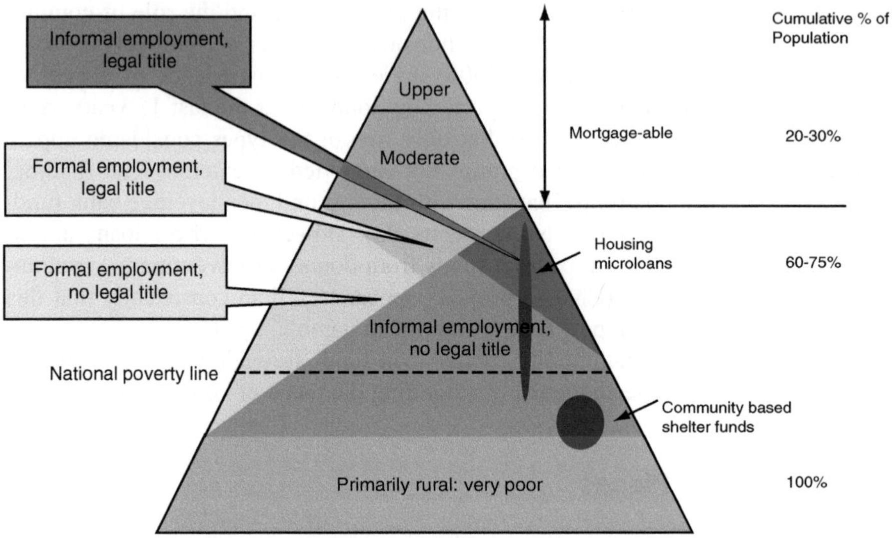

Fig. 7. Stylized profile of housing finance instrument usage in developing countries

Conclusion

A decade ago, the housing finance systems of many developing countries would, in Renaud's (1999) terms, have been considered missing, fragmented or unstable. Today, these systems have become much larger relative to GDP and more complete in the range of loan products offered. In middle-income countries it now seems likely that mortgage-to-GDP ratios above 15% will be common within a decade. In developed countries, the global financial crisis of 2007 has already fundamentally reshaped financial markets, including mortgage markets, but in most developing countries, it has at most slowed but not reversed the underlying growth trend. Even at slower rates, the continued expansion of housing finance systems in developing countries will carry vast implications for the financial systems as well as the real economies of these societies.

Notwithstanding the growth, this chapter has highlighted the limited reach of formal housing finance in developing countries today: typically, a third or less of households in middle income countries has effective access to mortgage finance. Formal housing microfinance has the potential to reach the next third or so of the income spectrum, but access is limited by its small scale in most places, even though it is now growing fast in some. Measures to move the mortgage access frontier beyond the top third and expand the scale of home improvement lending

Microfinance." The important question of how to best provide housing subsidies to low- and very low-income households is the subject of the chapter by Hoek-Smit.

within the middle group are necessary and important if access to housing finance is to improve significantly, even as volumes of home loans grow.

This chapter has sought to demonstrate the value of clearly segmenting the groups which have access to different financial instruments such as mortgages and microloans. This type of analysis permits a realistic assessment of the current and future limits of housing finance and may help to focus the targeting and composition of housing subsidies.

However, despite the new surveys and survey techniques described here which have become available in the past ten years for some countries, compiling information on the reach of financial instruments on a consistent basis across a broad sample of countries remains no easy task. Indeed, the effort required simply to assemble the cross-country data for this one-off analysis of eight countries supports one firm conclusion: systematic collection of key housing finance data would be highly useful for policy makers and researchers. While international housing practitioners have long recognized the usefulness of such information for in-country purposes, financial regulators now recognise this as well: "The trend towards globalization (in housing finance assets), particularly in the investor base, will require more international information exchange" (CGFS 2006:3).

Two distinct but related data sets would be especially useful in this regard:

- *Market level data,* containing overall measures pertaining to housing and housing finance markets, such as those used earlier in this chapter. Indeed, this chapter was intended to explore which data provide a useful and consistent picture. In EU markets, the European Mortgage Federation is increasingly playing this role by publishing cross-country data, but there is no equivalent for emerging markets.[34]

- *Lender or portfolio performance data:* there is currently no consistent means of collecting data on the size, nature and performance of housing loan books, although some industry associations collect and publish data provided by their members. Rating agencies are the conventional guardians of loan portfolio performance data and increasingly play this role in the larger emerging economies. Yet it may also be useful to create a central repository for the collection and aggregation of confidential reports from individual housing lenders which focus on the low end of the market at a country, regional and global level. In the microcredit sector, The Mix Market, publisher of the authoritative *MicroBanking Bulletin* (www.themix.org), has played this role but as yet has no special categorisation or reporting system for low-income housing loans since its focus is different.

[34] The scale of the task of collection and maintenance of large cross country data sets should not be underestimated. A previous effort to collect and update city-level data on housing markets, the Global Urban Observatory, was started by the World Bank in 1990s, and taken over by UN Habitat. However, much of the data is now old and the site was not even available on-line in mid-2006.

No information source yet provides consistent tracking of these types of indicators across developing countries. New efforts like Hofinet, a web resource site managed by the International Housing Finance Program at the Wharton School, represent a move in this direction.

Better comparable information can inform clearer policy, and perhaps even support improved risk judgments by private housing finance providers. However, better information alone will not curb housing finance bubbles. In some developing countries, the gathering flood of housing credit may yet become a torrent, eroding the very hillside of social and economic stability on which it stands. This risk would materialize if there was an inadequate supply-side response. More finance would then simply drive up existing property prices, enriching the upper and middle classes. The fallout from the US sub-prime lending crisis provides a salutary warning to financial regulators who stand back too long as credit bubbles form; and to housing lenders which ignore prudent lending standards. In one sense, the US sub-prime crisis marked the high water mark of an approach in which access to credit was long prioritized over prudential concerns. As the waters from that particular flood recede, the challenge for developing countries remains how to increase access substantially without compromising financial stability. Both are clearly necessary. However, success in international housing finance can no longer be measured by the volume of lending alone, as in the past: now increased access and loan quality must be taken into account too.

The international study of housing finance is a relatively new sub-field of international finance: like microfinance, it is perhaps ten to twenty years old at most. As microfinance has done, international housing finance needs to develop and espouse consistent standards of practice and to spread knowledge more widely. The recent move to place financial inclusion near the center of international policy approaches carries the risk that housing finance may be relegated to the status of a narrow technical niche, rather than seen as a key sector within the financial inclusion framework, alongside SME, micro-savings and others. In response, this chapter has sought to demonstrate how housing finance can and should be located in the heart of the emerging agenda.

References

ACCION (2002) "ACCION Poverty Assessment Framework", *Insight* No 1

ACCION (2003) "Poverty Outreach findings: MiBanco, Peru", *Insight* No 5

ACCION (2004) "Developing Housing microfinance products in Central America", *Insight* No 12

Baumann, T. and D. Mitlin (2003) "The South African Homeless People's Federation—investing in the poor" in *Small Enterprise Development Journal* Vol 14 No 1

Beck, T. and A. de la Torre (2006) "The Basic Analytics of Access to Financial Services", Working paper March 2006

Buckley, R. M. (2003) "Housing's Role in Wealth and the Economy", presentation delivered at the Fannie Mae International Housing Finance Symposium Sept 17, Session 1

Buckley, R. M. and J. Kalarickal (2005) "Housing Policy in Developing Countries: Conjectures and Refutations", World Bank Research Observer

Collins, D. (2006) "Housing and the finances of the poor", special paper prepared for this conference, available via www.financialdiaries.org

Collins, D. et al. (2009) Portfolios of the Poor: How the World's Poor Live on $2 a Day, Princeton: Princeton University Press

De Soto, H. (2001) The Mystery of Capital, New York: Basic Books

Fay, M. and A. Wellenstein (2005) "Keeping a Roof Over One's Head", Ch 3 in Fay, M. (Ed.) The Urban Poor In Latin America, World Bank

Fay, M. and C. R. Laderchi (2005) "Relying on Oneself: Assets of the Poor", Ch 6 in Fay, M. (Ed.) The Urban Poor In Latin America, World Bank

Field, E. and M. Torero (2006) "Do Property Titles increase credit access among the Urban Poor? Evidence from a Nationwide Titling Program", mimeo available from www.tinyurl.xx

Ferguson, B. (2004) "An update on Housing Microfinance and its importance to home lenders", Presentation at IUHF Conference, Brussels 23 June 2004

Ferguson, B. and P. Smets (2009) "Finance for Incremental Housing: Current status and prospects for expansion", Habitat International, doi:10.1016/j.habitatint.2009.11.008

Helms, B. (2006) Access for All: Building Inclusive Financial Systems, Washington: World Bank

Hokans, J. (2008) "Maximizing Choices: Models and Challenges in Housing Microfinance", USAID Micro Note

Kuyasa Fund (2005) "Delft Area Housing Needs Analysis", August 2005, research supported by FinMark Trust, available from www.finmarktrust.org.za/research

Lea, M. et al. (2005) "More than Shelter: Housing as an Instrument of Economic and Social Development", Housing Finance International May 2005

Lea, M. (2006) Presentation to 2006 Wharton International Housing Finance Course, Wharton, Philadelphia PA

Low, S., A. Dübel. and M. Sebag-Montefiore (2003) "Study on the Financial Integration of European Mortgage Markets", Study commissioned by the European Mortgage Federation to Mercer Oliver Wyman. London/Brussels, available via www.hypo.org

Matul, M., E. Durmanova. and V. Tounitsky (2006) "Market for Microinsurance in Ukraine: Low-Income Households Needs and Market Development Projections", Mimeo Submitted to Microinsurance Centre, commissioned by KfW & Microinsurance Centre

Melzer, I. (2006) "The access frontier for housing finance in South Africa: how low can you go?", report prepared for Finmark Trust, available via http://www.finmarktrust.org.za/documents/2006/July/AccessFrontierTool.pdf

Murray, J. and R. Rosenberg (2006) "Community managed loan funds: which ones work?", *CGAP Focus Note* No 36

OECD (2004) "Housing Markets, Wealth and the Business Cycle", Ch IV in *OECD Economic Outlook*

Pearson, R. and M. Greef (2006) "Causes of Default among Low-income Housing Loan Clients", Report commissioned by FinMark Trust, NHFC, RHLF and DBSA, available via www.finmarktrust.org.za

Porteous, D. J. (2005) "The Access Frontier as a Tool in Making Markets Work for the Poor", Paper commissioned by DFID

Porteous, D. J. (2008) "Applying the Access Frontier", *Enterprise Development and Microfinance,* Vol 19 No 2, June, pp. 137–153

Prahalad, C. K. (2004) *The Fortune at the Bottom of the Pyramid,* Philadelphia: Wharton Press

Renaud, B. (1999) "The Financing of Social Housing in Integrating Financial Markets: A View from Developing Countries", *Urban Studies,* Vol 36, No 4, April 1999, 755–773. *Special Issue: Social Housing Finance in the European Union*

RHLF, NHFC & MFRC (2005) "Housing Microlending: a financial performance analysis", unpublished report

Rutherford, S. (2000) *The Poor and their Money,* Delhi: OUP

Rutherford, S. (2002) *Money Talks: Conversations with Poor Households in Bangladesh about Managing Money,* IDPM Working Paper No 45

Rutherford, S. (undated) "Uses and users of MFI loans in Bangladesh", MicroSave Briefing Notes on Grameen II No 7, available via www.microsave.org

Segel, A. and N. Meghji (2005) "Patrimonio Hoy: A Groundbreaking corporate program to alleviate Mexico's housing crisis", mimeo Harvard Business School

Stickney, C. (2006) "Habitat for Humanity LAC", note prepared for CGAP Housing Microfinance group

Struyk, R. (2005) "Home Purchase Affordability and Mortgage Finance", Ch 5 in Hegedus, J. and R. Struyk (2005) *Housing Finance: New & Old Models in Central Europe, Russia and Kazakhstan,* available via www.mri.hu

UN Habitat (2005a) *Financing Urban Shelter: Global report on Human Settlements,* available via http://www.unchs.org/pmss/getPage.asp?page=bookView&book=1918

UN Habitat (2005b) "Homeownership through Mortgage Finance", available via www.unhabitat.org

General Data Sources

World Bank, *World Development Indicators*, accessed via website by country for various years

Country Sources

Armenia

Source: published material, with input and comments from Mher Yerdigaryan (Bank Akademie) and Smbat Nasibyan (Conversebank)

Rabenhorst, C. and R. Struyk et al. (2005) "*Development of a Sustainable Market for Housing Finance:Feasibility Study",* prepared for KfW, 2005

Ghana

Source: Jim Hokans (consultant) working with in-country consultant

Hokans, J. et al. (2004) "Strategic Assessment of the Affordable Housing Sector in Ghana", report from the in-country assessment team, CHF International, available via http://www.chfhq.org/content/general/detail/1428/

India

Source: Dev Goel, HDFC

Deutsche Bank Research (2006) "Building up India: outlook for India's real estate markets", available via www.dbresearch.com

IUHF (2006) Country fact sheet downloaded from http://www.housingfinance.org/Content/ContentIndex.php?Interest=Factsheet&plus=%%

NHB (2004) "Report on Trend and Condition of Housing in India", available via http://www.nhb.org.in/Publications/default.htm

Mexico

Source: Alan Elizondo, SHF

Babatz, G. (2005) "Housing Microfinance: Mexico's Experience and Attempt to Scale the Program", presentation at the African Microfinance conference, Cape Town 2005

Pakistan

Source: Mehmood Bughio, HBFC

Serbia

Source: published materials, with advice and input from Ljubica Gelev, NKOSK; and Mirjana Zakanji, ProCredit, Serbia

Elliot, T., A. Jovic. and J. Pupovac (2006) "A Rising Star: The National Mortgage Insurance Corporation of Serbia (NKOSK)", *Housing Finance Internationa*l

Roy, F. (2006) "Mortgage Lending and Risk management in Serbia", presentation delivered in Bucharest, 5 April

South Africa

Source: Kecia Rust, FinMark Trust

Zambia

Bank of Zambia, Website: www.boz.com

FinScope Zambia (2006) see www.finscope.co.za

Annex A

See Background description in Box 2

Table 6. Completeness diagnostic

		Criteria used	Weight	Changes from original MOW Comments
A.	**LTV, Borrower & Purpose**		35%	Kept the same
A1.	*Maximum LTV*		10%	
	<80%	0		
	80%–89%	1		
	90%-99%	2		
	>100%	3		
A2.	*Borrower/purpose*		25%	
	0 – no availability; 0.5 – limited availability; 1 – readily available			Same
		Young household <30		
		Older household >50		
		Low equity		
	Access criteria	Self certified income		
		Previously bankrupt		

		Criteria used	Weight	Changes from original MOW Comments
		Credit impaired		
		Self employed		
		Government sponsored		
		Second mortgage		
		Overseas holiday home		
		Rental		
		House equity release		
		Shared ownership		
B.	**Product**		50%	
	0- no availability; 0.5–limited availability; 1- readily available			
		Variable (any)		
		Variable (Referenced)		
	Rate structure:	Fixed for life of loan		Changed from 'discounted'
		Capped		
		0–5 years		
		5–10 years		
	Range of fixed term	10–20 years		
		20+ years		
		Amortizing		
		Interest only		
	Repayment structures:	Flexible		
		Fee free redemption (during fixed period)		
				Left out 'Yield maintenance fee on fixed' and reweighted category accordingly
C.	**Distribution channels**		10%	
	1- at least 5% of mortgages distributed through it			
		In branch		
		Tied advisor		
	Channels	Independent advisor		
		Direct		
		>80%	1	
	Concentration: % through primary channel	55%-80%	2	
		<55%	3	

		Criteria used	Weight	Changes from original MOW Comments
D.	**Information quality**		5%	
	Quantity and quality of information to the consumer			
	Score of 1–5, assigned based on answers to questions below:			
		Are there laws governing disclosure of information on mortgage contracts?		MOW score in this category was largely subjective;
		Are mortgage contracts and terms standardized?		I used these further questions to determine score
		Is borrower education available?		
		Is borrower education required for first time home buyers?		
	TOTAL		100%	

Comments:

1. The MOW framework is a useful one, but does require:
   a. A common explanation of certain terms used;
   b. Some standardization about the difference between 'readily available' and 'somewhat available' mean: certain scores were reduced following further questioning.
2. Missing product categories relevant to developing countries which were not included:
   a. Mortgages linked to foreign remittances;
   b. Mortgages offered in local and a foreign currency option.

Table 7. MOW features per country

A. LTV, Borrower & Purpose	Armenia	Ghana	Honduras	India	Mexico	Pakistan	South Africa	Serbia
Maximum LTV								
<80%	Yes							
80%-89%				Yes		Yes		Yes
90%-99%			Yes		Yes			
>100%		Yes					Yes	
Availability for:					General			
Young household <30	Limited	Limited	Readily	Readily	Readily	Limited	Readily	Limited
Older household >50	Limited	Limited	Limited	Readily	Readily	None	Readily	Limited
Low equity	None	Limited	None	Readily	Readily	Limited	Readily	None
Self certified income	Limited	Limited	Readily	Limited	Readily	Readily	Limited	Limited
Previously bankrupt	None	Limited	Limited	Limited	None	None	Limited	None
Credit impaired	None	None	Limited	Limited	Limited	None	Limited	None
Self employed	Limited	Limited	Readily	Limited	Readily	Readily	Limited	Limited
Government sponsored	None	Limited	Readily	Readily	Readily	Readily	Limited	Limited
Second mortgage	None	Limited	Limited	Readily	Readily	Limited	Readily	Limited
Overseas holiday home	None	Limited	Readily	None	Limited	Limited	None	None
Rental	Limited	Limited	Readily	None	Limited	None	Readily	Limited
House equity release	None	Limited	Limited	Limited	None	None	Readily	Limited
Shared ownership	None	Limited	None	Readily	Limited	Readily	None	None
B. Mortgage Product Features								
Variable (any)	Limited	Limited	Readily	Readily	Limited		Readily	Readily
Variable (Referenced)	None	Readily	Readily	Readily	Limited		Readily	None
Fixed	Limited	None	Limited	Readily	Readily		None	None
Variable but capped for life of loan	None	None	None	Readily	Readily	Readily	Readily	None
0–5 years	Limited	None	Readily	Readily	Readily		None	Readily
5–10 years	Limited	Readily	Readily	Readily	Readily	Readily	Limited	Readily
10–20 years	None	Readily	Readily	Readily	Readily		Readily	Readily
20+ years	None	None	Readily	None	Readily		Limited	Limited
Amortizing	Limited	Readily	Readily	Readily	Readily		Readily	Readily
Interest only	None	None	None	Readily	Limited		Limited	None
Flexible	None	Readily	Limited	Readily	Readily	Readily	Readily	Limited
Fee free redemption (during fixed period)	Limited	Limited	None	Readily	Readily	Readily	None	None

C. Distribution channels	Armenia	Ghana	Honduras	India	Mexico	Pakistan	South Africa	Serbia
Is as least 5% of new mortgages originated through the channel below:								
In branch	Yes	Yes	Yes	Yes	Yes	Yes	Yes	Yes
Tied advisor		Yes	Yes	Yes	Yes		Yes	
Independent advisor		Yes		Yes	Yes		Yes	
Direct	Yes	Yes	Yes	Yes				Yes
What is the % of new mortgages originated by the primary channel:								
>80%	Yes	Yes	Yes		Yes	Yes		Yes
55%-80%				Yes			Yes	
<55%								

D. Information quality	Armenia	Ghana	Honduras	India	Mexico	Pakistan	South Africa	Serbia
Are there laws governing disclosure of information on mortgage contracts?	No	Yes	Yes	Yes	Yes	Yes	Yes	No
Are mortgage contracts and terms standardised?	No	No	Yes	No	Yes LI	Yes	Yes	Mostly
Is borrower education available?	No	Yes	Somewhat	Yes	No	Yes	Yes	Yes
Is borrower education required for first time home buyers?	No	No	No	No	Yes	Yes	No	No

Source: Country correspondents, see References for sources

CHAPTER 3

Government Policies and Their Implications for Housing Finance*

Marja C. Hoek-Smit

Wharton School, University of Pennsylvania

Introduction

This chapter develops a framework to clarify the roles of the private and public sectors in expanding formal housing finance markets. It examines the reasons for government intervention in housing markets and the types of regulatory and subsidy interventions that may improve market outcomes for different market segments.

This is in fact a propitious time to focus on the role of government in the housing finance sector in developing and transition countries. The recent crisis in housing finance, while affecting advanced economies most severely, holds important lessons for government policy for all countries. In the decade before the crisis, a growing number of developing countries experienced sustained macroeconomic stability, sound economic growth, and lower interest rates which offered opportunities for governments to begin to address legal and structural issues that hindered the expansion of the sector and that have proven to make it less vulnerable to upheavals in international credit markets.[1]

Improved macroeconomic conditions increased private sector interest in expanding the scale and extent of mortgage and consumer lending for housing and in accessing domestic and foreign capital market funds for the housing sector in countries such as Mexico, Colombia, Chile, Malaysia and Korea. The global liquidity crisis that morphed into a global economic crisis brought a temporary halt to the expansion of private mortgage lending and many countries reverted to government sponsored mortgage systems. However, progress made by many govern-

* This article was initially written in late 2006 and revised in May 2010 to reflect relevant, recent developments, including the impact of the financial crisis.

[1] A 2006 IMF study showed the importance of structural reforms for the financial sector as a whole in terms of benefits for growth and stability, drawing on a large sample of countries (Kose et al 2006).

D. Köhn and J.D. von Pischke (eds.), *Housing Finance in Emerging Markets: Connecting Low-Income Groups to Markets*, DOI 10.1007/978-3-540-77857-8_3,

ments in strengthening the legal infrastructure for housing finance has continued. Improvements include better land titling and property registration systems, transferability of titles, and stronger enforceability of contracts, including foreclosure procedures and reforms in judicial systems biased in favor of the underdog.[2]

But there is still a long way to go; mortgage loans and other types of housing finance products remain accessible only to a small portion of the population in most developing and transition economies. Often not more than 10 or 20 percent of housing transactions involve credit. High real interest rates or the lingering volatility of inflation continue to limit long-term lending in several countries (e. g. in Latin America and Africa), while in others current low rates add pressure on house prices (e. g. in China, Singapore and Korea) thus limiting affordability. Private lenders are reluctant to expand into underserved markets that are considered more risky, because mechanisms to deal with those risks are inadequate. Households below the 70th or 60th percentile of the income distribution or those employed in the informal sector rarely have access to mortgage finance.

Also, major structural problems remain or have worsened in many countries due to the crisis. The large role of government-owned housing finance institutions, central banks and finance ministries that often led to unanticipated liabilities to the state while hindering private entry into the sector has further increased in countries where such systems are prominent (e. g. Mexico, Brazil, US). Trends to commercialize or privatize the many state-supported or state-owned housing finance systems and to curb deep institutional and non-transparent subsidies have been temporarily halted. Structural reforms are difficult in the best of times.[3] The current crisis has reinforced the perception by governments and housing ministries in particular that the state is more efficient in allocating scarce housing credit to large segments of society than the private sector. Indeed, the risk that governments will change the rules and regulations governing private lenders' compliance is another reason why banks are reluctant to enter.

Many governments in developing and transition economies therefore face a fourfold challenge in improving the housing finance system. They have to facilitate:

- improvements in institutions and regulatory environments to allow down-market expansion of real estate markets,

[2] Comparative data for European countries compiled by MacLennan et al (1999) indicate that asymmetries in market structure, institutions and tax policies affect the degree of competition in the housing finance system. These imperfections and their related extension of housing finance are more important than relative income levels and have far-reaching macroeconomic policy implications. Other studies show that micro-level housing finance policies have a greater impact on (formal) home ownership rates than the income level of countries in their sample (Chiuri and Japelli 2003).

[3] Subsidized housing finance institutions fear loss of their privileges and can be powerful opponents to change. This phenomenon has been observed by Rajan and Zingales 2003 for the financial sector in general.

- reforms of subsidized state housing finance institutions as a prerequisite for creating a more competitive and efficient housing finance system,
- the provision of institutional incentives (mostly regulatory but also through subsidies) to strengthen the private housing finance sector and stimulate efficient lending without exposing the state to excessive risk or moral hazard, and
- the reform of household subsidies to improve their targeting to specific household groups and well-defined housing problems.

These transformations require that the consumer subsidies – often implicit and poorly targeted – that now flow through state-owned lending or land institutions should be rationalized. The complexity of this process makes it necessary to have high-level political and administrative commitment for a multi-year and multifaceted reform program.

We focus here on the general reasons for widespread government interference in the housing finance sector, followed by an exposition of current thinking about the best ways for government to engage in the private housing finance sector.

Why Do Governments Intervene in Housing Finance?

Social and Political Reasons for Intervention

Nearly all governments intervene in housing finance markets, primarily for social and political reasons. Housing finance is a critical component of a housing system. Housing is one of the largest investments in an economy, one of the biggest parts of household budgets, and a key barometer of social well-being. When societies urbanize and real incomes increase, housing expectations and standards also increase. But standard housing is expensive relative to household incomes or investor resources, and the degree of access to long term financing to pay for a house over time is especially important unless the state takes on that responsibility. Lack of an efficient system of housing finance that includes existing houses impedes low- and moderate-income housing markets in particular. Without access to debt finance, whether long- or medium-term, households have to build their homes over long periods or settle for a lower quality structure, often extra-legal.

In addition, the absence of ready buyers means that households will not be able to sell their homes at prices that permit them to recover their investment. This impediment to sell hinders mobility and has a negative effect on the quality of urban neighborhoods and hence the fiscal situation of cities, which limits service provision in low-income areas. This creates a vicious cycle in many countries. It perpetuates informal settlements and overcrowding. There is therefore a private and political urgency to provide access to at least medium-term, fairly priced debt finance. For these reasons, housing finance is often more prone to government intervention than are other types of finance.

However, the political urgency to intervene in housing finance systems may also make lenders reluctant to expand mortgage lending. For example, if foreclosure in the event of loan defaults is not accepted and governments fail to protect creditor rights, banks cannot accurately price credit risk. They would also be exposed to reputational risk when they try to sell a foreclosed property. Or, when the government puts caps on interest rates for mortgage lending for similar reasons (as in Colombia), the effect may be a shrinking rather than an expanding mortgage market. Lenders will simply not enter "politically" risky markets.

Economic and Market-Based Reasons for Intervention

Intervention is also frequently inspired by efforts to rectify the imperfections and incompleteness of housing finance markets, both in mortgage lending and microfinance lending. Debt finance for housing, especially mortgage finance, emphasizes relatively large loans and long repayment periods because:

- housing usually retains value longer than industrial equipment or automobiles, for example,
- it can be collateralized more easily because it is an immobile asset, and
- spreading payment over a longer term permits the acquisition of more housing.

This makes lending for housing more complex and risky than lending for many other goods. It has caused governments to regulate mortgage lending and to put in place the basic institutions for mortgage lending. It has also caused governments to assume or share some of the risks that buyers of housing finance services or lenders may not be well positioned to deal with. For example, macroeconomic conditions may cause interest rate shocks and make borrowers' monthly payments unaffordable because incomes do not adjust at the same pace. In this situation, governments often assume some of the residual credit risk faced by borrowers and lenders, as in Brazil and Mexico. In fact, government involvement in the mortgage sector tends to be particularly strong during periods when macroeconomic or financial sector conditions inhibit the expansion of private mortgage credit as the recent crisis shows.[4]

The social and political importance of housing and the reluctance of lenders to provide loans when risks are perceived to be too high has led governments in many countries to take over mortgage funding or the lending function altogether. Examples include special labor tax funds or other closed housing funds created in many Latin American and some African countries and the government housing banks in Asia and Africa.

---

4 The public cost of such interventions is often correlated with macroeconomic instability and may expand its amplitude.

The situation is similar in housing microfinance. Consumer loans used for home improvement or incremental home construction are often larger and of a longer duration than other consumer or microfinance loan products. Unlike microfinance loans for entrepreneurial activities, housing microfinance loans are not "secured" by future income from the investment. The combination of the higher risk of this type of lending and the effort to expand it to a large scale in countries where the majority of households do not qualify for mortgage loans creates pressure for government intervention. The establishment of special government or charitable lending institutions funded from non-market sources was and still is often chosen as the fastest way to provide microfinance at scale. These institutions or programs are not sustainable in most cases and fold when program funds dry up.

In the past, the impact on the private market of such politically and socially driven interventions was seldom questioned: long-term mortgage lending was not attractive for the private sector and was at best provided to upper-middle and high-income clients. Nor were these interventions questioned on the basis of their distributional effects, since they were often not perceived as subsidies. Currently, there is a much deeper appreciation of the dangers of addressing social goals through subsidies embedded in the financial system. These subsidies are often "through the back door," while the stated goal of the government is to improve market efficiency.

The appropriate role of government interventions is now widely accepted to be the improvement of the functioning of the housing and housing finance markets and to directly address the housing problems of households that are not yet served by private markets, rather than to provide finance through government entities,[5] even though the current crisis necessitates a temporarily increased government role in some countries.

However, for government interventions to improve the efficiency and stability of housing finance markets, the reasons for market inefficiencies must be understood in considerable detail.[6] Designing new incentives and institutions with the objective of improving market functioning is complex: it is just as easy for such interventions to create negative effects on markets, particularly if subsidies are used.[7]

---

[5] See Mayo, S.K. (1993) *"Housing, Enabling Markets to Work – with Technical Supplements",* A World Bank Policy Paper, The World Bank: Washington DC , Angel, S. (2000) *"Housing Policy Matters, A Global Analysis"*, Oxford University Press: New York and Renaud, B. (1999) "The Financing of Social Housing in Integrating Financial Markets: A View from Developing Countries", *Urban Studies.* 36(4): 755-773.

[6] Mayo, S.K. (1999) *"Subsidies in Housing*", Paper prepared for the Sustainable Development Department Technical Paper Series", Inter-American Development Bank: Washington DC.

[7] Some authors maintain that subsidies cannot improve market efficiency because of their unavoidable deadweight losses. Deadweight loss is the inefficiency that a subsidy creates as people allocate resources according to the subsidy incentives rather than the true costs and benefits of the goods and services they buy and sell. Others explicitly include subsidy measures to address market failures.

If subsidies are essential for the achievement of social goals, they are best designed as household subsidies that are transparent, efficient, and well targeted, even if they use the finance system for disbursement and collection. For example, the development of mortgage insurance may benefit from some risk sharing by government in a public/private mortgage insurance enterprise or, more transparently, government may pay the mortgage insurance premium for selected households through private mortgage insurance companies. Subsidies that address social goals should target households that are not served by the private sector because land or housing finance markets do not yet work at their level.

Where to Start? Assessing Housing Problems and Their Causes

The housing systems and housing finance institutions of advanced economies have evolved gradually over an entire century. Policy issues usually involve only modest incremental changes in existing systems. In contrast, developing and transition economies have to deal with fundamental questions such as property rights, public regulations, and structural problems in the housing finance sector. At the same time, they face political pressure to do something about housing conditions that are perceived as unacceptable for a large proportion of urban households. The multitude and depth of these problems can overwhelm policy makers. All too often, the response consists of ill-advised attempts to adopt practices from other countries that may be inappropriate for the housing problems in the country concerned. Another frequent reaction is to request more subsidies for the housing sector. In reality, subsidies to the housing sector are already high in most emerging markets, but are hidden and are neither efficiently nor equitably allocated.

Many countries could benefit from an in-depth, broad-scale inquiry into the nature, breadth and causes of their housing problems. Similar wide-ranging reviews of private markets are necessary, covering their current and potential reach and constraints and their existing subsidy programs. Reviews should address the depth of subsidies and their beneficiary groups. Based on such analyses, governments can define long-term policy goals as well as medium- and short-term programmatic actions – a roadmap – to achieve greater private sector participation. Strategic goals should address the housing problems of those not yet well served by market forces, even with government incentives. Korea, Latvia, Mexico and Morocco offer examples of countries that have recently implemented such exercises, followed by a medium-term strategic plan for the sector.

Such straightforward exercises would create, within a short period of time, the general basis for initial housing policy analysis. Pertinent housing issues are aired for discussion at various levels of government and among government and private sector agents in the housing market. Such an analysis and analytical framework would identify the gaps in access to formal housing and housing programs for different income groups. This approach can be especially useful for policy makers who are not aware of important issues because of the hidden nature of many subsidies.

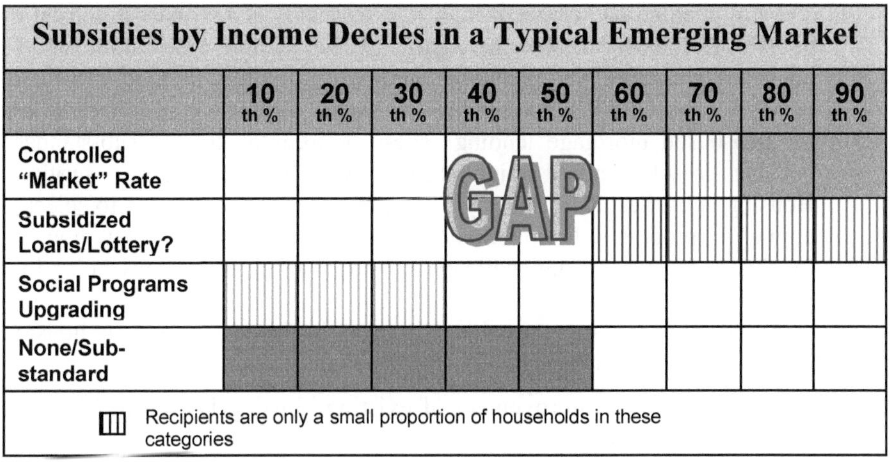

Fig. 1. Gap analysis

The outcome of this initial analysis would ideally be the identification of specific market segments for different types of housing and for housing finance products and their frontiers, i. e. the margin beyond which specific demand and supply constraints limit expansion of and access to these markets.

The following classifications incorporate the usual broad market segments to which government interventions may most fruitfully be directed and the areas where expansion of opportunities are most likely.

1. The middle- and lower-middle-income market segment consists typically of the 40th or 50th percentile and above in the income distribution. Household incomes would be adequate to obtain formal moderate-income housing, but most people in this group live in unauthorized or substandard formal housing. The frontier for expanding the formal housing market downwards for this segment is not so much constrained by low incomes, although that is certainly part of it, but by lack of access to finance. Limited access is related to a) informal employment, b) lack of wealth or savings, c) uncertain collateral because of poor land registration and cadastre systems, d) alternative types of property rights or neighborhood risk factors, e) inefficiencies and incompleteness of housing finance markets and, importantly, f) lack of appropriate housing products offered by the market. In some countries, housing finance-linked subsidy programs enable households at the top of this income bracket to obtain new formal sector housing. But real regulatory constraints and controls on rental markets often form barriers to expansion of formal housing for the unassisted part of this market segment. Upward mobility out of unauthorized or substandard formal housing is limited.

2. The low-income or perceived high-risk segments of the market consist of households below the 40th percentile of the income distribution and/or households that are not considered creditworthy. These include informally or self-employed households whose collateral is considered inappropriate for lien-based mortgage lending. These households live in sub-standard housing or sub-standard neighborhoods with limited access to services. Housing subsidies accessible by these groups are often limited to selected upgrading programs. Formal housing markets seldom deliver new housing for this segment, and the challenge is how to bring more households into the formal sector.

   The frontier for the expansion of formal, healthful low-income housing is often two-dimensional:

   - the frontier for improvement of existing housing is confined by lack of infrastructure, the absence of formally registered property rights, inadequate regulations and lack of access to consumer or microcredit for home improvement;
   - the frontier for new low-income housing is constrained mostly by a combination of a) regulatory issues, b) non-functioning land markets, c) poor permitting procedures, d) low incomes and e) lack of access to appropriate financial instruments. Microfinance, even if it is available, is not the solution for large scale development of new housing for this market because of its rate structure. Expansion and strengthening of existing credit cooperatives or mutual credit unions is a more promising strategy.

The relative proportions of households in each category will differ in each country and so will the specific causes of housing problems.[8] It is, however, not uncommon in emerging market economies to find that approximately 60 to 70 percent of new households coming into the market each year cannot afford to pay for the lowest cost house produced in the formal sector, even if finance were available. When urban growth rates are high, upward filtering[9] will be insufficient to fulfill demand for housing when new housing can be produced only at this income level. An example will clarify this point.

Table 1 shows a stylized "affordability" distribution of a fairly typical emerging market country. It calculates the house price that households at each income decide can afford if they use either mortgage credit or consumer or microcredit at nominal market rates. It shows a distribution similar to the stylized market figure in the chapter by David Porteous in this volume.

---

[8] For example, in transition economies the second market segment may not exist or it may take the form of substandard condominiums or rental units (or mixed rental/ownership buildings) for which it is difficult to attract improvement loans.

[9] Filtering is the process by which successively lower-income households move gradually into better quality existing housing when the supply of new housing allows those with relatively higher incomes to move into standard new housing.

Table 1. Example of income and finance affordability

Affordable Loans / House Price Scenarios for Household Expenditure Decentiles, Using Different Nominal Interest Rates and Loan Conditions

Urban Households	10th%	20th%	30th%	40th%	50th%	60th%	70th%	80th%	90th%
Monthly income, based on expenditures	310	450	510	610	770	840	1,085	1,285	1,775
Borrowing capacity	10%	15%	20%	20%	20%	20%	20%	20%	20%
Monthly pmt.capacity	31	68	102	122	154	168	217	257	355
Term	2	5	7	15	15	15	15	15	15
Interest rate-nominal	30%	30%	20%	17%	17%	17%	17%	17%	17%
Affordable loan	554	2,086	4,593	7,927	10,006	10,916	14,100	16,699	23,067
Savings effort/down-payment	10%	10%	20%	20%	30%	30%	50%	50%	50%
Afford w/loan alone	554	2,086	4,593	7,927	10,006	10,916	14,100	16,699	23,067
Afford w/down-payment	616	2,318	5,742	9,909	14,295	15,594	28,200	33,398	46,134

* The lowest cost house in the formal market for new housing was $25,000 at the time the survey was conducted

At the time this calculation was made, the lowest priced house in the formal urban housing market in a city approximately 40 km outside one of the main metropolitan areas costs USD 5,000. It could be afforded only by the 75th percentile of the income distribution and only with a 50 percent down payment. The supply of this type of house at a national level was only a tiny fraction of the yearly increase in the number of households in the 70th percentile group alone! As a consequence, only a small part of the annual requirement for new housing could be fulfilled by constructing standard houses and the subsequent filtering up of lower-income households – possibly from the 50th percentile – into vacated houses. This situation often translates into pressure on government to subsidize housing for middle-income families, often through finance. In this case, deep interest rate subsidies were available to select formally employed members of labor tax funds. But allocations were unstable from year to year, hindering the development of that segment of the real estate market.

The bottom half of the income distribution has no access to adequate new housing nor can it finance the purchase of existing housing. Many countries have small upgrading programs and deeply subsidized but often small government-funded new housing programs, but low-income households have no choice other than to build their own dwellings in unauthorized settlements. In the example above, the central government subsidized developers and lenders who would construct and finance a USD 10,000 house. This "market" was viable only when developers used serviced land donated by local governments with fairly high development standards. Households between the 30th and 40th percentile qualified for an upfront subsidy up to a maximum of USD 4,000. This is an extremely deep total subsidy (both land and upfront cash) for the lucky few – and one that does not expand the basic functioning of the lower-income housing market.

How can this vicious cycle be addressed? To begin, it helps to be clear about the three components of housing affordability:

- The level of income and its distribution. This is a matter of macroeconomic outcomes and a "given" from the housing policy perspective.
- Access to and cost of debt finance. Finance dramatically expands affordability as the example above shows, and can be improved by private and public initiatives. This is particularly the case for the lower-middle-income segment.
- The supply elasticity of housing, which is linked to both the operation of land markets and the organization and financing of the construction industry.

Lower-income housing markets in most emerging market countries cannot expand without drastic improvements in the land market and the regulatory system governing land use. When serviced land supply is inelastic and does not respond to price signals caused by increasing demand for housing, and when efforts are made to increase access to finance or the provision of subsidies, prices of formal housing will increase relative to incomes.

It is essential that all parts of the housing delivery system – finance, land and infrastructure, and construction – work well. Successful approaches to expand the current frontiers of the two housing market segments distinguished above must deal with all critical supply bottlenecks in order to create the filtering of households into better quality formal housing appropriate for each income level. While normal market forces will gradually expand these frontiers, in most emerging market countries four types of government action are required to accelerate this process:

- improving the regulatory and institutional environment for the housing development and construction sector;
- improving regulations and institutions for the housing finance sector (improved regulations for the housing finance sector are discussed in the chapter by Dübel);
- using well-targeted subsidy incentives to improve the efficient supply of housing finance; and
- providing well-targeted subsidies to households.

Each of these imperatives is discussed below.

Expanding Formal Housing Frontiers: Reforming Land and Real Estate Markets

Without new land and new housing, improvements in housing finance merely generate price effects. In its 1993 programmatic shelter paper, "Enabling Housing

Markets to Work," the World Bank undertook a comprehensive review of land conversion and servicing multipliers globally.[10] The analysis revealed inefficiencies of supply processes in much of the developing world. Negative market outcomes are now evident in countries experiencing housing finance system expansion arising from lower interest rates and macroeconomic stability, while serviced land supply and development finance are stagnant. South Africa is an example.

Box 1: South Africa – Public Service Delays Jeopardize Private Sector Housing Finance Access Program

South Africa's private sector lenders committed to provide housing finance to households earning between SAR 1500 – R 7500 per month (USD 200-USD 1000). Yet, as reported by the South African Banking Association, there is an increasing dearth of properties to buy within the reach of households in that income range. The annual delivery of houses in 2005 costing less than SAR 200,000 (USD 27,000) was about 19,000 units, whereas the shortage was estimated at 661,000 units. Similar figures were estimated for later years.

The report cites three main reasons for the failure to close this gap:

- the failure of public land management to mobilize reasonably located and priced public land for low-income housing purposes, and the high prices of private land;
- major and increasing delays in land conversion and land servicing – reportedly the process had lengthened from 12–18 months to between 30–59 months over the last few years;
- land title transfer and building permit processes have extended the housing delivery process from 5 months to 19 months. In addition, other input costs such as material and labor have risen substantially.

Source: "Housing Supply and Functioning Markets," SABA, December 2005

What principal constraints in land and real estate markets prevent optimal investment in land? Why are returns on such investments often lower than for other assets, even in markets where house prices in general are increasing rapidly? Much has been written about these issues and we will summarize the main areas of reform. There are at least four main sources of market failures in land and real estate markets:

---

10 See Mayo, S. K. (1993) *"Housing, Enabling Markets to Work – with Technical Supplements"*, A World Bank Policy Paper, The World Bank: Washington DC and Angel, S. (2000) *"Housing Policy Matters, A Global Analysis"*, Oxford University Press: New York.

- Government control over large tracts of land and residual government control over ownership of land may create an uncertain investment climate.
- Information asymmetries, lack of well defined property rights, and the high transaction costs of property registration and transfers create risks and reduce incentives to trade.
- Inefficiencies in input markets such as developer finance, infrastructure and construction markets limit investment options.
- Policy distortions in the regulatory system or tax system prevent market expansion.

Government Control over Land and Land Ownership

Local and federal governments, often through land agencies, own large tracts of land or real estate assets, often in prime urban locations that face an uncertain future. When these lands are allocated at no cost or at below market prices for social housing, they distort land and housing markets and may impose high externality costs for surrounding developments. Moreover, the real cost of the land is usually not taken into consideration in the market assessment and subsidy calculation of these projects. These costs can be extremely high. For example, land subsidies in Iran amount to 5 percent of GDP,[11] much higher than any subsidy provided through the financial system.

The purposes and operations of public land management agencies in many emerging markets have conflicting mandates; among those are fiscal motives (sales price maximization), social motives (swapping land into housing for their own development programs) and political motives. For example, the Turkish Mass Housing Agency, which has large urban land holdings, prefers to develop its land for social housing purposes through land-to-housing swaps, rather than selling it into a market undergoing rapid land price increases. The result is distorted land and house prices and often extremely high but implicit subsidies to non-priority groups. Moreover, such systems are universally prone to corruption.

While it is critical to mobilize public land resources, particularly in high-growth urban areas, the efficiency of land allocations can be greatly improved by auctioning parcels of government land into the market, with or without development guidelines for their use. Government can then use well-targeted, transparent subsidies to reach housing goals for specific disadvantaged groups.

Another investment constraint is the residual control by central or local government over privately held land. For example, governments may expropriate land without compensation or put ceilings on land ownership; they may fail to enforce property rights in the case of illegal settlements; and once such settlements are

[11] Refer to World Bank (undated, assumed 2004/05) *"Islamic Republic of Iran: Housing Sector Strategy"*, The World Bank: Washington DC.

established, governments may or may not recognize settlers' de facto occupancy. While some government control over private land is necessary – for example to acquire land for public uses and environmental protection – government should exercise such powers within a well established legal system using transparent mechanisms to clarify and improve the credibility of its commitments and ensure the fair resolution of disputes.[12]

Property Rights and Information Systems

It is not uncommon to find that 30 to 50 percent of households in urban areas of developing countries lack secure ownership of their house and the land it is built on. Lack of property rights is associated with low investment in housing and fairly large equilibrium house price differentials when compared to housing in formal sector areas.[13] Also, investments in infrastructure and other public goods are generally lower in non-titled neighborhoods, which is, among other things, related to the lack of formal taxes or difficulties in their collection in informal areas (Hoy and Jimenez 1996).[14] An interesting case of property rights as a catalyst for infrastructure investment is provided by the national titling program in Peru. Residents of informal areas who received title can now connect to individual services at their own cost. Mibanco, a microfinance lender, has initiated a lending program for that purpose which has grown enormously.

Property rights that allow collateralization and transfer of the property are also considered important to expand access to mortgage credit. For example, De Soto's *The Mystery of Capital* (2000) focused on unlocking the "dead" assets of the poor through granting property rights and improving access to credit. The increase in mortgage lending after the implementation of titling programs has been limited, however, at least in the early years (see the experimental studies done in Argentina by Galiani and Schargrodsky 2006 and in Peru by Field and Torero 2006).[15] The likely reasons are that mortgage loans are not appropriate for low-income households with informal employment, and housing assets in recently formalized areas are not considered good collateral for a mortgage loan.

[12] See Galal A. and O. Razzaz (2001) "Reforming Land and Real Estate Markets", Policy Research Working Paper 2616, The World Bank, Washington DC.

[13] See Jimenez, E. (1984) "Tenure Security and Urban Squatting", *Review of Economics and Statistics*. 66(4): 556-567.

[14] Granting formal rights may not be feasible in all informal areas. For example, in urban India where plot sizes in informal areas are very small and densities are high, existing plots cannot meet formal standards. Similarly, formalization of rights is impossible in physically risky areas.

[15] An effect of property rights perceived in the 2002 study by Erica Field in Peru was that participation in the labor force increased among households that obtained a property title. Such an outcome increases the "affordability" of home improvements.

However, the growth of microfinance loans in countries with well-established microfinance institutions is often facilitated by secure but not necessarily freehold land titles, since proof of ownership of the land and possibly the house is often necessary to obtain such loans or to obtain a better rate on such loans for housing or for business purposes. For example, BRI in Indonesia, MiBanco in Peru[16] and several microlenders in Bangladesh require proof of property ownership as part of the underwriting or residential verification process before issuing a micro loan.

Property rights are not synonymous with freehold title. They are best perceived as a bundle of different types of "rights" ranging from de facto claims[17] to formal rights to exclude others from occupying the land, using it and building on it, and/or the right to collateralize or transfer it, which requires state guarantees. Investment in housing and in relative house prices may differ according to the bundles of rights and the perceived security of such rights.[18] The registration of rights – any type of right – is often more important to stimulate investment in housing and infrastructure than the issuing of freehold ownership titles *per se*.

The development of property rights and registration systems is, therefore, a critical area of reform. It includes a) the constitutional protection of property, b) laws and regulations defining rights and obligations to property, c) means of assignment of rights to property, and d) institutional arrangements which register and enforce such rights.[19]

Several countries have implemented broadly based property right formalization projects (e. g. Indonesia, Thailand, Peru, Colombia) and many others have provided titles as part of specific upgrading projects. Experience in countries that have established comprehensive title registration systems has shown that these systems

---

16 COFOPRI, the commission to formalize informal settlements in Peru, issued 1.5 million titles between 2000 and 2006 and saw an increase in the use of credit. But it is inconclusive whether this was due to the titling program or the overall improvement in the economy (2006).

17 See Razzaz, O. (1993) "Examining Property Rights and Investment in Informal Settlements: The Case of Jordan", *Land Economics.* November 1993.

18 For example, Hoek-Smit and Hoek (1998) found that investment in urban housing in several African countries was higher in tribal areas than in areas with a limited bundle of formal rights, but highest in areas with freehold titles, all things being equal. However, the use of debt finance was limited to consumer finance on tribal land and on land with a user license only, while mortgage debt was common on freehold land.

19 See Galal A. and O. Razzaz (2001) "Reforming Land and Real Estate Markets", Policy Research Working Paper 2616, The World Bank, Washington DC and Butler, S. B. (2006) *"Broadening Mortgage Markets by Attending to Legal Fundamentals"*, Lecture notes for the Wharton International Housing finance Program, University of Pennsylvania.

- are best integrated with the cadastre (which includes the value of the land and the improvements on the land for taxation purposes) within a single public corporation;
- should be considered a public good that may be based on the principle of cost recovery for its services, but not as a profit or tax center because high expenses of using the system can easily defeat its purpose;
- should give open access to all parties;
- are best designed not to eliminate all risks, but to provide some conditionality with the provision that the state will indemnify users for registration errors; and
- should be accompanied by an ongoing public education campaign focused on the benefits of title registration.[20]

Main Infrastructure Provision and Servicing of Residential Land

The provision of trunk infrastructure for opening up land for development seriously lags behind demand in many developing and transition countries. The example of South Africa noted above is but one of many. The lack of funds at the local government level is often noted as a major impediment to local infrastructure extension. But in reality it is often the lack of strategic planning and delivery capacity, and the weak political priority given to low-income developments that is the cause of these problems. For example, federal government transfers to local governments in Mexico include dedicated funds for infrastructure provision. But because of the low priority accorded to lower/middle-income residential development, limited planning capacity, and the short time horizons of the three-year local government political cycle, few of these resources are used to develop land for affordable housing.[21]

Equally, the provision of on-site residential infrastructure and services is often a long process and is difficult to coordinate among different entities. These include suppliers of electricity, water and sanitation, and roads, which are often independent agencies. The results are major delays and cost overruns. Detailed examples of countries as different as Zambia, Mexico and Indonesia show similar patterns.

---

[20] See Butler, S. B. (2006) *"Broadening Mortgage Markets by Attending to Legal Fundamentals"*, Lecture notes for the Wharton International Housing finance Program, University of Pennsylvania and Butler, S. B. (2003) *"Housing Finance In Emerging Markets: Policy and Regulatory Challenges"*, Paper presented at the World Bank Conference on Housing Finance in Developing and Emerging Economies. March 2003.

[21] Interviews by the author with experts in 2003-2006.

Thailand offers a positive example. The government made a concerted effort in the late 1980s and 1990s to open up new land and to allow urban development at simplified and lower cost standards. Private developers and investors were attracted to this new market and built large scale, low-income housing apartment complexes with units as small as 20 square meters. Consumers were initially reluctant to purchase these houses because of lack of transportation infrastructure, but this changed gradually along with ongoing efforts to clear slum areas. Moreover, because of improved access to finance, supply systems remained affordable for this segment even through the 1997 real estate and financial crisis which was linked to an overheated higher income housing market. The challenge now is to improve internal residential infrastructure in order to maintain the value of such developments.[22]

Regulatory Systems

As demonstrated in Thailand, another major constraint in expanding new housing construction at the two market frontiers is inappropriate regulatory regimes related to land management, development and construction. Standards for subdivision of land, infrastructure requirements and building standards are often unnecessarily rigid and out of balance with household incomes. The second impediment to residential construction is the excessive time and cost often required to obtain permits for development and construction. In several countries where data were collected, it was not uncommon to find that 20 to 35 percent of the cost of a lower-middle-income house was the formal and informal payments required to obtain permits. The process would often take several years and be fraught with uncertainty. Lastly, lack of coordination among different institutions involved in land development and infrastructure provision adds to the uncertainty of the development process and therefore to its costs.

Detailed studies, particularly in the US and the UK, have established the negative effects that regulation has on construction costs and house prices, both for ownership and rental housing, as well as on the standards of construction.[23] Prices were found to be higher and construction standards lower in urban areas with a higher degree of regulatory stringency (controlling for other market fundamen-

---

[22] See Hoek-Smit, M. C. (2002) *"Implementing Indonesia's New Housing Policy: The Way Forward, Findings And Recommendations Of The Technical Assistance Project–Policy Development For Enabling The Housing Market To Work In Indonesia"*, The World Bank: Washington DC.

[23] See Gleaser, E., J. Gyourko and R. Saks (2005) *"Why have House Prices Gone up?"* NBER Working Paper 11129; Quigley, J. M. and R. Steven (2004) "Is Housing Unaffordable? Why isn't It More Affordable?" *Journal of Economic Perspective* 18(1) winter 2004: 191-214; Gleaser, E. and J. Gyourko (2003) "The Impact of Building Restrictions on Housing Affordability, Policies to Promote Affordable Housing", *Economic Policy* (June) 9(2): 21-39.

tals). It was also shown that within cities the non-responsiveness of supply as a result of stricter regulations was greater for the low-income housing sector.[24]

Similar results were found in studies of housing markets in developing countries, for example in Malaysia as detailed in Malpezzi and Mayo's 1997 study. Other evidence is provided by a 2003 survey of the Centre for Urban Studies in Dhaka, Bangladesh, that found land prices from $27 to $60 per square foot (as high as peripheral land in many US urban areas) because of non-transparent land development regulations.[25] Buckley and Kalarickal[26] quote the example of Mumbai, where building height restrictions limit the efficient use of reasonably located, serviced land for housing, leading to extremely high costs that crowd out the poor to peripheral locations. The many examples on Alain Bertaud's[27] website tell a similar story.

Local regulators of urban land developments have to balance risks associated with building low-cost, higher density developments. One set of risks includes perceived health and environmental impacts, higher long-term maintenance costs, and political backlash. Another set consists of negative market outcomes such as the growth of informal settlements without infrastructure, or higher house prices in general. The trade-offs are seldom clear cut and are often framed in a political rather than a technical perspective, leading to unsatisfactory regulatory solutions. The best outcomes in attracting the private sector to the lower/middle-income market have been achieved in urban areas where high level political support was provided for relaxed regulations, fast tracking of development approvals and local government facilitation of off-site infrastructure provision (e. g. in Thailand, as discussed above).

In poor developing countries, the low-income frontier below the 30th or 40th percentile often requires a different approach. It is unlikely that private developers will enter the new housing market at this income level without comprehensive government support. New housing developments at this level will mostly be project based, and government often has to subsidize the serviced lot and/or a core house permitted by special regulations that allow small lot development and incremental construction. Similarly, government partnership arrangements are needed for high density, multifamily housing projects on infill land located closer to city centers.

---

24 In addition, a detailed comparative study of supply constraints in the UK relative to other European countries showed that supply inelasticity had a negative impact on the volatility of house-prices (Barker 2003).

25 Seraj, A. (2003) *"Solving Housing Problems through Private Sector Development"*, Water and Sanitation for Cities, Bangladesh Institute of Planners, Centre for Urban Studies: Dhaka.

26 See Buckley, R. and J. Kalarickal (2005) "Thirty Years of World Bank Shelter Lending – What have we Learned?" Directions in Development – Infrastructure. The World Bank: Washington DC.

27 http://alain.bertaud.com.

The challenge for central government is that most of these policies and regulations on the "real" side are in the political realm of local government, which is often under political pressure *not* to allow low-income developments. Local governments generally also have limited analytical capacities to assess the impact of deficient regulations and housing development processes. Benefits from the reform of non-transparent systems are often limited or even negative for local regulators and private title registration notaries, which makes change difficult. Central government subsidy incentives or conditions are often required for local governments to undertake the necessary enabling policies before they gain access to central government housing subsidies.[28]

Paradoxically, it often takes strong central government incentives to unblock local level housing markets for lower-income households, whether through sticks (conditional withholding of housing-related subsidies and transfers) or carrots (through capacity building support to local land and property institutions or subsidies for the development of residential serviced plots or multi-family housing for low-income households). The challenge for both local and central government is to make sure that all parts of the supply chain work sequentially for different market segments, i. e. improving the supply process for each market segment before finance and subsidies are used to expand demand.

Housing Finance Subsidies and the Expansion of Markets

A Changing Universe

In most developing and transition economies government intervention in housing finance systems is deep and based on a long tradition. Some countries inherited government-controlled housing finance systems from their colonizing country. Latin America inherited the French/Spanish government bank system. This was later adjusted to include a funding model based on taxation of labor rather than on voluntary savings (Mexico, Peru, Brazil, Colombia). Other traditions stem from the post-colonial period that espoused nationally-controlled financial systems that included the housing finance system as in most of Asia and Africa. Private mortgage lending through the commercial banking systems and mutual credit unions coexisted, but remained small in most countries. These government-controlled housing finance systems combined strict regulatory oversight with deeply imbedded subsidies. The poor performance of these government systems challenges their validity. At the same time, positive changes in the macro economy and financial sector in many countries over the last two decades has attracted the private sector to housing finance, the recent crisis notwithstanding.

[28] See also Mayo, S. K. (1999) *"Subsidies in Housing*", Paper prepared for the Sustainable Development Department Technical Paper Series", Inter-American Development Bank: Washington DC.

This shift has brought a new approach to regulating and subsidizing the sector, focused on:

- incentivizing private mortgage institutions to build up their portfolios while maintaining their stability;
- improving basic lending infrastructure;
- transforming the often dominant government systems; and
- reforming the deep subsidies imbedded in these systems in ways that create more transparent subsidies targeted at specific underserved market segments.

Housing Finance Problems, Causes and Subsidies

Constraints to the efficient growth of housing finance systems vary widely across countries and among mortgage finance and other types of housing finance.[29] There are at least four general categories of constraints:

- Constraints imposed by macroeconomic conditions or volatility (high and unstable inflation, volatile real wages) that encompass much more than the housing finance system *per se*.
- System imperfections due to market concentration problems or lack of a level playing field among financial institutions, and/or the existence of powerful gatekeepers that resist innovation and new entrants into the market.
- Constraints in the ways funding markets can manage liquidity or interest rate risks, thereby truncating lending options and possibly leading to destabilization of the housing finance system.
- Lending market failures or incompleteness due to lack of credit and property market information, high risk of loss given default because of poor foreclosure systems, lack of mechanisms to deal effectively with credit risk, lack of consumer protection, and high transaction costs of lending that prevent suppliers of credit from profitably serving all or a large portion of the housing market.

How can government intervention – specifically subsidies – help overcome such constraints? We start from the premise that subsidies are incentives to change behavior, either of consumers or producers of housing, relative to specific goals and objectives (Box 2). We focus here on subsidies as incentives to improve the effec-

---

[29] Imperfections such as asymmetric information, incompleteness of markets and moral hazard are endemic in housing finance systems. This means that second best solutions to those assumed by theories of complete and competitive financial market models are all one can hope for. Allen and Gale (2001) discuss such trade-offs for financial systems in general.

tiveness of housing finance systems rather than on subsidies to households. There are four general types of subsidies for housing finance systems:

- subsidies for research, information collection, or education programs targeting housing policy goals;
- provision of below-market funds for housing loans or insurance schemes;
- direct government risk sharing through financial intermediation at the retail or secondary market level; and
- regulatory controls on prices or credit allocations for housing finance.[30]

Box 2: Defining Subsidies

Subsidies are often perceived as giving or receiving something for free. That notion is misleading. From a broad perspective "a subsidy is an incentive provided by government to enable and persuade a certain class of producers or consumers to do something they would not otherwise do, by lowering the opportunity cost or otherwise increasing the potential benefit of doing so." (adapted from the US Congress 1969)

Specific incentives will of course depend on the existing housing finance system and the quality of the infrastructure, as well as on the type of housing finance system the country is moving towards. Possibilities include a system based on capital market funding through securitization or mortgage bonds, or a predominantly deposit-based system where non-bank financial institutions do not play a major role. Since subsidies are prone to misuse, particularly in the hands of powerful interest groups that control their delivery, the choice of subsidies will also depend to a large degree on the relative ability of the structure of the subsidy to contain misallocation and moral hazard by government.

Table 2 summarizes the main constraints in the housing finance sector outlined above and the types of subsidies that have frequently been applied, or that may be considered, to overcome the causes or effects of such constraints. The texts underlined flag the subsidies that induce high costs and that therefore should be avoided if at all possible. The following sections briefly discuss these very different subsidies and their positive and negative impacts on housing finance systems.

---

30 According to the definition used here, an intervention to improve the housing finance system is a subsidy even if government is compensated on the basis of some accepted measure of a suitable rate of return: the intervention lowers lenders' opportunity costs, whether private or state-sponsored. The all-in impact of the subsidies on financial intermediation will, of course, depend on the difference between the rate of compensation to government and the presumed "market" rate for delivering the service.

Table 2. Examples of system subsidies

Housing Finance System Constraints	*Possible Subsidy Measures*	*Issues*
1. Macroeconomic Constraints/Volatility		
System risk/ political risk	• Shift all or part of interest-rate risk to government, e. g. forgiving balances on inflation-adjusted loans, providing non-market sources of funds • Subsidized lending at fixed rates or capped adjustable rates by a government-sponsored/ owned financial institution for rental or ownership housing	• Unpredictable and often extremely high costs to government at times when it can least afford it • Government lending is often not phased out after macroeconomic stability is achieved, thus hindering private sector re-entry
2. Market Structure and Vested Interests.		
State or incumbent lenders have excessive market power **Incumbent lenders limit new entry, innovation and price competition**	• Remove subsidy and other privileges from state lending institutions • Support short-term alternative types of lenders, e. g. through liquidity funding • Increase competition by liberalizing the financial sector, especially encouraging access by foreign lenders (e. g. removal of hidden subsidies) • Remove price controls, e. g. caps on interest rates for micro loans or mortgage loans	• Vested interests resist removal of subsidies • Usually requires additional regulation of such lenders • Interest rate controls often decrease volume of lending to targeted groups
3. Funding Constraints and Risks*		
Limited/costly equity funding	• Provide equity capital for partially or fully state-owned housing lenders, without dividend obligations • Provide equity for non-profit financial institutions that on-lend for social housing, rental or owner-occupied	• Partial or full state control can lead to operational inefficiencies, reduced competition and excessive risk-taking
Limited access to or high costs of funds for lending	• Subsidize cost of funds through government credit lines, special tax funds or debt funds for social rental or ownership housing • Tax subsidies for funds channeled to housing finance (e. g. bonds, savings) • Public guarantees for lenders to access funds (public/private partnership) • Cash subsidies for funding for housing finance • Subsidized cash-flow guarantees for debt funds channeled to housing lenders	• This class of subsidies is often provided through special government-sponsored institutions, adding to the cost of the subsidies and possible inefficiencies in the housing finance market • Subsidizing ways to assist private lenders to obtain access to debt or capital markets carries less risk (see also below)
Liquidity risk	• Access to a (partially) government-sponsored liquidity facility (or secondary mortgage market) for all or a certain class of mortgage/microfinance lenders	• May be structured as a joint public/private venture to limit government risk exposure or political misuse

Table 2 (continued)

Housing Finance System Constraints	*Possible Subsidy Measures*	*Issues*
4. Lending Risks and Costs in Underserved Markets		
Credit risk/ collateral risk for mortgage lending	• Subsidize information collection and research on property and credit markets • Pay private mortgage insurance premium (overlap with household subsidies) • Pay for borrower education • Shift (part of the) credit risk to a (partially) state-sponsored entity • Provide (partial) guarantees for social rental housing loans	Additional government action needed: • Credit bureaus • Regulations allowing payroll deductions • Property information systems • Improved foreclosure methods • Community negotiations in case of default • Neighborhood investment plans to mitigate neighborhood risk (see below) Requires private lenders to invest in user-friendly servicing system
Credit risk related to construction lending	• Link household subsidies to specific developments to support market for housing production • Provide (partial) guarantees for construction loans	• Developer may capture a portion of the subsidy • Highly risky; requires safeguards on quality of construction, etc.
High transaction costs for loan origination and servicing	• Subsidize lenders' transaction costs for selected borrowers through cash payment or compensation for higher interest rate (can also be structured as part of a household subsidy)	Prerequisite: • Improved underwriting and servicing methods (see also under credit risk

Sovereign and exchange rate risk are not considered in this table.

Housing Finance Subsidies and Macroeconomic Volatility

Correcting adverse macroeconomic conditions mostly requires structural reforms of fiscal and monetary policy. Many countries have undertaken such reforms or are in the process of doing so. Structural reform often includes reduction of subsidies that are implicit, including housing subsidies. Such programs can improve the ability of the market to provide credit and ultimately the ability of governments to provide more efficient on-budget housing subsidies.

Instead, the historic tendency has been to use housing subsidies to compensate for difficult macroeconomic conditions. In particular, many governments with national housing systems[31] have attempted to soften the negative impacts of macroeconomic volatility on the housing and housing finance markets by assuming interest rate and credit risks in order to protect lenders (and borrowers) from the adverse prospects of lending during periods of volatile economic conditions. Many such systems offer not only subsidized rates but also provide fixed rate loans when market rates are likely to be quite volatile and uncertain – conditions under which private lenders are not willing to offer long-term fixed rate loans. Such interventions can be rationalized as promoting social goals or stabilizing the housing sector in the short term. However, these measures are often extremely costly and have a negative impact on the long-term efficiency of the housing finance sector. Yet, new government housing banks continue to be created to lend under conditions unattractive to the private sector, as in the Ivory Coast, Mali, Namibia and Senegal.

Housing Finance Subsidies, Market Structure and Vested Interests

When one or a few large lenders with vested interests gain excessive power over housing finance they unduly influence the pricing of loans, the types of loan products available and the market segments served. They also prevent new entry and innovations, often raising the costs of lending and imposing inappropriate limitations on access to loans. These structural and political problems arise in both public and private sectors.

Public Sector Induced Structural Problems in Housing Finance

Structural and anti-competitiveness problems frequently arise when specific institutions, often state-owned, are subsidized or when these institutions erect regulatory or political barriers to entry.

As mentioned above, many countries have housing finance systems dominated by state housing finance funds or banks, state conduits in the secondary market, state-owned mortgage insurance companies or state microlending institutions. These institutions usually have tax, funding or risk-bearing advantages and do not have the concerns about return-on-equity to their owners that guide private institutions. It is difficult for private lenders, insurers or guarantors to compete in the market segments dominated by such state institutions or programs. These state entities often hinder innovations, such as risk mitigation measures because of their profiles (Rajan et al. 2006). The first priority, and a prerequisite for the creation of a more competitive and effective housing finance system, is to eliminate the often hidden subsidies to state housing finance institutions, to provide these subsidies to

[31] Examples in Africa include Botswana, Egypt, Nigeria, Tanzania, Uganda and Zambia. Examples in Asia include Korea, Pakistan, and Thailand. Examples in Latin America include Argentina, Brazil and Mexico.

all qualified actors in the sector, or to re-orient these subsidies to leverage private sector participation.

This is not an easy task, particularly when these institutions are the largest sources of funds for housing finance and are supported by powerful constituencies. The Government Housing Bank of Thailand is one of the few state housing banks that successfully calibrated its operations to stimulate, not prevent, greater private sector participation in housing finance. Many other emerging economies are analyzing or trying out alternative options to dissolve, break up or change the function of state housing finance institutions. Korea and Peru have dismantled their special funds. Indonesia, Mexico and to a limited extent Brazil and Nigeria are seeking reforms, but the recent crisis has made this more challenging because of private sector withdrawal from mortgage lending.

When new public institutions are proposed to provide financial intermediation functions that the private sector cannot yet profitably deliver, such as mortgage insurance and capital markets access, an exit or sunset provision should be included to prevent these institutions from turning into gatekeepers that will discourage private sector entry later.

Private Sector Induced Anti-competition Problems in Housing Finance

In some countries the private housing finance industry may engage in anti-competitive behavior such as price-setting, collusion not to enter certain sub-markets, or lobbying to exclude other types of financial institutions from entering housing finance. There is often a lack of clear rules guiding structure and market conduct such as disclosure standards and competition. Government's first priority should be to improve such regulatory measures. But even during the period of financial sector liberalization, regulators frequently use price controls and credit allocation requirements to reach social goals for housing finance. These include interest rate ceilings whether for mortgage or micro loans, and quotas for lending to special groups or priority sectors.[32] This approach easily creates an undesirable system of hidden subsidies which may be more costly than the anti-competitive behavior the regulations are intended to address. Better results are generally achieved by repealing such controls and replacing them by positive subsidy incentives that reduce the cost of providing housing finance services to nascent markets.

Housing Finance Subsidies to Alleviate Funding Constraints

Capital markets in developing and emerging market economies are often not well developed or are dominated by government debt. This commonly occurs because the level of contractual financial savings such as from insurance and pensions are

[32] Malaysia has gone one step further, mandating below-market lending for lower-income households, which is partly cross-subsidized from lending to higher-income households. South Africa has also considered a similar plan.

low relative to the supply of long term credit. This situation is changing rapidly because of innovations in voluntary savings systems and other developments.

Governments may want to channel a larger share of these longer-term savings into housing to improve the efficiency of the housing finance system, the overall efficiency and stability of the financial system, or to serve social goals. Even if a country has vibrant primary lending institutions, they may be limited in scale by lack of stable funding. Or the funding risk may be high – the system may not have appropriate markets for managing liquidity, interest rate, and prepayment risks. If so, interest rates will be higher and more volatile, and loan maturities will be shorter than they would otherwise be.

Hypothetically, private investors might create institutional arrangements to best manage these risks. For example, Mexican non-bank financial institutions (SOFOLs) increased their funding options by tapping capital markets through securitization.[33] However, for a variety of reasons, this does not occur in many developing and transition countries even before securitization markets dried up as a result of the financial crisis. Investors often distrust investments in mortgages or mortgage-backed bonds. Yield curves on these investments may be less attractive than government or other paper, and cash flows are less predictable.

Under these circumstances government could support subsidies, even if they are usually not considered as such. These measures include efforts to improve access to capital markets, to increase funding options and to improve the management of risks related to long term lending. For example, government may establish a liquidity facility or a secondary market institution or provide cash flow guarantees or tax incentives for mortgage securities.[34] Such measures are important for the expansion of mortgage lending. They may be particularly relevant for microfinance systems when funding through a deposit base is either limited or impossible because most such institutions are non-banks.

The state may also try to reduce funding constraints and risks, not just to improve markets, but to reach social goals. It may provide subsidized equity funding, lines of credit, or other funding advantages to (state-owned) primary market lenders. The objective of these funding vehicles is to provide below-market loans to specific categories of borrowers, or to investors in social or private moderate-income rental or ownership housing. These institutional subsidies are often accompanied by equity investments and tax write-offs on interest costs, indirectly reducing the cost of rental housing for lower-income groups. Such systems are often established with assistance from international development institutions. However, the costs and distortions imbedded in such special non-market funding sys-

---

[33] The crisis in the residential mortgage backed securities market has sharply reduced this market, however, and the government liquidity and secondary market institution (SHF) has stepped up its funding activities to fill the void.

[34] See the section on government funding windows.

tems have to be carefully assessed. Their long-term impact on the sector is often more harmful than beneficial.

Another issue arises when government's aim is to sell their often poorly performing subsidized mortgages into the capital market to generate more funds for housing. The costs of over-collateralization and other investor incentives such as tax breaks may be extremely high relative to the benefits. Experiences in Colombia and Nigeria have demonstrated how costly such transactions can be. Also, these "deals" are not necessarily helpful in creating a secondary market because investors are either "forced" to buy such paper or because the incentives are unsustainable and difficult to phase out.

These different ways to subsidize funding for mortgage or microfinance loans have very different long term costs, market effects and potential to support low-income housing. While they can increase the flow of finance to the housing sector and can be beneficial and efficient, their advantages often diminish with each additional transaction.[35] At best serving to distribute goods and services more equitably, they often hinder market efficiency when not phased out. Not originally designed for equity purposes, these subsidies are often inefficient in reaching distributional goals: their hidden costs to the financial systems and the economy are often high and they are poorly targeted. Policymakers should carefully examine alternative ways to reach distributional goals, e. g. through transparent household subsidies.

Subsidies to Address Lending Risks and High Transaction Costs

An evolving subsidy objective for housing finance is based on lending risks and transaction costs. The strategy is to encourage agents in primary or secondary markets to expand into housing finance markets that are not well served due to political or practical difficulties, to price differentially for risks and uncertainties – which often cannot be insured – or high transaction costs.

The first priority for government, jointly with the private sector, is to improve the regulations, institutions and information infrastructure that affect the mortgage or consumer/micro lending sectors. This initiative takes the form of creating or upgrading a) appropriate standards, b) property registration systems and cadastres, c) information and research on the housing sector, d) a credit information system and credit bureaus, e) improved foreclosure methods, f) reforms of usury laws, and g) improved underwriting and servicing methods by the industry. Government may also share some of the lending risks or cover high origination and servicing costs. Ideally, as the risks in these markets are better understood and controlled and transaction costs are reduced, government can decrease or phase out such support.

Information and Research. Information collection and research is essential for an efficient housing market, but is often lacking because of the nature of a public

---

[35] Van Horne, J. C. (1973) *"Financial Market Rates and Flows"*, Prentice Hall, Englewood Cliffs, NJ (second edition).

good, i. e. a private entity cannot capture the benefits. Examples of such useful public good data and research topics include a) comprehensive property information, b) consolidated credit information across financial institutions for credit scoring or development of mortgage default insurance or securitization markets, c) research in standardization of mortgage procedures, d) new credit instruments, e) reasons for default, f) default trends and the scale of and reasons for losses after default occurs, and g) trends in house prices. The rewards from developing expertise in housing and housing finance issues are extremely high, given the huge amount of resources that most governments and societies invest in housing.

Credit risks. The most basic lending risk is credit risk, which is often the main source of private sector reluctance to enter underserved markets. Interventions that share credit risks can improve the overall efficiency and stability of the system, and can be designed to fulfill social goals.

One proven intervention is subsidizing the establishment of a credit information system or a credit bureau. Government can go a step further and support the establishment of private credit insurance, or share some risk in a public-private insurance scheme, or even establish its own credit insurance system, although it creates moral hazard.

The type of credit insurance program will depend on the goals set by government. For example, insurance may be priced at or below market; it may be universal or applied to targeted households; or it may cover part of the risk or take on all of the risk; it may be designed for long-term mortgage credit or shorter-term microcredit. Government may also consider paying the mortgage insurance premium for selected households rather than sharing the credit risk directly. A combination of such measures was adopted by SHF in Mexico. SHF established a mortgage insurance scheme targeted to the lower middle income market which qualifies for an upfront subsidy. The insurance rate charged is somewhat concessionary and the premium is paid as an additional subsidy for those households that receive their mortgage through private lenders. A major concern is that whenever the state assumes risk, moral hazard easily arises, i. e. participants will be prone to commit fraud or take excessive risks. The design of the administrative and control systems are therefore as important as the insurance system itself.

A proven way of decreasing credit risk is to educate borrowers before they receive loans, not just on the rights and duties of borrowing, but also on home maintenance. Government can subsidize such education. The effectiveness of this method has been shown in the US (Hirad and Zorn 2001) and by South Africa's HLGC and Mexico's SOFOLs, which have user-friendly servicing systems that pay immediate and personal attention when a borrower misses a payment. This is critical for reducing losses when a default occurs.

If the goal is to expand lending into marginal neighborhoods, partial mitigation of the credit risk is seldom sufficient. Much broader infrastructure and institutional support is often required to alleviate neighborhood risk effects on the value of the collateral.[36]

Development and construction lending creates a special type of credit risk. This type of short-term lending is relatively risky because of a) frequent construction delays, b) difficulty in enforcing quality controls, c) the uncertain collateral value of unfinished construction projects, and d) sensitivity to macroeconomic cycles or risks in the sale and transfer process to end users. Lenders are often reluctant to make such loans and will do so only with special guarantees. Government may develop measures to overcome this constraint to the construction of socially-important housing, perhaps by a) paying for guarantees offered through private guarantors, b) establishing institutions that guarantee quality controls, or c) taking on some or all of the risk by itself or jointly with private or international development institutions, with the necessary safeguards to control moral hazard.

Transaction costs. Aside from credit risk, the main reason that housing submarkets are not served is related to lenders' costs. Household income verification may be cumbersome because of the large proportion of self-employed households; loans are small and therefore the origination fee is either inadequate for the lender or excessive for the borrower; and loan servicing costs are high relative to loan size. Government may compensate lenders directly for these higher transaction costs in order to attract financial institutions into these markets, at least for an initial period. Colombia used this method successfully and phased it out as lenders gained experience in serving more risky markets.

Even with subsidies, mainstream mortgage finance institutions resist incurring set-up costs to reach lower-income, higher-risk customers. This reluctance has led many to conclude that it may be more cost effective to target this type of government support towards community-based or smaller mutual housing finance institutions. These lenders already have information systems in place to deal with less conventional clients because they operate at the community level.

Problems of Subsidies for the Housing Finance System

This discussion shows in general terms that system subsidies can play an important role in overcoming the inefficiencies or instability of housing finance systems. However, it also notes that subsidies have frequently created new problems. These poor outcomes are often due to faulty subsidy design, especially because key de-

[36] The single most important barrier to lending in low-income markets is the uncertainty of neighborhood factors that are critical in determining changes in house values. Lenders may require additional equity investments by third parties and agreements on an investment plan by local government before entering into low-income markets or neighborhood improvement ventures. In the US, the FHA insurance program was effective in stimulating investments in underserved neighborhoods, even without additional community support.

tails of guarantees or other schemes generate costs that are far higher than expected. Excessively deep intrusions into the market can also create strong distortions elsewhere in the growth of the financial system. An essential element in avoiding this outcome is to have political commitments to remove these interventions over time – which may prove difficult – or incentives to induce markets eventually to take over the functions provided by subsidy programs.

Probably a bigger source of problems derives from a lack of clarity in the purpose of a subsidy. Some housing finance system subsidies focus on improving the stability and efficiency of the housing finance system. Others are purposely introduced to seek redistributional goals. These include providing housing finance services at below-market prices to lower the cost of housing – usually through either funding financial services or direct provision – risk sharing or regulation. Some aim to do both.

Even when intended simply to increase efficiency, many system subsidies serve equity goals through the "back-door." This occurs when the original pricing of efficiency-oriented subsidies is not adjusted, or when the subsidy is not phased out when no longer required to improve the private market. A good example is the implicit government guarantee of secondary market entities in the US which has proven a major liability for the government in the recent crisis and which is still to be resolved. The subsidy mechanism is often the same irrespective of the goal. The distinction between market efficiency and equity goals is important, mostly in the way system interventions are priced, adjusted and phased out when the market can take on the risks and costs covered by the subsidy.

But if social goals are the primary purpose for initiating subsidies through the housing finance system, the long term and hidden cost of these types of subsidies and their redistributive effects would have to be compared with alternative subsidies provided directly to households. It often turns out that both their cost efficiency and equity outcomes are second best. The superior alternative is to use transparent household subsidies such as upfront grants in the form of down payments, land grants or savings-linked grants, payment for upfront mortgage insurance premiums, and monthly payment buy-down subsidies.[37]

Conclusion

The liberalization and development of financial systems over the past decades deeply touched the housing finance sector in many emerging market economies. It created momentum for reform, which continues in many countries despite the downturn. A growing demand for urban middle- and lower-income housing has fueled the urgency to expand housing finance systems. One area of critical rethinking, and a frequent bottleneck in system expansion, is housing finance subsidies. These are by far the most prevalent housing subsidies in all countries, although

[37] For a discussion of household subsidies see Hoek-Smit and Diamond 2003.

they are not generally recognized as such. Many finance subsidies have had a negative impact on the development of housing finance markets, and the impact on social goals is mixed. Goals and specific objectives, often not well defined, lead to dysfunctional subsidy design.

The second major bottleneck is inefficient land markets for lower- and middle-income groups. Even when finance is available, the regulatory system often makes it unprofitable or unfeasible for private developers to operate in middle-income markets. Low-income markets certainly require subsidies for serviced land, preferably targeted to individual households.

The challenge for policymakers is to identify the housing problems of different types of households, the land and housing finance system constraints that prevent expansion in underserved markets, and how current regulations and subsidies alleviate or worsen such constraints. Based on this knowledge, clear policy goals could be established and multi-year strategies developed to implement regulatory and other support systems to address these limitations and problems.

This chapter has provided a framework to assist such analyses. Household subsidies can be efficiently applied only when systems work well for the majority of people. The overview of broad categories of subsidy interventions and delivery mechanisms noted here exclude the numerous variants found in practice. The aim here is two-fold. The first is to present the most prevalent "old generation" housing finance subsidies. The second is to explore the gradual reforms and alternatives that may be considered as a result of growing awareness of the importance of transparency in financial markets, sound risk management in financial institutions, and redress of growing housing inequities worldwide. The recent crisis has dramatically highlighted the relevance of those factors.

References

Accion (2003) "Building the Homes of the Poor – One Brick at a Time: Housing Improvement Lending at Mibanco", Insight, No 4. www.Accion.org/pubs.

Allen, F. and D. Gale (2001) "Comparing Financial Systems", The MIT Press: Cambridge, Massachusetts.

Angel, S. (2000) "Housing Policy Matters, A Global Analysis", Oxford University Press: New York.

Barker, K. (2004) "Delivering Stability: Securing our future housing needs", HM Treasury: London.

Bertaud, A. (http://alain.bertaud.com)

Blood, R. (2003) "Key Policy and Regulatory Issues for Credit Insurance and Guarantee Schemes", presentation at the World Bank Conference on Housing Finance in Emerging Markets. March 2003.

Buckley, R. and J. Kalarickal (2005) "Thirty Years of World Bank Shelter Lending – What have we Learned?" Directions in Development – Infrastructure. The World Bank: Washington DC.

Butler, S. B. (2006) "Broadening Mortgage Markets by Attending to Legal Fundamentals", Lecture notes for the Wharton International Housing Finance Program, University of Pennsylvania.

Butler, S. B. (2003) "Housing Finance in Emerging Markets: Policy and Regulatory Challenges", Paper presented at the World Bank Conference on Housing Finance in Developing and Emerging Economies. March 2003.

Chiuri, M. C. and T. Japelli (2003) "Financial Market Imperfections and Homeownership: A Comparative Study", European Economic Review. 47(02): 857–875.

COFOPRI (2005) "Peru pais de Proppietarios", Lima, Peru.

de Soto, H. (2000) "The Mystery of Capital", Basic Books: New York.

Diamond, D. B. (1999) "The Transition in Housing Finance in Central Europe and Russia: 1989–1999", The Urban Institute: Washington DC.

Diamond, D. B. and M. C. Hoek-Smit (2000) "Unblocking Finance For Affordable Housing", Report for the National Housing Finance Corporation of South Africa, International Housing Finance Program, Wharton School, University of Pennsylvania.

Dipasquale, D. (1999) "Why Don't We Know More About Housing Supply?" Journal of Real Estate Finance and Economics. 18(1): 9–23.

Duebel, A. (2000) "Separating Homeownership Subsidies from Finances – Traditional Mortgage Market Policies, Recent Reform Experiences and Lessons for Subsidy Reform", The World Bank, Final Draft, mimeo.

Duebel, A., J. Brzeski and E. Hamilton (2006) "Rental Choice and Housing Policy Realignment in Transition: Post-Privatization Challenges in the Europe and Central Asian Region", World Bank Policy Research Paper, WPS3884. Washington DC.

Ferguson, B. (2004) "The Key Importance of Housing Microfinance", F. Daphnis and B. Ferguson, Housing Microfinance: A Guide to Practice, Kumarian Press: Bloomfield CT.

Field, E. (2002) "Urban Property Rights and Labor Supply in Peru", Department of Economics, Princeton University.

Field, E. and M. Torero (2006) "Do Property Titles Increase Credit Access Among the Urban Poor?" manuscript.

Franklin, A. and D. Gale (2001) "Comparing Financial Systems", The MIT Press: Cambridge MA.

Friedman, J., E. Jimenez and M. Stephen (1988) "The Demand for Tenure Security in Developing Countries", Journal of Development Economics 29(2): 185–198.

Galal A. and O. Razzaz (2001) "Reforming Land and Real Estate Markets", Policy Research Working Paper 2616, The World Bank: Washington DC.

Galiani, S. and E. Schargrodsky (2006) "Property Rights for the Poor", Manuscript.

Gleaser, E. and J. Gyourko (2003) "The Impact of Building Restrictions on Housing Affordability, Policies to Promote Affordable Housing", Economic Policy. (June) 9(2): 21–39.

Gleaser, E., J. Gyourko and R. Saks (2005) "Why have House Prices Gone up?" NBER Working Paper 11129.

Hirad, A. and P. M. Zorn (2001) "A Little Knowledge is a Good Thing: Empirical Evidence of the Effectiveness of Pre-Purchase Home-Ownership Counseling", Freddie Mac: Washington DC.

Hoek-Smit, M. C. (1982) "Improvement Strategies for Lower-Income Urban Settlements in Kenya", The Residential Circumstances of the Urban Poor in Developing Countries: Housing Conditions and Improvement Strategies, Praeger Special Studies: New York.

Hoek-Smit, M. C. (2001) "Home Ownership Assistance Programs for Thailand: A Feasibility Study", Prepared for the Ministry of Finance and the Government Housing Bank, Government of Thailand and The World Bank: Bangkok and Washington DC.

Hoek-Smit, M. C. (2002) "Implementing Indonesia's New Housing Policy: The Way Forward, Findings and Recommendations of the Technical Assistance Project–Policy Development for Enabling the Housing Market to Work in Indonesia", The World Bank: Washington DC.

Hoek-Smit, M. C. (2003) "Subsidizing Housing or Housing Finance?" Paper for the International Housing Conference on the occasion of the 50th anniversary of the Hong Kong Housing Authority, February 2004.

Hoek-Smit, M. C. (2004) "Making Sense of the Universe of Housing Subsidies", paper prepared for the Housing Credit Conference, Dubna, Russia, February 2004, IHFP, Wharton School, University of Pennsylvania.

Hoek-Smit, M. C. and D. Diamond (2003) "Subsidizing Housing Finance", Housing Finance International, June 2003, London UK.

Hoek-Smit, M. C. and J. J. Hoek (1998) "Property Rights and Investment in Housing in Botswana, Tanzania and Swaziland", unpublished manuscript.

International Monetary Fund (2004) "The Global House Price Boom", World Economic Outlook, Chapter II, Washington DC.

Jimenez, E. (1984) "Tenure Security and Urban Squatting", Review of Economics and Statistics. 66(4): 556–567.

Kose, M. A., E. Prasad, K. Rogoff, and S-J Wei (2006) "Financial Globalization: A Reappraisal", IMF Working Paper 06/189, Washington DC.

Kritayanavaj, B. (2002) "Financing Affordable Homeownership in Thailand: Roles of the Government Housing Bank since the Economic Crisis", Housing Finance International, (December): Chicago.

MacLennan, D., J. Muellbauer and M. Stephens (2000) "Asymmetries in Housing and Financial Market Institutions and EMU", in T. Jenkinson (ed.) Readings in Macroeconomics, pp. 74–98. Oxford University Press: Oxford.

Malpezzi, S. and S.K. Mayo (1997) "Getting Housing Incentives Right: A Case Study of the Effects of Regulation, Taxes and Subsidies on Housing Supply in Malaysia", Land Economics. (August) 73(3): 372–391.

Mayo, S.K. (1993) "Housing, Enabling Markets to Work – with Technical Supplements", A World Bank Policy Paper, The World Bank: Washington DC.

Mayo, S.K. (1999) "Subsidies in Housing", Paper prepared for the Sustainable Development Department Technical Paper Series", Inter-American Development Bank: Washington DC.

Mayo, S.K. and D. Gross (1987) "Sites and Services – and Subsidies: the Economics of Low-cost Housing in Developing Countries", World Bank Economic Review. 1(2), 301–335.

Meen, G. (2002) "Why Do Mortgage Markets Matter?", Economic Outlook. 24:4, 12–17.

Mills, E.S. (1987) "Has the United States Overinvested in Housing", Real Estate Economics. 15(1): 601–616.

Quigley, J.M. and R. Steven (2004) "Is Housing Unaffordable? Why isn't It More Affordable?" Journal of Economic Perspective. 18(1) winter 2004: 191–214.

Razzaz, O. (1993) "Examining Property Rights and Investment in Informal Settlements: The Case of Jordan", Land Economics. November 1993.

Rajan, R.G. and L. Zingales (2003) "The Great Reversals: the Politics of Financial Development in the Twentieth Century", Journal of Financial Economics. 69: 5–50.

Renaud, B. (1999) "The Financing of Social Housing in Integrating Financial Markets: A View from Developing Countries", Urban Studies. 36(4): 755–773.

Seraj, A. (2003) "Solving Housing Problems through Private Sector Development", Water and Sanitation for Cities, Bangladesh Institute of Planners, Centre for Urban Studies: Dhaka.

Van Horne, J.C. (1973) "Financial Market Rates and Flows", Prentice Hall, Englewood Cliffs, NJ (second edition).

World Bank (undated, assumed 2004/05) "Islamic Republic of Iran: Housing Sector Strategy", The World Bank: Washington DC.

World Bank (2008) "Housing Finance in Emerging Market Economies", The World Bank: Washington DC.

CHAPTER 4

Regulation and Access to Finance

Hans-Joachim Dübel

Principal, Finpolconsult.de

Abstract

Notwithstanding the financial crisis, housing finance remains a booming industry globally with strong growth potential in developing economies. Especially in the subset of countries dubbed 'emerging markets', the sector's risk environment and available risk management options have changed dramatically in the past two decades reflected by low inflation, the development of funding markets, deregulation, the IT and communications development, and the globalisation of financial services. However, elevated global house price risk and mortgage loan defaults that already materialise in some of the new markets are the price to be paid for fast growth, while access to housing finance for low-income households still remains at a nascent stage.

Financial regulation and state intervention must be designed to support a consistent strategy for access to housing finance. This should include greater institutional diversification and specialisation; product innovation; effective mobilisation of collateral; appropriate client information, consumer protection and financial education; as well as adequate borrower screening and monitoring.

With a few exceptions, commercial banks in developing economies are traditionally reluctant to enter lending to low-income customers, reflecting high transaction cost, perceived low creditworthiness of low income borrowers and inadequate product and underwriting imposed by regulatory barriers, and lack of competition associated with subsidies for a few incumbents, and cartel-style market structures. Lending institutions suited to low-income housing finance need cash flow based lending models and with it a fine-tuning of regulations reflecting different charters and risk profiles.

Regulatory limitations or biases in mortgage lending often make housing unaffordable to low-income groups. Classic examples include requirements for very long-term fixed-rate lending and prohibition of inflation-indexed lending instruments. Tight usury ceilings and foreclosure protection show the trade-off between consumer protection and access to formal finance for low-income groups. An appropriate approach is to improve consumer protection from the perspective of of-

D. Köhn and J.D. von Pischke (eds.), *Housing Finance in Emerging Markets: Connecting Low-Income Groups to Markets*, DOI 10.1007/978-3-540-77857-8_4,

ten risky informal sector practice, rather than aligning standards to those of developed markets for a small almost non-existent formal sector, which is normally out of reach for the poor.

The emphasis of real estate collateral as an instrument for expanding housing finance to low-income households should be de-emphasised. Rather, real estate collateral should be part of a broader underwriting concept utilising consumer credit risk assessments supported by IT and know your customer relationship management. Many collateral-focused mortgage regulations that historically served their purpose in Europe or North America have proved questionable in the context of the ongoing financial crisis. Collateral-focused mortgage lending is particularly ill-suited for newly emerging mortgage markets, which are characterised highly cyclical property markets. Regulation in developing economies should diversify from bricks and mortar regulation towards improving tools effectively assessing personal borrower solvency. This is consistent with a renewed focus on relationship approaches including microfinance or neighbourhood banking, which provide invaluable data mines about low-income household behaviour and risk exposure that gradually improve these models.

Two messages are important in framing public support strategies for low-income housing finance: first, policymakers should avoid replicating top-down approaches from the developed world, such as public housing banks. Rather they should develop their own public-private partnership approaches as done in Mexico or Thailand, and help bottom-up lenders rooted in communities or regions to access relevant broader market data, risk management and risk transfer technology through appropriate apex or service institutions.

Second, despite low political visibility, officials should not neglect badly needed investment in the mortgage market's infrastructure – they should promote a) markets by improving price and market intelligence; b) financial education for consumers; and c) access to justice systems, modern communication, and land registers and information to consumers. Such investments promise greater social returns for low-income housing than direct lending and regulatory interventions.

This chapter is organised as follows: The first introductory section briefly describes the risk and infrastructure constraints of mortgage finance that have been addressed by many countries in the past. It gives a short historical overview of the booms and crises of Housing Finance Regulations since the 1980s. The second part of the chapter starts out by introducing the reader to the prerequisites for broad and sustainable access to housing finance, before dealing with three separate issues: First, the importance of institutional diversification and specialisation, or charter competition for access to housing finance is discussed. Second, the appropriateness of mortgage-specific lending rules in defining loan instruments and the use of real estate collateral is presented. Third, consumer information and protection policies and their nexus with financial regulation are addressed. A concluding section discusses how the information opacity of low-income households can be addressed by laws and regulation.

Introduction

A Supportive General Risk Environment

Housing finance has been a booming industry globally and is likely to remain so, despite the severe setback that hit developed markets in the context of the ongoing financial crisis. Growth has picked up first in developed markets since the 1990s. Table 1 exhibits BIS (Bank for International Settlements) research for the subset of emerging markets. This development is the result of many countries' efforts in the past two decades to address the following risks and infrastructure constraints of mortgage finance which adversely affected demand and supply:

- *Macroeconomic risk:* The global high inflation of the 1970s and 80s depressed the availability of long-term capital and undermined the development of financial markets. Housing finance emerged only after successful reduction of inflation, followed by a phase of high real interest rates that lasted well into the 1990s in developed markets. In many emerging markets, this period of high real interest rates continued well into the 2000s (e. g. Poland) and still goes on (e. g. Brazil, Turkey). In the future, the financial crisis may even lead to higher macroeconomic risk in some developed economies, exceeding those of emerging economies.
- *Interest rate risk*: With macroeconomic stabilisation, the more successful countries have boosted their domestic financial markets. Reforms often included the introduction of mortgage-backed securities for example in Chile, Colombia, the Czech Republic, Hungary, Korea, Malaysia and Mexico.[1] Reliance on foreign capital imports, in contrast, was accompanied by severe setbacks. For example, in June 2006, Turkish mortgage rates almost doubled within two weeks following turmoil in the foreign exchange market. In October 2008 lenders ran into funding problems for their foreign exchange denominated loan portfolios in Hungary and Poland. While emerging economies in Asia and Latin America, have fared better than in the past during the global financial crisis in maintaining private capital inflows, the deepening of domestic and regional long-term capital markets remains an imperative for financial market resilience.
- *Credit risk and access:* Until the late 1970s, even most developed country mortgage markets were underdeveloped by regulation that curbed mortgage lending, imposing excessive product standardisation and high asset quality criteria, and limiting banks' ability to enforce mortgage collateral. Such regulations often imposed unnecessary credit constraints on households.

[1] In developed markets, the picture is more mixed. Spain and France reached higher market penetration with a capital market development strategy, while Portugal, Ireland and the U. K. reached significant growth rates mainly through deposit mobilisation.

Housing Finance Regulation Booms and Crises since the 1980s

Developed markets in the 1980s dominated by 'pro-market' government policies brought about a regulatory 'big bang' for the mortgage industry. The U. S., the U. K. and other European countries removed many regulations. Yet, deregulation had adverse side-effects in the form of additional credit risk. For example in the U. K., the absence of long-term fixed-rate instruments and high loan-to-value ratios led to vulnerability and to macroeconomic shocks for mortgage borrowers. This culminated in a market crisis in the early 1990s, when interest rates increased as a result of the massive capital demand associated with German reunification. In the U. S., federal state usury interest rate ceilings were removed in the early 1980s when prime mortgage interest rate levels started exceeding those limits. When interest rates dropped, this enabled the creation of the subprime mortgage market.

Persistently low interest rates, and an increasingly aggressive and less prudent housing finance system gave rise to enormous house price inflation and subsequently high levels of credit default during the 2007 subprime crisis. More than the U. K. experience, the U. S. subprime crisis revealed deregulation excesses, in particular in weakly regulated capital market financing (securitisation, derivatives) and finance company lending. In contrast to the U. K., where the right-to-buy for low income borrowers was official government policy, the U. S. government had not emphasised such efforts, leaving the initiative to the private sector, which abused the deregulated environment in providing high risk products to unfit borrowers.

Meanwhile, a number of emerging economies improved their legal and regulatory system for mortgage finance by liberalising outdated lending constraints that directed credit to governments or corporations and thus proving households lasting access to housing finance by commercial banks. As reflected in Table 1, the discovery of consumer households by banks was stimulated by privatisations and alternative capital market funding for corporations which freed bank capital for household and consumer lending. Improved information systems and the globalisation of financial services are important recent trends that are creating new options for utilising consumer-related information and managing risk on a global scale. These opportunities attract investment capital to the far corners of emerging markets. With this tailwind, the mortgage industry, historically one of the more parochial segments of financial services went global. The viability of this trend however requires high risk recognition, underwriting and modelling skills.

In this context, increased availability of housing finance in emerging markets has not universally created better access to housing finance. It has often added to house price inflation, resulting less in improved affordability for households with access to finance, and a drop in affordability for those who had hitherto no access. Crises associated with high loan default rates have already have materialised in Latvia and Ukraine.

A coherent strategy to improve access to housing, as opposed to housing finance only, has to also address inefficient housing supply in land markets, planning sys-

Table 1. The housing credit boom in emerging markets

Composition of bank credit[1]

	Housing credit			**Consumer credit**			**Business credit**		
	1994	**1999**	**2004**	**1994**	**1999**	**2004**	**1994**	**1999**	**2004**
Latin America									
Argentina		18	7		15	7		38	17
Chile	13	17	21	8	9	12	79	74	67
Colombia		7	11		15	14		56	39
Mexico	17	16	9	7	4	13	62	36	28
Venezuela		4	1		18	7	44	55	47
Asia									
India			10			12		7	7
Hong Kong SAR	7	15	15	2	3	3	86	76	73
Singapore	14	20	26	13	12	15	60	51	39
Indonesia		5	6		7	18		60	37
Korea		9	33		18	17		69	47
Malaysia	10	18	28		8	16		64	45
Thailand	9	7	10	4	3	6	64	71	68
Central Europe									
Czech Republic[2]		10	16		4	5		41	37
Hungary		3	17		6	8		62	46
Poland		2	10		21	23		44	35
Israel	0	0	8	15	10	9			
Turkey	0	0	2	2	3	6	76	58	39

[1] Of commercial banks. As a percentage of toal domestic credit of commercial banks. [2] The data in the middle columns refer to 2002.

Source: BIS (2006a, p.15) based on national questionnaire data.

Note: Declining housing credit in Mexico is explained by an increasing role of non-bank financial institutions – see discussion below. Declining housing credit in Argentina is explained by the macroeconomic crisis in 2001 and the subsequent default crisis.

tems, and building standards and codes. Such strategies are still largely nonexistent in most developing countries.

Risks for emerging market housing finance also arise from the speed at which markets are expanding. China's ongoing property boom since the mid-2000s, the second after the Shanghai boom before the Asian crisis of 1998, shows that large capital flows into the sector may lead to price inflation even when supply is expanding. However, there are exceptions. For example, bottom-up entities such as co-operative and savings banks face a reverse access problem in the absence of access to the capital markets through apex institutions that could mitigate repricing risk and provide macroeconomic/house price risk protection.

A particularly important risk in emerging markets is the absence of efficient mortgage market infrastructure, consisting of registration systems, credit bureaus, effective consumer and investor information and protection, and enforcement mechanisms.

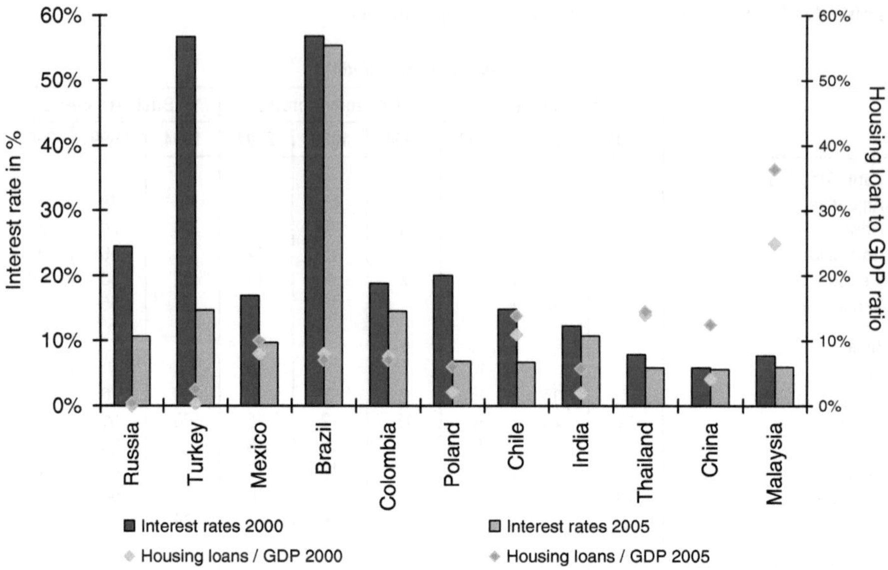

Fig. 1. Tumbling interest rates and housing finance growth in emerging markets

Source: Dübel (2008); Housing Loan to GDP ratios based on World Bank, Merrill Lynch and consultant databases. Lending rates based on IMF international financial statistics and other sources. Note: logarithmic scales.

Regulation at the Crossroads

"If I seem unduly clear to you, you must have misunderstood what I said."

Alan Greenspan

Broad and sustainable access to housing finance requires a combination of:

- institutional diversification and specialisation,
- product innovation, with reasonable risk mitigation,
- adequate consumer information, protection and education,
- adequate loan underwriting and monitoring based on borrower cash-flow,
- appropriate use of technology and information and efficient use of collateral, and
- access to funding beyond the risk appetite of banks through capital markets.

Financial sector regulation and consumer protection are frequently not supportive in promoting access to finance. This may reflect a general emphasis of regulation to protect depositors or consumers with less regard to market access and poor implementation of policies. In addition, many emerging markets have adopted regulation from developed markets without appropriate customisation to the country context.

Charter Competition

Charter Types

Mortgage finance is delivered by many different types of financial institutions that operate under different financial regulations, or charters. The most important are:

- Commercial banks;
- Insurers;
- Local or neighbourhood banks, such as savings and co-operative banks, and more recently microfinance banks;
- Mortgage specialists, including banks, insurers, finance companies and agencies that operate according to voluntary or mandatory operational specialisation and sometimes additional mandate restrictions; and
- Corporate distributors of financial services, ranging from brokers via correspondents to telecom companies.

Is the Role of Commercial Banks Declining?

Over the past two decades, some analysts took the view that commercial banks are either unable or too slow to provide finance in emerging markets, which makes it possible for other banks and non-bank financial institutions to grow. Data provided by a special study undertaken by BIS on the share of credit delivered by commercial banks in emerging markets, however, contradict this general view. While credit provided by non-commercial banks has been on the rise in Latin America and Central Europe, commercial banks still and increasingly dominate financial sectors in China and other Asian economies. The dominance of non-commercial banks, in particular finance companies, in the U. S., and here largely as a result of their role in consumer and mortgage finance, cannot be seen as a model for emerging markets.

"Non-commercial Banks"

'Other banks' includes institutions with close relationships to consumers and local communities: savings and postal banks as well as co-operative and microfinance lenders. Peachey[2] dubs the latter groups of banks 'bottom-up community based'

---

[2] Summarising the World Bank/Brookings conference findings of May 2006, Peachey, S. (2006b) "The Double Bottom Line – Making Access Profitable: Evidence from Microfinance and Savings Banking". A study for the World Bank and Brookings Institution Global Conference on Access to Finance. May 30–31, Washington, D. C.

Table 2. Credit delivered by different types of financial institutions in emerging markets

	Real aggregate credit[1]							
	Average growth rate		Share in aggregate credit					
			Commercial banks			Other banks and non-bank financial institutions		
	1995–99	2000–04	1994	1999	2004	1994	1999	2004
Latin America[2]	3.6	4.5	78	69	68	22	31	32
China	17.1	13.3	100	100	100	0	0	0
India	6.1	14.6			97			3
Hong Kong SAR, Singapore	1.4	3.4			97			3
Other Asia[3]	–0.3	4.7	62	70	74	38	30	26
Central Europe[4]	9.6	8.1		96	83		4	17
Total[5]	7.8	9.6	86	88	88	11	12	12
Memo: United States	*10.1*	*3.3*	*23*	*17*	*18*	*77*	*83*	*82*

[1] Referring to domestic credit by commercial banks, other banks (excl. central banks) and non-financial institutions (questionnaire). In cases where data are not available from the questionnaire. They have been taken from the IMF, IFS; deflated using annual percentage changes of the consumer price index; regional averages calculated using 2000 GDP PPP weights. [2] Argentina, Brazil, Chile, Mexico, Peru and Venezuela. [3] Indonesia, Korea, Malaysia, the Philippines and Thailand (columns 3 to 8 except Indonesia). [4] Czech Republic, Hungary and Poland. [5] Countries shown plus Israel, Russia, Saudi Arabia, South Africa and Turkey (columns 3 to 8 except Indonesia, Israel and Russia).

Source: BIS (2006a), p. 15.

banks, and identifies them as the most important distributors that have provided access to financial services for low-income households. Peachey estimates that savings and postal banks alone maintain 1.1 billion savings accounts globally, compared to 35 million in microfinance lenders and 50 million in co-operative banks. Yet, savings and postal banks in many markets such as Russia, China and the former British colonies of Africa and Asia provide similar restricted lending as commercial banks. Co-operative and microfinance institutions have started to fill the gaps in some of these countries. While such lenders may play an increasing role for low-income housing finance, reliable information is hard to obtain.[3]

Mortgage specialists, including specialised banks and non-bank lenders, have in many cases offered better financial access to low-income households than commercial banks. Finance companies have developed a specialised franchise that has often focused on low-income market segments, even in emerging markets. The case of Mexico's housing finance market development is insightful with regard to both potential and risks of the model.

[3] See Hassler (2006).

Box 1: The Emergence of Housing Finance Companies in Mexico

In 1994, Mexico was hit by a major currency devaluation that caused steep interest rate increases, a property price collapse, spiralling mortgage defaults and the withdrawal of commercial banks that had dominated the mortgage market.

The resulting gap, especially for moderate-income housing finance, was filled through of special-purpose finance companies, called Sofol (Sociedad Financiera de Objectivo Limitada). Sofols are nonbank lenders that are funded through long-term loans provided by the federal housing finance agency (SHF), and now also through bonds and securitisations. SHF has developed centralised bond issuance together with Hipotecaria Total, a joint venture of the George Soros corporation and the Danish securities technology firm VP. Hipotecaria Total has successfully issued mortgage bonds since 2008.

Funding through bonds and securitisations improved Sofols' asset-liability management by relieving it from liquidity and interest rate risks. Since 1995, a loan origination and servicing platform made it possible to lend to low-income households. In addition, loans were provided to construction companies.

New low-income household programmes have been launched recently in cooperation with Infonavit, the wage-tax funded mortgage agency. Infonavit loans now piggy-back Sofol loans and thus provide both credit protection for Sofols as well as greater outreach through lower down payment requirements. Fitch estimates that Sofols reach approximately a quarter of Mexican households having incomes above 800 USD/month, while Infonavit and other agency lending reach another quarter with incomes above 400 USD/month.

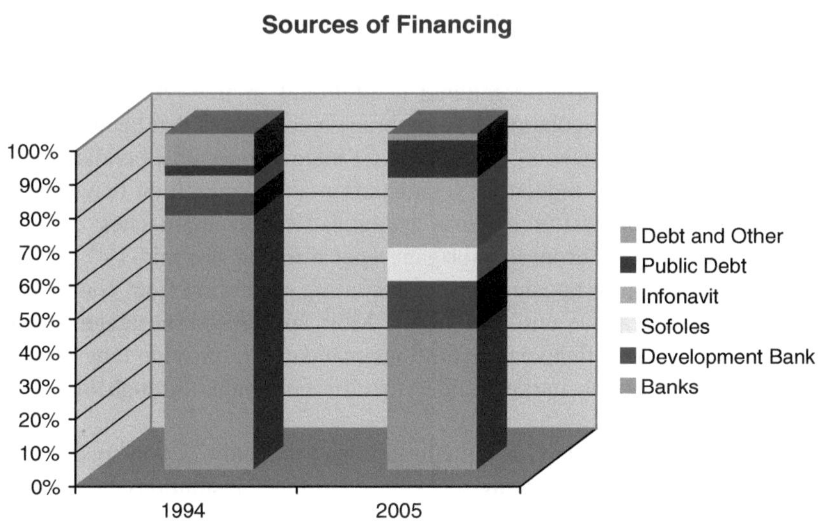

Fig. 2. Supply structure of housing finance in Mexico
Source: Campos (2006).

Despite their success, Sofols have been hit hard by the indirect impact of the U. S. subprime crisis and resulting substantial drop of business and bankruptcies. Fitch (2010) reports increasing defaults, especially for lending to the lowest income segments and loans underwritten at the house price peak in 2007. Delinquencies in Residential Mortgage Backed Securities (RMBS) originated by Sofols averaged 11% at the end of 2009, while those of banks were roughly half of this proportion. Sofol and Bank RMBS transactions dropped to 2005 levels in 2009, while Mexican public housing funds continued to expand. As real incomes dropped in 2009, the Mexican housing finance agency SHF began supporting the market by salary-inflation indexed swaps. SHF also funds Sofols directly. By 2010 Sofols will be regulated by the National Banking and Securities Commission CNBV and it is still unclear whether this leads to additional capital requirements, reduced competition and access for low-income groups.

Other Non-financial Institution Distribution Channels

Porteous[4] (2006) highlights the importance of the market entry of new distributors and of the creation of consumer access points. Indeed, banking through correspondents such as merchants, telecommunication companies/IT providers and other non-bank firms may significantly enhance the bank distribution network. For example, Brazil's correspondents exceeded bank outlets by more than 50% becoming the main mortgage delivery channel at the municipality level in 2005. In addition, loan brokers increasingly support loan originations in developed and emerging markets such as in Poland, where brokers originated one in five loans in 2006.

Charter Competition in Developed Markets – Lessons from Financial Crises

If greater access requires a differentiated institutional framework, what are the needs to modify banking regulations? To embrace mechanisms that become available from new types of financial institutions (i) integration cum liberalisation of banking regulation and (ii) regulatory segmentation and competition between different classes of financial institutions may appear as sensible approaches.

Since the creation of European mortgage specialists in the mid-19th century, regulatory segmentation of housing finance including separation from commercial banks was common practice until the 1980s. Most specialised mortgage finance institutions were the only financial institutions mandated to provide long-term finance and accessed capital markets under specific conditions through long-term deposits or bonds.

Since the 1970s deregulation, demutualisation and the entry of non-specialist financial institutions have pushed many specialised mortgage institutions either out of

4 See Porteous, D. 2006. "Banking and the Last Mile". Presentation at the World Bank Global Conference on Access to Finance, May 30–31, Washington, D. C.

the market or under the umbrella of commercial banks. Still, important institutions remain in housing finance, for example, German Bausparkassen that offer the tightly regulated Bauspar contract and British building societies.

In the U. S., the gigantic housing finance institutions Fannie Mae and Freddie Mac act as specialised capital market guarantors operating individually under separate charters and were collectively called 'government-sponsored enterprises' (GSE). With the collapse of the subprime market in the U. S. and the heavy losses, these GSE's are de-facto government-owned since October 2008. Both GSEs benefitted from advantages and suffered constraints compared with mortgage charters in the banking sector. For example, both GSEs were able to (i) sell their securities to U. S. investors without the corporate counterparty exposure constraints, (ii) obtain secure access to large U. S. Treasury credit lines. This regulatory support has pushed the U. S. GSEs' enormous growth, and ultimately has contributed to their failure. On the other hand, subsidies of this kind have supported mortgage lending to the U. S. middle-class credit in the form of 30-year fixed-rate mortgages as a very safe product compared to adjustable-rate mortgages routinely offered by commercial banks.

The special mortgage charter of the Bausparkassen in contrast represents very stable institutions that have rarely ran into crisis. The Bauspakassen operate independently from capital market conditions offering fixed interest rate loans, too, but suffer severe regulatory lending conditions and funding constraints that conflict with the objective of providing reasonable funding access to low-income households. A recent trend is to replace special charter regulations with special loan or funding product regulations, or treat special mortgage charter institutions more like universal banks.

Of the **neighbourhood banks, savings and postal banks** are often subjected to special banking charters operating under an explicit 'social contract' with governments. For example, savings banks in Europe are generally subject to regulated social mandates in exchange for subsidies, such as lower return on equity requirements or implicit guarantees provided by their public owners. Savings and postal banks are also more exposed to regulatory constraints in mortgage finance due to stability concerns. For example, severe constraints were imposed on U. S. savings and loans institutions in the 1990s due to their lack of long-term funding. The efficiency of such dual regulation is therefore questionable.

Another important special charter for low-income mortgage finance is **bond-issuing finance companies,** who primarily issue public debt under securities and exchange regulations. Falling outside the ambit of banking regulation that focus on protecting depositors, finance companies' operations are much less tightly regulated and in turn more scrutinised by their investors and rating agencies. In this way, Sofols, Spanish mortgage finance companies, U. S. finance companies and Indian housing finance companies have been able to focus on low-income housing markets and were able to contribute in breaking the price and distribution cartels of banks.

However, the 1998 crisis of Long Term Capital Management (LTCM) in the U. S. has raised concerns over the stability of the finance company bond-issuance model.[5] The LTCM collapse has prompted bank regulators to seek greater oversight and interventional jurisdiction over finance companies by bringing them under the banking charter.[6] The disastrous collapse of the originate and trade model, where finance companies in the U. S. subprime mortgage market crisis entirely depended on lifeline loans of investment banks, has recently further accelerated calls for tighter regulation. At least, the originators will have to have greater 'skin in the game' by permanently holding minimum parts of the securitised assets and legal responsibility for defaulted loans, which requires permanent funding at substantial capital cost. While the split between finance company and bank charter is unlikely to be removed altogether in the U. S., as for example in Germany under the Banking Act 'Kreditwesengesetz', the discussion on better regulation of these entities is still open. Clearly, the recent financial crisis has shattered the belief in good market ethics and practice and the ability of self regulation of markets and raised the concern over financial stability and the call for tighter regulation. The painful lessons in advanced economies may be of use when designing appropriate housing finance policies and regulation in emerging markets.

Charter Competition in Emerging Markets

As in developed markets, the picture in emerging markets is mixed, however for different reasons. For example, Mexico's government and banking regulator CNBV reacted to the funding crisis of their Sofol finance companies in 2010 similar to the German approach by passing a law to bring them under the banking act. Going in a different direction, Egypt in 2009 created a single regulator under the Financial Services Authority to keep non-bank financial institution and especially finance company regulations in separate charter from banking regulation.

As for the **regulation of microfinance institutions,** Meagher et al.[7] compare the framework in seven developing countries.[8] They find examples of both banking charter differentiation and special non-bank charters. As an example of the former, banking charters in the Philippines were in 1993 divided into commercial banks, savings banks (thrifts), rural banks and rural co-operative banks. Regulations are

---

[5] Even more problematic was the 'create and trade' model, where finance companies acted as undercapitalised fee originators supported with credit lines by investment banks. This widely used model has disappeared with the collapse of the U. S. subprime market.

[6] The EU Banking Codification Directive 2000, amended in 2006, defines those finance companies as banks, that fund themselves through permanent issuance of public debt.

[7] See Meagher, P., P. Campos, R. Christen, K. Druschel, G. Gallardo and S. Martowijoyo. 2006. "Microfinance Regulation in Seven Countries: A Comparative Study". Study commissioned by the IRIS center, University of Maryland.

[8] For a comprehensive overview of regulations in developing and emerging markets compiled from the perspective of, but not limited to, microfinance see http://www.microfinanceregulationcenter.org.

differentiated for capital requirements, loan loss provisions) and fixed costs reduced for neighbourhood banks (reduced minimum capital requirements, accounting and auditing costs) to meet the specific constraints of low-income household and micro and small business lending. However, limitations of services offered and certain stricter risk management requirements are the price to be paid. Indonesia follows a similar approach.

In Latin America, MFIs are largely regulated through special non-bank charters. In 1995, Bolivia brought no deposit taking MFIs and local lenders under the non-bank charter of 'private financial funds'. These entities benefitted from lower minimum capital (1/9th of the level of commercial banks) but were subjected to stricter risk exposure limits, such as a leverage ratio of only 10. Savings co-operatives were accepted in three different capital brackets. Minimum capital levels go as low as USD 200,000 for very low leverage limits. As a concession to access, concentration limits for the new lenders were relaxed to support local lending. However, general regulation and consumer protection rules as well as supervision remained broadly the same as for commercial banks.[9]

Another trend in emerging markets is to allow bank distribution networks to leapfrog traditional growth by accepting non-banks, and in this way indirectly extending regulatory coverage to non-banks. Since 1999, Brazil allows banks to co-operate with correspondents in areas with thin bank branch networks and such correspondents may include non-banks since 2003. Since 2006 India has allowed banks to appoint microfinance institutions and post offices as correspondents licensed to take small deposits and loans.[10]

End of Charter Competition via Regulatory Convergence?

The regulatory arbitrage opportunities arising from the extremes of strictly regulated special financial institutions and almost unregulated finance company charters culminated in the U. S. subprime crisis. While charter competition in emerging markets may not necessarily end up in financial crisis, the negative experience calls for a careful consideration of the opportunities and trade-offs between safety, competition and access to finance. The two strategies of (i) measured scaling-down and differentiation of bank regulation and (ii) upgrading of non-bank charters subjecting it to tighter banking regulation should lead to similar results.

On the safety side, stricter regulated institutions will have access to deposits and central bank safety-net operations that non-regulated entities will either not receive, or only under unpredictable ad-hoc emergency measures. With regard to competition and access, regulations need to accommodate sustainable business models targeted to the low-income households. Good examples for this approach can be found in the innovative regulation framework for microfinance.

---

9 The Interamerican Development Bank is currently supporting the expansion of the Bolivian experience in a project on Regulation and Supervision of the Andean Financial Co-operatives.

10 See Porteous (2006).

Going forward, regulatory convergence will also be brought about indirectly. The British Financial Services Authority (FSA) model of regulated mortgage contracts uses a special product focus rather than a special charter focus.[11] This approach binds *any* loan originator and servicer, including brokers and correspondents which in most markets are not regulated, to financial and consumer protection regulations.

The extent to which emerging mortgage markets should sustain special secondary mortgage market institutions, banks or finance companies, operating under special charters, is an open question. Those institutions have come under tremendous pressure in developed markets as a result of the crisis. Their benefits are obvious: (i) allowing greater focus on the mortgage sector's comprehensive underwriting and monitoring needs, (ii) selling long-term funds to investors, and (iii) supporting the maturity matching of primary banks and non-banks, and thereby protecting their solvency. However, the vulnerabilities of this model are also obvious: (i) principal reliance on capital markets, (ii) exposure to cyclical insolvency risk as the hedging with the profits of other business lines is absent. This calls for a public role in building those entities and a permanent role of bank or non-bank groups in sustaining them. Issuing long-term funding instruments, e. g. covered bonds, in primary banks and non-banks without such specialised institutions is an option that carries significant reputation risks. Restricting the issuance of long-term instruments to sound institutions and enhancing the level of expertise in the mortgage sector could be good reasons to continue with charter discrimination.

Product Regulation

Protection Against Macroeconomic Risk

Macroeconomic stability in most emerging markets has significantly improved since the high inflation of the 1970s and 1980s. Figure 3, however, shows that it is not at all unlikely that macroeconomic shocks generate significant interest rate

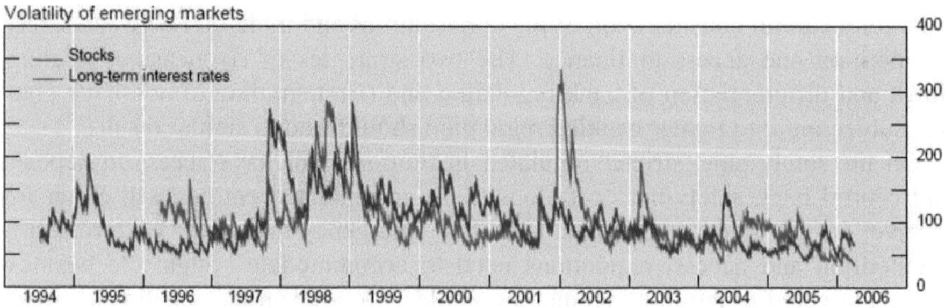

Fig. 3. Daily volatility of long-term interest rates and stocks in emerging markets (in %)
Source: BIS (2006), graph A2.6

[11] After the subprime debacle, the model is likely to be copied in the U. S., which had suffered from extreme regulatory fragmentation through multiple competing charters.

volatility and high inflation in the future. When regulating mortgage products, governments should strike a balance between concerns about consumer vulnerability, future interest rate shocks and affordability of mortgage products.

The Cost of Interest Rate Volatility Risk Protection for Mortgage Borrowers

Financial regulation frequently aims at minimising loan default risk. This may lead to favour high interest rate risk protection by promoting or requiring fixed-rate lending without consideration of associated costs for consumers. The U. S. housing finance market is a prominent example of a regulatory bias in favour of fixed-rate lending through the restrictive purchase policies of Fannie Mae and Freddie Mac. These policies have been adopted by some emerging markets such as the Philippines. Also, emerging markets dominated by national housing banks have tended to develop a fixed rate bias. In addition, many Islamic countries interpret fixed rates of return ('interest' is not permitted) for the financier under the typical fixed installment leasing contracts as a religious requirement, indirectly serving consumer protection purposes.

In volatile market rate environments, these policies may create severe maturity mismatch for lenders. For example, in Iran, which together with Libya has the strictest Islamic finance regulations, only fixed rate of return housing finance contracts are permitted. This contrasts with de-jure variable deposit rates, and similarly variable remaining funding base. The results are high risk spreads. Also, at rate of return levels of between 15% and 25% caused by high inflation risk levels, the high forward risk premiums embedded in fixed-rate contacts may be unaffordable to households.

Even developed markets bear a regulatory bias in favour of fixed rate loan contracts, often with severe consequences, as the example of the U. S. shows. The internal regulations of Fannie Mae and Freddie Mac, offer only a single product, which is also the most expensive – pre-payable 30-year fixed-rate mortgages. U. S. housing prices and the costs of mortgages had increased during the late phase of the house price boom between 2005 and 2007, leading to an explosion of mortgages. The new products such as adjustable-rate, frequently uncapped, zero or negative amortisation mortgages have produced the highest default rates when interest rates increased and house prices collapsed. A more affordable product than the 30-year fixed-to-maturity product would have been a fixed-to-term product, for 5 or 10 years, as practiced for example in Germany and Canada.

Amortization and Affordability – Standard vs. Inflation Adjustment

Amortisation standards are crucial, affecting mortgage affordability during macroeconomic instability. At interest rates exceeding 10%, loans that nominally amortise from the beginning may result in initial debt-service-to-income coverage ratios (DSC) that exceed tolerable levels. For example, in Iran, initial DSC ratios produced by the aforementioned interest rate levels of 15–25% p. a. may be as high as 50%, while the standard in developed markets lies at around 30–35%.

In high inflation economies, zero or even negative amortisation may lead to a time profile of the loan balance that better matches house price development and lower initial debt service is the main strategy used to mitigate the default risk under this product. Negative amortisation means the capitalisation of principal and even interest into the balance of the loan for later amortisation, following some defined payment deferral mechanism. An alternative is the use of loans denominated in foreign currency. The expected devaluation of the currency is an implicit mechanism to create negative amortisation of the loan balance in local currency.

Both types of **negative amortisation** strategies expose the borrower to mismatch between actual and anticipated house prices inflation and general actual and anticipated inflation or currency depreciation. Many emerging markets therefore apply regulatory barriers against such instruments, rather than trying to regulate such risks. Examples include prohibition or limits against foreign exchange denominated lending, especially after the most recent crisis in particular in Central and Eastern Europe (Ukraine, Hungary, Poland), bans on negative amortisation, as in many Islamic countries. For instance, Hungary has introduced in 2010 an LTV limit for Euro loans of 60% and for Swiss Franc loans of 45%, while Hungarian Forint loans remain unaffordable. As a result, the market for new mortgages has collapsed.

In contrast, many Latin American financial systems have learned to live with high interest rates and regulations have been adjusted to permit negative amortisation in a controlled fashion. The most popular product used in Chile and Colombia is price-level adjusted mortgages, which capitalise the inflation component of the interest rate into the balance of the loan and charge a real interest rate over that balance.[12] In fact, regulation in Latin America may have gone to the extreme in favour of negative amortisation. After a long phase of declining inflation, the Mexican agency Infonavit was permitted in 2009 to issue fixed-rate Peso loans.

Striking the Balance of Affordability and Risk Protection for Low-Income Borrowers

For low-income borrowers, more affordable products are a double-edged sword that requires adequate risk protection. Examples are protection against devaluation in the case of foreign exchange loans, or protection against real income risk in price-level adjusted mortgages that arises if prices rise faster than incomes, or protection against roll-over risk when rates are fixed for only 5 or 10 instead of 30 years. The key principle here is that borrowers should not bear the full downside risk of a shock. One approach increasingly adopted in the U. S., which is experiencing a

[12] Of lesser importance, but still relevant, are 'dual-indexed' mortgages. These let the loan balance grow with the price index while linking installments payable to a wage or other index that more closely matches affordability. While minimising affordability risk to the borrower, such products impose risks for the lender that full amortisation will not be achieved within the scheduled maturity. The mechanism has been abused politically. In Brazil a significant portion of public debt (about 10% of GDP) was created by the remaining principal outstanding at the maturity of such loans, which had to be financed by government.

surge of negative amortisation products, is to limit the maximum outstanding loan amount in local currency. A typical downside level in loan contracts in the U. S. is 20%.[13] With high house price inflation, higher levels could be acceptable.[14]

Limiting negative amortisation or interest rate shocks through caps ex ante may be a risky strategy for some lenders, but it should be preferable to the alternative of court interventions in favour of consumers after a shock occurs, let alone a default crisis. In Colombia in 1999, for instance, the mismatch between the price index used in mortgage lending and the house price index became so large that the Supreme Court required an ex post re-indexation of the entire mortgage portfolio of the

Box 2: Reforming Housing Finance Products in Turkey

The 2001 macroeconomic crisis in Turkey led to extreme interest rate surges and default levels of housing loans, many of which were adjustable-rate. After the crisis, the government decided to abolish adjustable-rate loans altogether and to permit only fixed-rate lending.

In the wake of this decision, the limited product range posed problems for both lenders and consumers. Lenders that lacked access to long-term fixed-rate funding in Turkish Lira either incurred large interest rate mismatches or had to resort to swapped EUR or USD funding, which made them dependent on foreign counterparties. Due to the funding risks involved, maturities shortened to 5–8 years. The additional amortisation burden cumulated with interest rates in the range of 15–20% into payment rates that made housing loans unaffordable.

At the same time, Turkish borrowers, remembering a 30% devaluation of the Turkish Lira in 2001, were loath to take loans in foreign currencies – a strategy to address affordability that is widely used in other emerging markets.

As interest rates declined in 2004 and 2005, the government began reforming housing finance, liberalising mortgage products, while introducing new consumer protection and foreclosure legislation. The new housing finance law allows adjustable-rate loans. However, the rate adjustments have to be linked to an official index and an interest rate cap is required for the three initial years of the loan. The cap levels relative to interest rates are not legally defined to limit the additional costs of the regulation. Yet, they must be advertised with the rate and are monitored by the central bank, which can intervene if the spreads between rates and caps become too wide. The market boomed since the introduction of the Law, supported by declining interest rates.

13 A problem with these loans in the U. S. has been that a 20% negative amortisation becomes a large number in a falling house price environment, which speaks for adjusting the ceilings depending on *realistic long-term* house price appreciation assumptions.

14 Any risk protection approach should include advanced risk disclosure techniques to consumers, such as asking foreign exchange lenders to add the swap rate that reflects expected currency devaluation to the interest quote. Enhanced disclosure is often difficult to communicate to consumers, though, and generally fails to protect against downside risk.

country, imposing significant losses on lenders. Turkey offers an attempt to strike a balance between affordability and consumer protection when liberalising mortgage products.

A complete absence of protection through fixed-rate mortgages is often as bad as lacking affordability. This is an issue in many emerging markets, including the British Commonwealth and China. Here, housing finance often relies on building societies funded by short-term deposits while only gradually introducing fixed-rate mortgages. Lower capital requirements for lower default risk, such as fixed-rate loans or adjustable-rate loans with caps may help create a mortgage market.[15]

Consumer Protection

Affordability and Access vs. Usury Rules – An Antagonistic Debate

There are two major conflicting concepts in consumer protection: the Rawlsian, which considers the least lucky individual's outcome to be the social outcome, and the Benthamite, which assesses the social outcome as the sum of individual utilities where a particular individual's outcome carries less weight. Jeremy Bentham's *"In Defence of Usury"*, written in 1789 in a social situation comparable to many emerging markets today, pushes his argument to the limit.[16]

Both concepts characterise extremes: but the question of what *are* usurious interest rate levels that might hurt the unlucky few is at the heart of the debate on low-income housing finance. The main purpose of usury law would be to limit default risk arising in a self-fulfilling fashion from high interest rate levels. The U. S. subprime mortgage market that arose after the removal of state usury ceilings has historically shown both significantly higher interest rate and foreclosure levels than in the U. S. prime mortgage market and has recently highlighted its instability in the ongoing crisis.[17] However, the subprime market has undoubtedly created access to mortgage finance for many previously underserved groups, such as immigrants. High defaults of subprime borrowers triggered the renewed emphasis on tighter regulation, although a reintroduction of usury rules appears unlikely.[18]

---

[15] Many housing finance systems also change the composition of adjustable/fixed-rate mortgage products with cyclical changes in the yield curve.

[16] As a rule of thumb, the Benthamite school, most popular in Anglo-Saxon countries, focuses consumer protection on information and transparency, while the Rawlsian school, prevalent in Continental and Eastern Europe and most emerging markets, stresses comprehensive consumer protection by limiting risk exposure in products and practices.

[17] The ongoing U. S. subprime crisis that originated in 2007 was preceded by an earlier collapse in the late 1990s. In contrast to public housing finance, which was almost entirely at fixed rates, the private subprime mortgage lending in the 2000s was largely made in risky adjustable-rate products, often introduced by low teaser interest rates that prompted high defaults once rates were adjusted upwards to the fully indexed and amortising levels. Also defaults increased reflecting widespread fraud violating prudent underwriting principles by overstating borrower income and house price values.

[18] See Saunders and Cohen (2004).

Taking the Benthamite position of *"the greatest good for the greatest number"* with its bias against comprehensive consumer protection, it seems that ethics and transparency standards, as well as financial education, form an acceptable minimum standard of consumer protection. In emerging markets, such a minimum

Box 3: Limiting Microfinance Outreach Through Usury Rules

Usury limits are challenging for MFIs, who offer rates between moderate commercial bank rates and high money lender rates. Because of high loan transaction costs for micro-size loans, lenders cannot get close to effective interest rates offered by commercial banks for much larger loan sizes.

For instance, annual effective interest rates charged by MFIs in the Philippines in 2003 exceeded those of commercial banks by 31–55% (Source: Helms & Reille 2003). Research published in World Development Indicators 2003 highlights the extent that interest ceilings undermine outreach of microfinance. In a sample of 23 countries, market penetration in countries with interest rate ceilings was only a fourth of the penetration in countries without ceilings. Table 3 summarises the type of interest rate ceilings. Mortgage finance often falls under special regulation that is excluded from such ceilings. However microfinance indicates the general approach adopted towards consumer protection.

Microfinance advocates favour lifting interest rate ceilings and focusing consumer protection on better disclosure and financial education. As an example, Campion, Kiran Ekkan and Wenner (2010) suggest that usury ceilings reduce the outreach to low income clients, especially women, as MFIs with a high proportion of women clients tend to charge higher interest rates. They ascribe this to women taking smaller loans, reflecting high management cost per loan. Table 3 shows that some emerging markets have exempted microfinance from their usury rules. But it is crucial for policymakers to establish an empirical link between levels of loan default and interest rates, and how MFIs can improve cost effectiveness without compromising client outreach.

Table 3. Emerging markets – interest rate ceilings and treatment of Microfinance

Interest rate controls		Usury limits		De facto controls
Algeria	Paraguay	Armenia	Honduras[a]	Brazil
Bahamas	Syria	Bolivia	Indian States	China
China	Tunisia[a]	Brazil[a]	Nicaragua[c]	Ethiopia
Libya	UEAC[b]	Chile	South Africa[b]	India
Morocco[a]	UMOA[a]	Colombia[b]	Uruguay	Laos
Myanmar		Ecuador[b]	Venezuela[c]	Pakistan
		Guatemala		Vietnam

Notes: [a] A separate regulation on interest rate ceilings exists for the microfinance sector.
[b] MFIs are excluded from interest rate ceilings, or authorised to charge additional fees.
[c] Ceilings apply only to institutions and individuals not regulated by banking authorities.

standard does not exist, leading to frequent court intervention that undermines the functioning of mortgage markets.

Ethics, Transparency and Financial Education – A Minimum Standard in the Lender-Consumer Relation

Ethics standards are often a first step in a completely unregulated environment impaired by conflict and scandals. The Russian Banking Association decided in 2006 to establish a Code of Ethics following Irish and to some extent U. K. examples. Standards include rules against conflict of interest (for example economic ties with developers), consumer information and most importantly internal complaints processes. This is followed by establishing formal transparency standards that enhance loan underwriting by requiring full and systematic information to consumers prior to signing a loan, separation of general advertisements and specific loan offers[19] and definition of standard contracts for loans.

Box 4: Consumer Protection for Mortgage Borrowers in Mexico

In 2002, Mexico introduced a law on minimum consumer protection for mortgage finance, focusing on pre-contract information exchange. Disclosure rules require comprehensive information of the total cost of credit and a list of documents providing minimum pre-contract information. Loan offers must be binding for a minimum of 20 days. Property appraisal standards are aligned with the requirement for public licensing of appraisers and minimum contents of contracts are determined. The Federal housing finance agency, SHF, is mandated to enhance transparency by providing regular market-comparative loan offer information to consumers.

As expected in an economy with a history of high inflation, the material consumer protection elements of the law concentrate on rules for interest rate adjustment. Variable rate contracts must follow a public reference rate. Spreads over the reference rate may vary only within contractually determined limits. Prepayment of fixed-rate loans is generally not cost-free. The Central Bank and the Federal Ministry of the Economy may jointly determine limits for conditions and fees payable for prepayments. Prepayment charges for variable rate loans, however, are limited by law to 1%. There is no usury ceiling for interest rates.

Source: World Bank Housing Finance Strategy, Chiquier and Lea (eds) (2009).

A lever to gain the acceptance of lenders for minimum standards of consumer protection is the insight that greater transparency and education not only help consumers but also promote fairness in competition among lenders. An example is the use

[19] For example, the standard information sheet adopted by most European mortgage lenders.

of effective interest rates in public advertisements and pre-contract communication, as opposed to nominal interest rates which invite abuse.[20] Effective rates consolidate any costs imposed on the consumer by the lender into a single interest rate reflecting the true cost of credit. Costs of third parties such as insurers may also be included.[21]

Lender Conflict of Interest with Third Parties

Ethics and transparency standards should cover also conflicts of interest arising from third party relations of the lender that could hurt borrowers. Examples are lender-developer and lender-insurer relations. For example, many borrowers finance property development with a direct project risk exposure through bank loans before project completion. To address this risk, legislation may require that deficiencies in the purchase contract – for example a building not being properly completed by the developer – translate into a deficiency in the loan contract between the consumer and the bank.

Some emerging markets took rather extreme legal positions. In Turkey, the lender is liable for building deficiencies for 5 years after completion, while Ukraine's legislation favours lenders by explicitly eliminating such liability.[22]

Addressing Consumer Heterogeneity

The heterogeneity of consumers is another issue to be addressed in low-income housing finance in emerging markets. The importance of investing in empowerment mechanisms for vulnerable groups, e.g. the financially less astute and educated, the elderly, or minorities is becoming widely accepted. Mechanisms include better financial education, access to advice and mediation and redress. Even in developed markets, many borrowers are unaware of the fundamental parameters of their loans, such as interest rate or repayment schedules. Studies in emerging markets point to deficient financial literacy, especially in rural areas, but financial literacy programmes have yet to prove their effectiveness in the long-run.

Access to credible and low-cost mediation and redress mechanisms, such as financial ombudsmen or consumer advocacy groups may be more immediately relevant. In South Africa, for instance, the microfinance lender association runs a successful consumer complaint hotline.[23] Ombudsmanship schemes are becoming increasingly popular in Central and Eastern European mortgage markets and independent advice, for example by consumer advocacy groups, is equally important.

---

[20] The U. S. first introduced the concept in the 1964 Truth in Lending Act. The effective rate is called the annual percentage rate of charge.

[21] In mortgage finance, caution is needed in defining effective rates. For example, loans are rarely held by the borrower until contractual maturity. Assuming contractual rather than empirical maturity may distort the effective rate computation. Empirical maturity is generally shorter than contractual maturity due to loan prepayments.

[22] Explicit builder warranty would resolve the issue by guarantees to consumers, assign cost to the risk, temper legal interventionism and reduce risk for lenders.

[23] See the discussion in Helms and Reille (2004).

Information Technology, Risk Modelling – New Perspectives on Credit Risk

Collateral – The Bricks and Mortar Workhorse …

The legal **ability to pledge collateral** to a creditor is central in achieving the dual goals of greater down-market penetration and low interest and default levels. The first institutionalised low-income lending business in European history, founded in 1452 in Perugia, Italy, used collateralised lending to break the practice of charging high interest rates to the poor, which was deemed usurious by its sponsor – the Catholic Church. Numerous similarly structured institutions followed, from pawnbrokers to modern cooperative mortgage lenders. De Soto's influential book, *The Other Path* (1990),[24] identified the mobilisation of properly titled real estate collateral as a key empowerment strategy for the poor and moved it from the fringe into the centre of the development debate.[25]

Several preconditions required to achieve the desired credit enhancement are discussed below. One conclusion is straightforward: mortgage lending cannot be limited to narrow construction and housing finance purposes if the broader goal of empowerment is to be pursued. Yet, financial regulation in many emerging markets limits the use of mortgages to the acquisition or construction of a home. Mortgages may be more widely used as multi-purpose credit enhancement for investments in income generation, old age retirement equity withdrawal and housing. This would require a wider definition of admissible purposes. There are also limits to this argument; over-indebtedness of households through high levels of home equity credit and excessive use of credit for consumption must be avoided.

… Relies on an Effective Judiciary

The most important condition for mortgages to function as effective credit enhancement is a functioning legal system, consisting of workable laws and regulations and low cost enforcement. Figure 4 shows the close relationship between contract enforcement and credit to the private sector.

Laeven and Majnoni[26] estimate that judicial efficiency, in addition to inflation, is the main driver of reducing interest rate spreads and the cost of borrowing. An improvement of property rights protection in emerging markets to a level of G10 countries would "achieve a reduction of banks' lending spread, net of inflation, of about 2.0 to 2.5 percentage points." Consequently, mortgage development programmes in emerging markets have focused on improving property rights through land title provision, property and mortgage registration, and execution of collateral.

---

24 See de Soto, H. 1989. "The Other Path: The Invisible Revolution in the Third World", Harper and Row. New York.

25 See The Economist (2006c) discussing case studies from Argentina and Peru that question the sufficiency of land titling for access to housing and finance.

26 See Laeven, L. and G. Majnoni. 2003. "Does Judicial Efficiency Lower the Costs of Credit?" World Bank Policy Research Working Paper 3159, October. Washington, D. C.

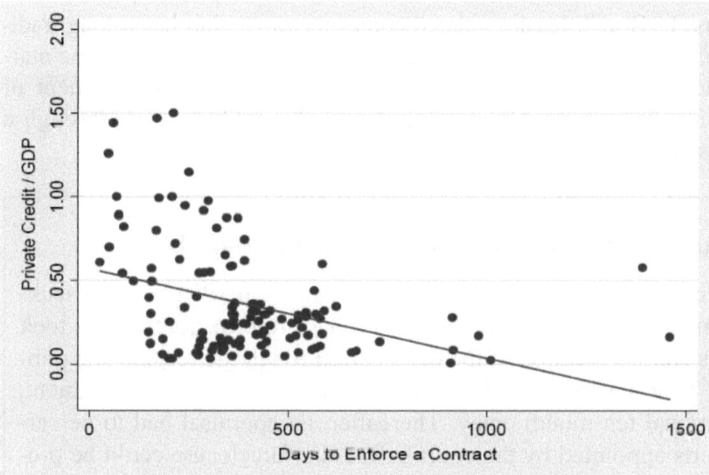

Fig. 4. Contract enforcement time and private credit to GDP
Source: Beck (2006).

Of the complexities arising in the creation of credible real estate property rights, the cost of collateral enforcement is probably the most important issue for lenders and consumer protection groups alike. Strategies here have focused on standard foreclosure reform, but also widened towards issues of particular relevance for emerging markets. Egypt's ongoing mortgage reforms,[27] for example, not only focus on improving the law governing the eviction of defaulting mortgage borrowers but also provide for training of judges to secure proper implementation.

Also low-cost non-judicial enforcement of collateral and/or the limitation of appeals options for consumers have become areas of reform. Rather than limiting appeals legally, their financial costs can be made explicit, discouraging frivolous appeals that only delay the process. In India, for instance, according to Butler (2003), "a debtor who disputes any action of the creditor pursuant to the law has 45 days in which to lodge an appeal with the Debts Recovery Tribunal. A condition of appeal may be that the debtor posts an appeal bond with the tribunal of 75% of the creditor's claim, unless a lower amount is set by the Tribunal."

While such limitations may appear unfavourable for consumers at first sight, alternative mechanisms are far less favourable for consumers. For example property leasing is so widespread in emerging markets that it dominates retail finance in places as Brazil, Egypt and Russia. Butler[28] describes consumer protection in Russia, where courts forced creditors to write leasing contracts in similar content to

---

[27] Sponsored by USAID.

[28] See Butler, S. 2003. "Enforcement of Mortgage Rights in Housing Finance."Paper presented at the conference on Housing Finance in Emerging Markets: Policy and Regulatory Challenges, World Bank, Washington, D. C., March 10–13.

mortgage contracts. In Brazil, leasing-related consumer protection has a long tradition and is even more elaborated than mortgage consumer protection. In some markets such as Chile, leasing has had particular relevance for the development of low-income housing finance since it did not require the creditor to go through a foreclosure process in case of a default.

Box 5: Introducing Extrajudicial Foreclosure in Colombia

After the 1999 crisis, Colombia embarked on mortgage market reforms tackling the problem of long foreclosure delays. Prior to reform, foreclosure took up to three years and notification of the defendant through the responsible public office could take a year. The defendant could then appeal the judgment, causing an additional ten month delay. Thereafter, an appraisal had to be carried out by experts appointed by the court before the foreclosure could be processed by the court, causing an additional year of delay.

The reform streamlined the foreclosure process to less than a year: notification of the defendant could be by certified mail sent by the lender, appeal to the sentence was eliminated, and the lender could present an asset appraisal equivalent to either the open market value or the value set by the local tax authorities. Foreclosure is now carried out by a commissioner mostly through auctions in the Chamber of Commerce. Courts are still used, but less frequently.

Source: Cadenas (2006).

There Are Many Reasons Why the Workhorse May Stumble

Starting with the worst case of **credit default**: pre-foreclosure techniques such as free-handed ('short') sales or debt workouts may be favourable for consumers and lenders alike. This is especially relevant in emerging markets, where even under normal market circumstances bricks-and-mortar forced sale often lead to erratic recovery values and losses. In crises, massive sales of foreclosed housing may exacerbate the decline, as in Mexico following the Tequila crisis in 1995. Developed markets, such as the U. S. and Spain rely on short sales and debt modifications to avoid foreclosure and run public support programmes for low-income borrowers.

Many developed markets' laws require that prior to foreclosure the lender must demand the debtor to cure his default in a reasonable period. In France's Rawlsian juridiction, this procedure is a prerequisite for allowing the lender to demand acceleration of the loan repayment. But also in Benthamite jurisdictions, pre-foreclosure has been recognised in the default management of the U. S. public insurer FHA, or British mortgage industry practice.

Turning to loan underwriting: **appraisal standards** often generate a bias against low-income households, such as the costs of mandatory external appraisal as in Poland. Often, collateral that is readily available cannot legally be used to support mortgage lending. The possibility of financing progressive housing construction, the standard approach in underdeveloped financial markets associated with low access to finance and high costs of finance, is particularly adversely affected by rigid definitions. Even in developed markets, appraisal standards differ. It is common for a German bank to finance a progressively built home in instalments disbursed after checking construction progress, usually with a mortgage on the land. Such lending has become less common in commoditised mortgage markets in the U. S. or the U. K., and there is little reason to exclude the financing of progressive housing construction from the menu of options.

Financing progressive housing can be delicate, however, if the builder-lender relationship is distorted through high housing prices and strong developer lobbies, like those existing in Istanbul, Cairo or Kiev. Here, developers offer consumers unfinished apartments to be completed with consumer loans that are rarely secured by mortgages. Developers and banks are frequently jointly owned, raising consumer protection concerns over conflict of interest to the detriment of borrowers.

Even more problematic are **valuation techniques** that rely exclusively on open market price observations. In a market with cartel-like developer market structures, as in Kiev, estimated developer margins lie between 50% and 70%. Hence, open market valuations reflect high profit ratios of cartels and not scarcity of land and construction. Appraisers' fees that are based on the price of the house establish a conflict of interest against the buyer. Appraisal rules that focus on construction or replacement costs, as practised by the Sociedad Hipotecaria Federal in Mexico, seem to be a reasonable alternative. Such an approach can also be applied to progressive housing construction.

Regulations that rely heavily on collateral value to determine loan limits must be regarded with scepticism, especially in the low-income market. Loan-to-value limits focus on the expected recovery ratio in case of a default, while neglecting the drivers of the probability of default.

Also **rigid loan-to-value** (LTV) rules do not work in the high interest rate environments. For example, a 70% LTV ratio may imply a 30% initial debt-service coverage (DSC) ratio in a low-interest (and inflation) rate environment and a close-to-default 50% initial DSC ratio in a high interest (and inflation) rate environment. In addition LTVs must be adjusted to accommodate payment shock risks, where a loan with negative amortisation or potential repricing risk (such as a foreign currency and or variable interest rate loan) should have lower LTVs than an amortising mortgage issued in local currency with interest rates fixed to maturity.[29] In 2010, Hungary introduced legislation that differentiates LTV by currency of the loan – Swiss Franc, Euro or Forint.

Historical experience suggests that strong house price cycles appear with the sudden expansion and contraction of credit available for housing. Such cycles are exac-

---

29 This critique also applies to the 'Anglo-Saxon division' of the mortgage finance universe between lenders and insurers, which hinges on rigid LTV rules. Also problematic are the LTV rules that govern in continental Europe. For example, the Czech Republic and Hungary adopted 70% and 60% maximum LTV limits for mortgage loans.

erbated by LTVs which often produce ad hoc, pro-cyclical limitations on mortgage lending. A prominent example is Fannie Mae's 80% maximum LTV loan purchase rules that became highly restrictive once U. S. house prices collapsed in 2008/9 and made refinancing into cheaper loans impossible, despite historically low mortgage rates. Housing markets in developing countries are particularly vulnerable to the resulting credit crunch, such as in Thailand after the 1997 crisis from which recovery took almost a decade.

The Spanish regulatory approach of **dynamic provisioning** adopted in 2002 tries to counter the cyclicality of regulations by forcing lenders to accumulate reserves in good times, especially when interest rates fall rapidly and lending is booming. Such excess capital reduces the need for regulatory tightening when interest rates and defaults rise. However, such measures may not be sufficient in a large house price cycle and the proliferation of risky short-term adjustable-rate loans, which have combined to substantially degrade mortgage portfolio quality in Spain in 2010.

Prospects and Limitations to Information Technology and Risk Modelling

The emerging mortgage markets of the past two decades have ironically adopted the bricks-and-mortar approach to regulation precisely when developed markets were decisively abandoning it. These regulators had instead started to focus on a comprehensive information- and risk-based approach to the lending process, a trend that has accelerated by the mortgage market crisis in the U. S. and Europe.

The crisis constitutes a severe setback to the widening use of complex mathematical models to estimate risk with large databases. The rise of empirical techniques that trace determinants of credit losses had received recognition through their incorporation into the regulatory frameworks. These measures included Basel II for banks and Solvency II for insurance companies, as well as internal risk and pricing models of larger mortgage lenders, and to a lesser extent into default models of rating agencies. It was conceivable that mortgage-related regulation such as loan-to-value lending limits, and consumer protection such as limitation to certain products, were to be remodelled based on these empirical techniques.

In developed mortgage markets, increasingly reliable information helped to convert the unbankable into bankable borrowers. The development of subprime or non-conforming markets would have been unthinkable in the U. S. and the U. K. without such techniques.[30] Scoring models attempting to summarise the creditworthiness of borrowers in single figures was seen as a powerful tool to overcome low-income constraints that were absolute barriers to access.[31]

Many scoring and credit risk models, however, lacked empirical verification of their ability to predict default, and proved to perform poorly during the ongoing U. S. subprime and European mortgage market crisis. Errors are inherent to the models' rejection of bankable borrowers while approving non-bankable borrowers.

[30] A *different* question is, whether such markets should have grown to their actual size, which requires an analysis of alternatives such as private or public rental housing.

[31] Fannie Mae and Freddie Mac demonstrated this in numerous studies.

In addition, weak understanding and predictability of the depth and length of house price cycles, and their reinforcement through risky loan products, showed the severe underestimation of risk and limitations of the models. Strategic defaults of perceived prime borrowers resulting from negative equity increased default rates to unprecedented levels. The crisis also highlighted massive errors of adverse incentives, fraud, manipulation and abuse of borrower information that entered scoring systems.[32]

Clearly, the high reliance of loan underwriting on statistical models in advanced markets has proven to be misleading. This experience sends a strong message of caution for scoring models in information-poor and governance-poor environments, such as in some emerging markets.

Yet, empirical data collection and processing remain important, and high data consumer protection standards have a significant adverse impact on the size of a mortgage market for low-income borrowers. Many emerging markets – such as Mexico – limit credit bureau data coverage to negative default or impairment information, while positive information on successful credit or rental payment histories is essential to improve access to finance through high credit scores.

Relationship Banking Remains Key

The ongoing crisis in developed markets has highlighted the overarching importance of relationship lending as practised by local banks, savings and loan cooperatives, building societies and even microfinance institutions in information-poor environments. These neighbourhood relationships help limit fraud when data collection is outsourced to brokers. Credit histories, as well as important information about living and working conditions collected, verified and processed by the lender, has proven to be far more reliable in understanding the behaviour and financial circumstances of borrowers. In many emerging markets, these are most often the only reliable methods.

To limit the disadvantages of high per unit administrative costs and the limited outreach of this approach, relationship lending has to make effective use of client information techniques and needs to be appropriately reflected in prudential regulation of housing finance.

It is important to reflect data quality in financial regulation, requiring robust testing of empirical models or accepting the higher quality of data generated by arms-length relationship approaches.

Determinants of Default – Experience from Emerging Markets

How risky is low-income housing lending in emerging markets empirically, and what are the determinants of default? To begin with, the vulnerability of low-income households to specific shocks is higher than in the case of middle-income households, as figure 5 suggests for South Africa.

---

32 For example, brokers received higher fees for originating "more profitable" subprime loans compared to prime loans, and consequently sold many prime borrowers subprime loans.

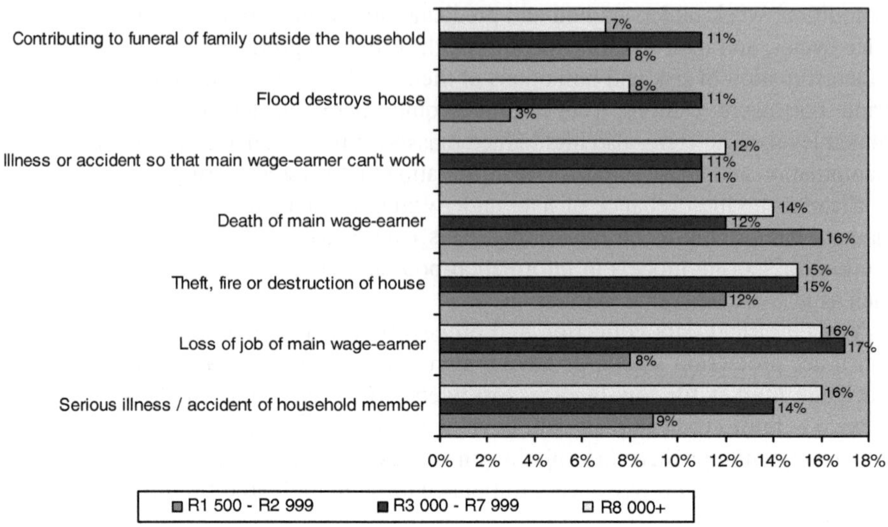

Fig. 5. Vulnerability of low-income households to various default triggers in South Africa
Source: National Housing Finance Corporation (NHFC) (2003). Note: Survey based on self-assessments.

The Importance of Decentralised Mortgage Servicing

Evidence suggests that the approach to mortgage servicing, i. e. loan administration and monitoring of borrowers, especially in an arrears situation, is critically important. For example, data from housing banks using a centralised mortgage servicing approach depict a significantly higher default risk for low-income groups than in decentralised servicing.

In the Brazilian Cartera Nova, originated after the restructuring of the housing finance system between 1993 and 1999, the housing bank Caixa's arrears of over 90 days by cohort of origination were three to five times higher than the arrears of the private savings bank system SBPE.

Similar results are found in South Africa. A study by the NHFC[33] determined that mortgage servicing deficiencies were determinants of defaults. In almost one quarter of cases, there was no immediate lender reaction after the borrower had fallen into arrears. In 2004 Fannie Mae undertook a similar review of servicing practices of South African lenders and found that institutions suffering from high defaults often had limited physical presence within their targeted communities, that few decision-makers were familiar with the target market, and that some lenders had not developed appropriate contacts for the low-income market. These

33 See study NHFC/South Africa. 2003. "Reasons for Non Payment of Mortgage Loans and Municipal Services". Discussion paper. Houghton, South Africa.

points support the relevance of a functioning, and potentially costly, relationship approach to gather sufficient information about low-income borrowers.

The importance of a workable servicing model is bolstered by recent research undertaken by Fitch for Mexican Sofols, which serve a lower-middle income market. Figure 6 shows the default drivers for Sofol RMBS pools as of September 2009, with defaults at elevated levels two years after the house price peak. The results support the typical assumptions holding for credit risk pricing in developed markets, i. e. a positive correlation of default risk with the loan-to-value ratio and negative correlation with the house price level (approximating income and thus unemployment and wage shortfall risk).

The recorded default levels are roughly twice the average level of prime mortgage pools in Mexico as approximated by bank portfolio default rates. However, they are far lower than the U. S. subprime portfolio default rates.

Delinquencies by Income Statement

Income Segment	Delinquencies 90+ Day (%)	Delinquencies 180+ Day (%)	No. of Loans in Sample
Social/Economic	11.62	6.41	39,508
Middle	8.48	4.47	23,971
Residential	7.85	4.40	4,184
Total	9.60	5.22	67,663

Note: Social/Economic is defined as property value up to MXP412,000; Middle is defined as property value form MXP412,00–MXP1.03 million; and residential is defined as property value greater than MXP1.03 million.

Delinquencies by OLTV

OLTV (%)	Delinquencies 90+ Day (%)	Delinquencies 180+ Day (%)	No. of Loans in Sample
0–59.99	3.18	1.59	5,810
60–69.99	4.53	1.86	4,687
70–79.99	5.50	2.73	7,666
>80	11.23	6.22	49,500
Total	9.60	5.22	67,663

Fig. 6. Delinquency profile of Mexican Sofol mortgage pools by income and loan-to-value ratios at September 2009

Source: Fitch (2009), based on Sofols' RMBS data. Note: OLTV = original loan-to-value ratio.

Various rating agencies have started to develop low-income housing finance default models for emerging markets such as Mexico and South Africa.[34] The availability of ratings is likely to help attract international capital to these markets, even though rating after the financial crisis will be likely of lesser relevance than before. The development of borrower databases is a central element in such methodologies: Fitch's approach to Sofols in Mexico, for instance, requires that borrowers are scored by FICO, the U. S. scoring company that has developed a service for SHF, the Mexican federal housing agency.

Regulation in the Information Society: The Future

There is vast differentiation along the lender spectrum in housing finance. While the dominance of regression banking is receding again after the financial crisis, supporting lending decisions via empirical modelling analysis will remain pivotal. The dominant approach to regulation is a 'widows and orphan's' protection approach focusing on the safety of deposits with simple rules. But this paradigm is about to disappear. Basel II's revised approach to bank regulation and also its parallel in insurance, Solvency II, address both issues by explicitly accepting empirical credit risk modeling techniques (Pillar I), by strengthening supervisory review (Pillar II), and by accepting a market assessment (Pillar III) of intermediary solvency. Basel III and other responses to the crisis will generally increase capital levels and introduce operational limitations for banks and insurance companies, but will not fundamentally alter this approach.

The change in approach has strong implications for emerging markets. First, most lenders and regulators in emerging markets will continue for some time to use the standardised approach for capital requirements, or possibly fail to implement Basel II and its successor Basel III. Yet, the mere prospect of a data-based option for credit assessments will revolutionise data collection, loan pricing and servicing standards. While lenders in emerging markets are severely challenged by foreign market entrants with better data processing capabilities, those who confront the challenge will have the chance to leap over decades of stagnation in coverage and service quality that have characterised many developed markets.

Second, the availability of data and improvements of process will keep attracting investors other than banks and others not subjected to similarly strict rules. Much depends on the response of bank regulation to the financial crisis, which will likely restrict bank consumer lending and lead (partly desirably) to higher credit costs. While highly leveraged, capital market access-based lending business models such as bond-funded low-income housing finance companies face challenging market and regulatory environments.

Alternative models backed by higher levels of equity may fill the gap. These will operate with higher costs than before, but will still command greater lending

34 See Fitch (2006) and Fitch (2003).

flexibility than banks. Also, rental housing finance, a quasi-corporate lending approach to housing finance, is likely to become more attractive to investors: rental investors de-facto operate as housing finance companies taking credit risk (non-payment of rents) and to some degree also interest rate risk. Rendering such models feasible in the long-run requires an overhaul of investment regulations for pension funds, insurers, mutual funds and other investors in housing assets, including equity. Many of these investors have been confined for liquidity risk reasons by regulation to capital market instrument investment, a costly aberration in hindsight. A long-term approach also requires a holistic approach to housing lending regulations and stricter regulation of finance companies, rental investors and other risk intermediaries to protect both investors and consumers.

Third, while it is likely that a coexistence of bank regulation and capital market control will prevail, because investor protection per se can be seen as a public good, the weights will shift towards market control. Questions about data quality and optimal models, about who sponsors rating agencies – investors or issuers – as well as to what extent bank-style credit risk intermediation ('skin in the game') is needed to further support mortgage-backed financings, will dominate the debate in both developed and emerging markets. Emerging market governments can facilitate the process by providing data and organising its collection, and by making it available for credit assessment purposes. Developed economies will hopefully support this by re-organising their markets after the crisis around 'gold standards' for mortgage-backed instruments, such as mortgage-backed securities and covered bonds.

An important issue is just getting started to be systematically and globally tackled by regulation. This issue is the vulnerability of mortgage lender solvency in the presence of market risk, such as interest rate and liquidity risk. By not covering capital charges for interest rate risk, which is an important source of solvency risk for mortgage lenders, Basel II has continued to place lenders who are funded long-term in the capital markets at a disadvantage compared to universal banks and other deposit-funded institutions.

A number of emerging markets have nevertheless reviewed experience from previous crises and changed the focus of their regulations to avoid mismatches in mortgage finance. These include Mexico after 1995 and Colombia after 1999. Also, the severe liquidity risk imposed by funding a long-term asset such as a housing loan needs to be addressed. Currently, regulations are drafted that would severely penalise liquidity risk on bank balance sheets. In that regard, with the Danish system of mortgage credit institutions, a hybrid of mortgage-backed securities and covered bonds exists, which allows banks to pass interest rate and liquidity risk to institutional investors. These are less vulnerable to both types of risk. The Danish system has made its first appearance in Mexico under the Hipotecaria Total project (see Box 1).

Finally, the same information generation and processing approaches applied to banking regulation should help to improve consumer protection rule-making. These rules are frequently still not empirically based. Once in use, databases can be pooled to calibrate relevant default incidences, e. g. for product or usury limitations. Unfortunately, pooling of data at the national or even international level is not an easy task, given a plethora of legal and institutional impediments in consumer and corporate data protection.

Box 6: New Mortgage Loan Risk Management Systems and Regulations for Colombia

After a default crisis, Law 546 of 1999 enforced a change in the Colombian system of mortgage indexation to relieve consumers. With this change, lenders came under renewed pressure due to mismatches arising from their costs of funds, prolonging the crisis.

The Colombian government reacted by creating a new capital requirement and risk management framework for mortgage finance, under which – in analogy to the Basel II approach – financial institutions were to make their own risk evaluations and determinations of provisions and risk-based capital. A new system of evaluation and administration of credit risk (SARC) was introduced. Exposure to market risk (interest rate, exchange rate, inflation, etc.) was to be addressed with a value at risk concept that would determine an additional capital requirement.

In total, capital requirements were raised to 9% of risk-weighted assets, and undercapitalised lenders were given a transition period of 3 years to reach that goal or to close or merge. For those lenders unable to develop their own internal risk models, Superfinanciera, the regulator, offered a benchmark model.

Conclusion

Throughout this chapter, three main messages are presented to financial regulators, consumer protection lawmakers and others involved in configuring the mortgage sector in emerging markets:

First, the tendency to regulate and protect commercial banks, and their resulting attitudes to low-income lending, creates adverse impacts on the costs to access mortgage finance and on cartel-style market structures in emerging markets. The regulatory response to the recent financial crisis is likely to reinforce that situation. Lending institutions that are subjected to capital market control (such as finance companies or rental housing companies), or lighter prudential regulation for MFIs should engage in direct charter competition with commercial banks.

Second, regulatory limitations in mortgage products may constitute important access barriers in emerging markets because they raise credit costs. Where lower credit costs coincide with higher default risk, e. g. due to possible payment shocks as in the case of adjustable-rate and foreign exchange lending, sufficient safeguards such as interest rate or negative amortisation (exchange rate) caps should be a firm part of prudential regulation. Some consumer protection, such as on usury ceilings and foreclosures, is a double edged sword, driving many lenders into informality, leading to even less protection for consumers.

A better approach that would benefit low-income households would reward improvements in risk protection relative to existing practices: for example, even a fast-track foreclosure law for mortgage lending often provides greater consumer protection than leasing, and a usury ceiling censoring strong deviations from an observed empirical interest rate average is better than a rigid absolute ceiling. However, well-understood consumer protection limiting high-risk practices and products and financial education are essential to ensure fair lender competition and transparency while limiting consumers' risks. These should by no means be seen as a luxury good available only in the developed world.

Third, the ability to mobilise real estate collateral remains a unique instrument for access to finance with the potential to keep interest rate levels affordable. However, the U. S. subprime crisis has shown that its importance has been overrated and partly ill-suited to emerging markets in the absence of more robust cash flow based debt service assessments of the borrower. Emerging markets are characterised by progressive housing lending, by limitation to loan-to-value ratio applicability and by problematic approaches to foreclosure.

Emerging markets and their developed country counterparts should improve bricks-and-mortar standards by embracing proven new techniques. Information opacity facing potential borrowers is perhaps the single most important access constraint in emerging markets. Based on relationship lending information, technology may offer opportunities to remedy that opacity and enhance access to mortgage finance, while technology-based underwriting should be discouraged.

Regulation and supervision in emerging markets, as much as in developed markets, can generally be improved by closer interaction with capital markets – a new approach that is already partly formalised under the Basel II framework. While the ability of a global capital market to properly underwrite and price risk must be put in doubt after the financial crisis, the case for domestic capital market development in emerging markets came out reinforced. Local markets proved highly crisis-resilient and may gradually break the cartel of universal commercial banking, supporting a combined institutional, product, collateral and information mobilisation strategy that can deepen access to mortgage finance for low-income groups.

References

Bank for International Settlements (2006a) "The Banking System in Emerging Markets: How much Progress has been Made?" BIS Papers No. 26. Basel.

Bank for International Settlements (2006b) "The Recent Behaviour of Financial Market Volatility". BIS Papers No. 29. Basel.

Beck, T. (2006) "Creating an Efficient Financial System: Challenges in a Global Economy." Paper for the G20 Seminar on Economic Growth in Pretoria, August 2005. The World Bank. Washington, D. C.

Bentham, J. (1789) "Introduction to the Principles of Morals and Legislation", Utilitarianism and Other Essays. Penguin Classics. London.

Butler, S. (2003) "Enforcement of Mortgage Rights in Housing Finance."Paper presented at the conference on Housing Finance in Emerging Markets: Policy and Regulatory Challenges, World Bank, Washington, D. C., March 10–13.

Cadenas, M. (2006) "The Regulatory Experience of Colombia after the Mortgage Crisis". Presentation at the World Bank Conference on Housing Finance in Emerging Markets, Washington, D. C., March 15–17.

Campos, M. (2006) "The Expansion and Future of Sofols in Mexico." Presentation given at the conference on Housing Finance Systems in Emerging Economies: The Role of the Specialized Housing Lenders, World Bank, Washington, D. C., March 14–15.

Chiquier, L., and M. Lea (eds.) (2009) "Housing Finance Policy in Emerging Markets". The World Bank.

de Soto, H. (1989) "The Other Path: The Invisible Revolution in the Third World". Harper and Row. New York.

Dübel, A. (2009) "Consumer Information and Protection" In: Chiquier and Lea (eds) 'Housing Finance Policy in Emerging Markets'. The World Bank.

Dübel, A. (2008) "Does Housing Finance Promote Economic and Social Development in Emerging Markets?" Study commissioned by the International Finance Corporation. Washington, D. C.

The Economist (2006c) "The Mystery of Capital Deepens". August 26th.

Fitch Ratings (2010) "Mexican RMBS Performance Update". Residential Mortgage Mexico Special Report. February.

Fitch Ratings (2009) "Mexican RMBS Performance Update". Residential Mortgage Mexico Special Report. September.

Fitch Ratings (2006) "Mexican Low-income Housing Construction Bridge Loans Methodology". International Criteria Report. April.

Fitch Ratings (2005) "Mexico Low-income Housing RMBS Methodology". International criteria report. October.

Fitch Ratings (2003) "South African Residential Default Model". Criteria Report. August.

Hassler, O. and B. Renaud (2009) "State Housing Banks". In: Chiquier and Lea (eds) 'Housing Finance Policy in Emerging Markets'. The World Bank.

Hassler, O. (2006) "Going Up Market to Serve Low-income Groups". Presentation at the World Bank Conference on Housing Finance in Emerging Markets, March 15–17, Washington, D. C.

Helms, B. and X. Reille (2004) "Interest Rate Ceilings and Microfinance". CGAP Occasional Paper No. 9. Washington, D. C.

Campion, A., Kiran Ekka, R. and M. Wenner (2010) "Interest Rates and Implications for Microfinance in Latin America and the Caribbean". IDB Working Paper Series IDB-WP-177. Washington, D. C.

Laeven, L. and G. Majnoni (2003) "Does Judicial Efficiency Lower the Costs of Credit?" World Bank Policy Research Working Paper 3159, October. Washington, D. C.

NHFC/South Africa (2003) "Reasons for Non Payment of Mortgage Loans and Municipal Services". Discussion paper. Houghton, South Africa.

Meagher, P., P. Campos, R. Christen, K. Druschel, J. Gallardo and S. Martowijoyo (2006) "Microfinance Regulation in Seven Countries: A Comparative Study". Study commissioned by the IRIS center, University of Maryland.

Peachey, S. (2006b) "The Double Bottom Line – Making Access Profitable: Evidence from Microfinance and Savings Banking". A study for the World Bank and Brookings Institution Global Conference on Access to Finance. May 30–31, Washington, D. C.

Porteous, D. (2006) "Banking and the Last Mile". Presentation at the World Bank Global Conference on Access to Finance, May 30–31, Washington, D. C.

Saunders, M. and A. Cohen (2004) "Federal Regulation of Consumer Credit – the Cause or the Cure for Predatory Lending?" Joint Center for Housing Studies, Harvard University. Working Paper Series BABC 04-21. Cambridge, MA.

CHAPTER 5

Institutions and the Promotion of Housing Finance

Hans-Joachim Dübel

Principal, Finpolconsult.de

> *"Take a method and try it. If it fails, admit it frankly and try another. But above all, try something."*

Franklin D. Roosevelt, U. S. President 1933–1945, describing the New Deal programmes

> *"To look upon these programmes as the result of a unified plan was to believe that the accumulation of stuffed snakes, baseball pictures, school flags, old tennis shoes, carpenter's tools, geometry books, and chemistry sets in a boy's bedroom could have been put there by an interior decorator."*

Raymond Moley, Advisor to Franklin D. Roosevelt

Abstract

Two messages are important in framing public support strategies for low-income housing finance: first, policymakers should avoid replicating top-down approaches from the developed world, such as public housing banks. Rather they should develop their own public-private partnership approaches as done in Mexico or Thailand and help bottom-up lenders rooted in communities or regions, to access relevant broader market data, risk management and risk transfer technology through appropriate apex or service institutions.

Second, despite low political visibility, officials should not neglect badly needed investment in the mortgage market's infrastructure and promote markets through improving price and market intelligence; financial education for consumers; and access to justice systems, modern communication, and land registers and information to consumers. Such investments promise greater social returns for low-income housing than direct lending and regulatory interventions.

D. Köhn and J.D. von Pischke (eds.), *Housing Finance in Emerging Markets: Connecting Low-Income Groups to Markets*, DOI 10.1007/978-3-540-77857-8_5,

Introduction

Privately organised financial markets have historically developed bottom-up institutions that serve low-income households in their self-interest – be it for profit or community development. Such institutions have generated more complex products over time, such as mortgage finance, and the apex and specialist bond issuer structures for their funding and risk management. As this happened in Europe and North America, such bottom-up development is now well underway in emerging markets. Examples include co-operative and savings banks, and more recently microfinance institutions.

Innovation in information and communications technology, globalisation of financial markets and new products such as securitisation have accelerated financial sector sophistication changed in emerging markets in the last two decades. Top-down market penetration has been seen as a realistic approach as banks and investors seek new profitable niches.

However the financial crisis has frustrated the hopes of a great leap over gradual improvements of housing finance and brokers, rating agencies, investment banks and uninformed investors have proven to be closely associated with the failure. Liquidity suddenly stopped and left the market in chaos. Yet, emerging and developing countries have shown greater resilience to the crisis and remain keen to accelerate financial market development. The massive failures of the private financial sector in advanced economies raises the question of the role of government in supporting and creating access to finance.

This section explores why governments have frequently intervened by developing public housing finance institutions and what key lessons have been learned. In view of this experience we discuss how appropriate public policy can be formulated to support sound development of mortgage markets. A new strategy needs to begin with the analysis of private market failure and a focus on a differentiation of both the instrument set and the intensity of public intervention, or public-private partnerships.

Public Banking and Credit Direction

Learning from Mistakes of Public Intervention

Public intervention in the institutional structure of housing finance is as old as the industry itself. Some argue that without such intervention, the industry would not exist. For instance, in France in the 1860s and the United States in the 1930s, public interventions were so strong, enabling the creation of mortgage markets. However, in light of the success of the private sector-based British building society model or the German/Scandinavian mortgage bank models, this cannot be said universally.

Emerging mortgage markets initially inherited the legal and institutional structure, including public interventionism, from more advanced countries. The French housing bank and directed credit model have been copied in Spain, the African Francophonie and Latin America. The British building society system has shaped mortgage finance around the Indian Ocean and in North America, and the German/Scandinavian corporate bond model was copied in Eastern Europe. After World War II, the American agency system of the 1930s was adopted by Western Europe and the Philippines.

Simple transplants of institutional models and laws have proven questionable. Fundamental flaws embedded in the original model are transferred, and are often magnified by the local risk environment. The main problems are:

- public sector retail lending often permanently replaced private sector lending rather than playing a subsidiary or partnership role, and
- concurrently, directed credit regulations embedded governments' excessive influence over private credit.

The emergence of the housing bank approach through Credit Foncier de France (CFF) in the 1850s can therefore not be separated from the directed credit policies of the early 19th century whereby financing of the public debt de facto eliminated private sector housing loans. Initially, France established an apex bank as a mortgage bond issuer following the German Pfandbrief model. CFF became a retail lender that dominated the French housing finance system for more than 100 years. Spain, Chile, Argentina, Uruguay and Brazil followed early on in copying this model. In a second wave a number of African and Asian countries, including Algeria, Egypt, India, Nigeria, Pakistan and Thailand, established government housing banks serving retail clients with an authoritarian planning and development approach in the 1950s and 60s. Even today, state housing banks continue to be created or revived as in Afghanistan, Congo, Gabon, Ivory Coast, Mali, Namibia, Rwanda and Senegal.[1]

The performance of public sector retail lending institutions in developing countries has generally been poor. Caprio et al.[2] stress complex governance issues arising from insufficient transparency and accountability, poor performance incentives, and inefficient management and regulation, suggesting privatisation or alternatively supervision of public lenders under the same framework applied to private lenders. This conclusion is similar for most housing banks, some of which suffered large losses that contributed to debt crises in their countries. For instance, Brazil's Caixa Economica Federal, the national mortgage bank, is estimated to have incurred public recapitalisation costs of $50 billion.[3] In 2001, Banco Hipotecario del

1 Source: Hassler and Renaud (2009) for a survey of housing banks in emerging markets.

2 Source: Caprio, G., Fiechter, J, Litan, R. and M. Pomerleano. 2004. "The Future of State owned Financial Institutions". World Bank/IMF/Brookings Emerging Market Series, Brookings Institution Press. Washington, D. C.

3 Source: Finance Ministry estimate of 2002 quoted in Caprio et al (2004), see also Alberdi and Dübel (2000) for related discussion.

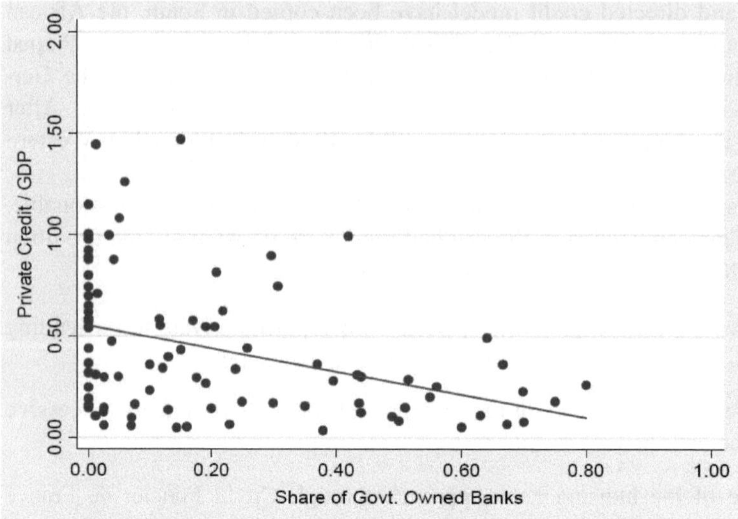

Fig. 1. Share of government-owned banks and credit to the private sector
Source: Beck (2006)

Uruguay reported a non-performing loan portfolio of 40% as well as considerable losses related to asset-liability mismatches. The bank collapsed during the Uruguayan financial crisis of 2002 and remains dormant. A recapitalisation today would require an estimated \$1.5 billion, or 93% of the loan portfolio outstanding in 2001.[4]

Apart from governance problems, an important cause of poor performance was the ill-designed attempt to conduct centralised retail lending. For example, Brazil's Caixa Economica, was created in the late 1980s from Banco Nacional de Habitação, which had operated as a second tier lender for Brazilian savings banks and local finance agencies. This step of introducing retail services reflects an erroneous policy role for Banco Nacional. Retail lending ceased during the 1980s because of government intervention in mortgage instruments (benefiting borrowers) and the adverse impact of hyperinflation, and because of a failure of retail lenders. As the government intervened, private financial institutions further withdrew from the mortgage markets, further worsening Brazil's fiscal problems and extending the crisis into the 1990s.

In contrast, the Government Housing Bank of Thailand, despite public subsidies, can be cited as an example of good performance, because it has systematically identified and addressed earlier governance and design flaws. The House Building Finance Corporation of Pakistan, another poorly performing government owned housing retail lender, was turned around in the late 1990s through the professionalisation of management and systems and the development of new prod-

[4] Source: Hassler and Renaud (2009).

ucts. Partial privatisation is being considered in enhance corporate governance. In Argentina, Banco Hipotecario Nacional was partially privatised successfully in 1999. The Mexican contractual savings agencies Infonavit and Fovisste have been modernised over the past decade and played a stabilising role during the ongoing crisis, when private issuance of debt and securitisations was severely reduced.

While we find some recent successful turnaround stories, many public lenders still lack an exit or conversion strategy when they have fulfilled or failed to fulfil their mandate. A successful case is Mexico's FOVI, (the Government Housing Finance Fund), a public lender that converted into an agency with a diversified programme and product menu.

There are some interesting models for the convertion of public lenders from specialised lenders to guarantors. However there are many badly performing public housing lenders in emerging markets that attempt over-ambitious simultaneous turnarounds of their performance and their mandates. For such institutions privatisation or greater private participation in risk-sharing and performance management may be the best choice.

Box 1: Government Housing Bank of Thailand (GHB): Turn Around After Recapitalisation

GHB was established in 1953. After a costly recapitalisation in 1973, it started a new life as a commercially oriented and managed institution. The bank is now subject to strict corporate governance rules, focuses on the quality of its portfolio, and posted profits of USD 62 million in 2006 on assets totaling USD 16 billion.

GHB operates as a decentralised savings bank with more than 120 branches country wide. Decentralised management has increased loan origination and servicing quality. Another reason for its good loan portfolio quality has reportedly been achieved through the pass-through of GHB's favourable funding conditions to beneficiaries resulting from low bond spreads, the absence of dividend payments and, until very recently, lower capital requirements than private lenders.

GHB has a diversified low-income housing loan portfolio that includes funding of social housing and slum upgrading programmes as well as leasing – targeting households that the financial system would not otherwise serve. During the 1997–2001 financial crisis GHB helped stabilise the market. While lending by commercial banks dropped, GHB's lending remained constant and its market share increased from 29% to over 35%. In addition, GHB supported the mortgage market infrastructure through its involvement in establishing the first Thai retail credit bureau, a real estate information centre, and a mortgage insurance scheme.

Source: Lea (2005)

Another interesting public sector exit model might be 'socialist competition' preceding privatisation. In 1998 Hungary created FHB, a public mortgage bank mandated to compete with OTP, a quasi-monopolistic state-owned savings bank to invigorate a small market. FHB was privatised in 2004.

Similarly, public agencies funded on a project-by-project basis can improve competition or develop regional markets – with a future privatisation perspective. An example is the Russian regional housing finance agencies, whose lending operations are refinanced by the central government-sponsored Agency for Home Mortgage Lending. While the activities of the regional agencies are occasionally fraught with problems, their existence has led to a more balanced regional development of mortgage lending than in other emerging economies.[5]

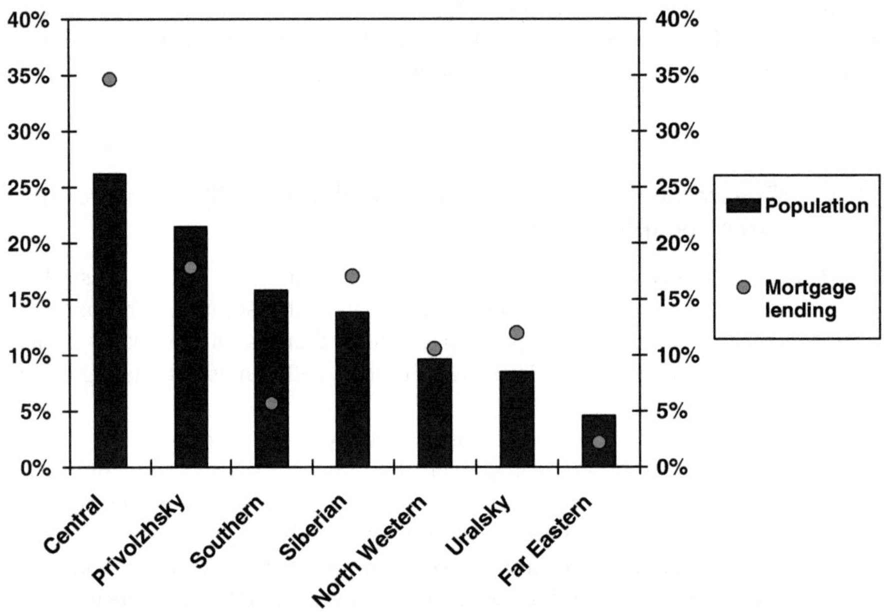

Fig. 2. Distribution of population and new mortgage lending in Russia 2006
Source: Dübel (2008)

A more recent and promising approach for retail lending is public-private partnerships to help create primary lenders for affordable housing. Successful examples are HDFC in India and Delta BRAC in Bangladesh. HDFC, established in 1977, was initially supported by public guarantees, the direction of funds to insurance companies, and incentives for banks to finance the company. HDFC has grown strongly since and acted as a promoter of other finance companies, which now

[5] See Dübel (2008).

Box 2: The Mandate Failure of Brazil's Directed Savings Bank System

The Brazilian housing finance system, Sistema Financiera Habitacional, consists mainly of the housing bank, Caixa Economica Federal – funded largely by a wage tax, and a private savings bank system, Sistema Brasileiro de Poupanca e Emprestimo (SBPE) – funded by tax-preferred deposits. SBPE was mandated by a directed credit rule to invest deposits in price-level adjusted mortgages, which protect borrowers from the impact of inflation.

However, the initial mandate was undermined by politicians who during the 1980s intervened regularly into mortgage products by determining lower payment rates, linked to a multitude of wage indices. The result was surging housing loan debts that, at their maturity, had to be taken over by a government fund, Fundo de Compensação de Variação Salarial (FCVS). Because Brazilian public debt service capacity was already limited, the savings banks were directed to finance the debt, leading to illiquidity of savings banks in the 1990s.

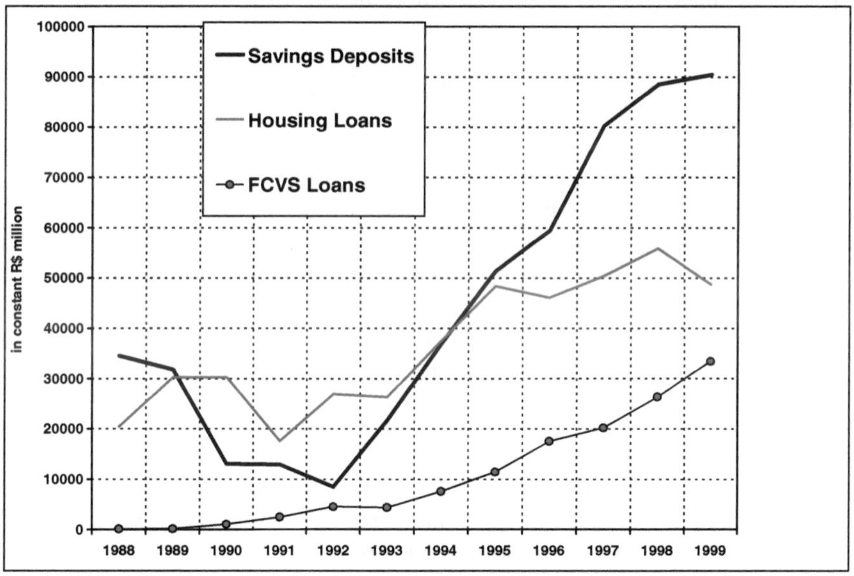

Fig. 3. Balance sheet positions of Brazilian savings banks 1988–1999
Source: Alberdi and Dübel (2000)

The government thus provided tax incentives for the soft funding of its own debt. The savings banks were happy with the procedure because public bond investments returned more on a risk- and cost-adjusted basis than mortgage lending. Mandate performance in consequence imploded as the financing ability of the system for new construction was eliminated.

form an industry catering to India's growing middle class. Delta BRAC, a promotion abroad, brought HDFC together with two Bangladeshi insurance companies and BRAC, a microcredit NGO. Delta BRAC uses both standard and microfinance origination and servicing techniques.

The HDFC example indicates that regulatory direction of credit – the Indian Priority Sector Lending – may have benefits as an instrument providing long-term capital in the absence of a functioning corporate bond market, which was the Indian situation in the 1980s. Yet, directed credit has also been one of the most abused and problematic interventions, especially in retail lending. It has more frequently been used against rather than in favour of housing finance. For example, in the early 19th century, the French and British governments de facto nationalised their low-income depository systems – Caisses d'Epargne and Trust Savings Banks – by investing their savings deposits in public debt. This has left deep traces in numerous savings and postal banks globally that continue to be severely constrained in their consumer lending and subjected to credit mandates. An example is the Japanese postal service that was reformed in 2004. In emerging markets, directed credit systems have lead to spectacular mandate failures, such as SBPE, the Brazilian savings bank system.

Targeting Specific Private Market Failure and the Lack of Infrastructure

In the presence of considerable interest from a variety of private sector institutions, fewer arguments are left for strong and lasting direct public intervention in the mortgage market. Despite the crisis in some developed markets, such conditions are present in many emerging markets that promise a genuine growth perspective, attracting large amounts of capital. The most promising strategies for public support are those that try to address private market failure directly and with targeted approaches. The relevant areas are:

- Bottom-up institutions often lack scale, i. e. of access to data pools (such as credit bureaus), interest rate risk management and risk transfer mechanisms which may pre-empt them from offering housing loans and managing their risks. In particular, they may want to provide low-income borrowers with fixed–rate products – an important lesson not only from the U. S. subprime crisis, and they lack the ability to issue same maturity bonds.

- Many commercial and investment banks show often only an opportunistic and cyclical commitment to the low-income market. This problem could be addressed by incentivised 'social contracts' that softly direct credit, as opposed to hard ratio-based credit direction. Opportunistic cross-border capital flows into emerging markets need to be particularly carefully monitored, and eventually discouraged, given the relative scales of source and target economies and the potential for serious imbalances. Public lending capacity should be retained to augment private flows in times of crisis and for reduced credit availability.

- The absence or underdevelopment of mortgage market infrastructure is a very legitimate area for public intervention. This includes a) access to communication infrastructure that could reduce transaction costs, public property and mortgage market information systems that can stabilise market expectations and create comfort with higher risk areas, and b) better accessibility to public litigation systems and support for consumer groups.

Support in Upscaling Bottom-Up Lenders

In many emerging markets, an array of microfinance institutions can or could develop housing finance products if a proper environment existed. Lea[6] points out that microfinance institutions in Bolivia (BancoSol), Chile (Banco del Desarrollo) and India (Sewa Bank) have developed into successful housing finance institutions. Some, such as BancoSol, are even tapping the bond market to fund their low-income lending. Moreover, in poor countries where little formal finance is available, microfinance institutions have been the only ones providing 'middle-income' lending. Examples are Delta BRAC in Bangladesh and the Home Finance Corporation in Ghana.

Peachey and Roe as well as Hassler[7] note the relevance of savings and loan and co-operative banking institutions in emerging markets. As in the historic European and American models, both types of lenders have developed mortgage lending, but first required a savings mobilisation phase for prospective clients before issuing larger loans. A recent example of this model is the Nyesigiso savings and loan network in Mali, which has 47 member institutions with 200,000 accounts. It has made mortgage loans since 2002 with mortgage insurance provided by the Mali Guarantee Fund. Loans have maturities up to 20 years, with competitive interest rates. In Rwanda, the Union des Banques Populaires has 150 co-operative banks and 360,000 accounts. It is Rwanda's second largest housing loan provider. The Populaires offer 15-year housing loans and contract savings-for-housing schemes. In Paraguay, the main housing finance providers are Cooperativas de Ahorro y Credito and closed membership "Cajas Mutuales." Hardly any housing finance is offered by commercial banks. Co-operatives have conquered 18% of the credit market.

In Europe and the U. S., most bottom-up institutional groups created apex institutions that provided risk management and capital market access. In 1901, Bohe-

---

6 Source: Lea, M. 2005. "Attracting Private Capital to Low-Income Housing Finance", Paper presented to Harvard Joint Center for Housing Studies International Housing Conference. Bellagio/Italy.

7 Source: Peachey, S. and A. Roe (2006a) "Access to Finance – What Does it Mean and How Do Savings Banks Foster Access?" A Study for the World Savings Banks Institute. Brussels and Hassler, O. 2006. "Going Up Market to Serve Low-income Groups". Presentation at the World Bank Conference on Housing Finance in Emerging Markets, March 15–17, Washington, D. C.

mian savings banks developed the first European secondary mortgage market by jointly creating a Pfandbrief issuer. Similar institutions followed in Switzerland (Pfandbriefzentrale) in 1922, in the United States (Federal Home Loan Banks) in 1928, and later in Germany, France and Spain. With the notable exception of British building societies and German Bausparkassen, all bottom-up lender groups in Europe today own or correspond with apex institutions.

The same pattern will surely develop in emerging markets: the Rwandan Banques Populaires are supported by an apex bank. In Mali, the mortgage lending of the Nyesigiso S&L (savings and loan) network is supported by a jointly-owned guarantee fund. Yet, the slow pace of the historic European process in which the savings banks took several decades to develop their own apex institutions seems hardly acceptable today. Also, the IT revolution offers large benefits by accelerating all processes with scale economies: credit information sharing, integration of payment systems, joint risk management systems. But the investment costs are high, making public support helpful.

The Mexican federal housing agency SHF has completely reversed its strategy, now enabling risk management and funding for bottom-up lenders, as well as developing market infrastructure, as explained in Box 3.

Box 3: Sociedad Hipotecaria Federal/Mexico – A New Type of Public Mortgage Agency

The former housing finance fund (FOVI) was turned around after the Tequila crisis. From being an inefficient direct public lender it became a multifunctional public agency that addresses various market failures and provides public goods for the entire mortgage market.

SHFs main financing function today is as a guarantor of bonds issued by housing finance companies and banks in the middle-income market. It played a major role in supporting the emergence of the Sofols over the past decade. SHFs guarantees are government backed through 2013; after that, credit enhancement offered by the institution will depend, inter alia, upon its credit standing.

At the retail level, the company offers mortgage loan insurance and a swap programme that covers borrowers against mismatches between nominal minimum wage development and payments due under the predominant price-level adjusted type of mortgages. The fund backing the swap can sustain a 25% deterioration in real wages over a 30-year period.

In addition to its financing activities, the agency works to improve the information environment of the Mexican market by introducing a mortgage credit scoring mechanism and offering consumer information on the loan offers in the market. SHF is finally active in developing the legal-regulatory aspects of mortgage finance in Mexico.

Establishing Social Contracts with Banks

Many European savings bank networks, such as Spanish cajas or German Sparkassen, operate under implicit or explicit social contracts that trade subsidies or ownership-related advantages against a lasting and regulated commitment to low-income finance. Social contract approaches have had a very mixed performance, depending on their formulation and enforcement mechanisms. In the German case, the savings bank commitment is broadly enshrined in state law and supervised by state finance ministries; it is not enforced with hard targets due to the political conflicts of interest of the public owners, resulting in suboptimal performance.[8] In Spain, in contrast, Cajas must fulfill statutory social dividend targets in proportion to their profit – in 2005 the system disbursed over 1 billion Euros in cash for a variety of local social and cultural purposes.

Still, many relationship lenders with well-defined constituencies, such as member-owned co-operative banks and many types of microfinance institutions, do not need explicit social contracts to stay focused on their mandate.[9] For many of these institutions subsidies are anathema due to the dependency and conflicts of interest they create.[10] Despite occasional demutualisations and privatisations, these groups appear to be sufficiently stable to deliver services over the long term.

A well-defined and targeted social contract approach still appears to be worth trying in emerging markets in some constellations. In South Africa, the 2003 Financial Sector Charter established a lending commitment by the four big commercial banks to issue a certain volume of low-income housing loans within 5 years. As noted above, the goal is in jeopardy due to rising housing costs, but the approach itself has worked and produced a boom in low-income lending. In Chile, the government offers origination subsidies for lenders disbursing small construction or modernisation loans, which compensate for the additional costs.

Targeted social contracts can have a significant effect on servicing capacity. This was the case in Slovakia, where consumers saved in the form of contract savings for housing schemes (Bausparen). These became subsidised in 1992. The small loan self-targeting of the schemes forced lenders to develop the capacity to serve low-income households that were the most likely group to draw on the loan entitlements, e. g. in modernising their homes. Yet, all subsidy programmes face a risk of moral hazard. The abuse of the subsidy is demonstrated by the initially identical programme in the neighbouring Czech Republic. Czech lenders could place their accumulated savings in mortgage bonds issued by high street mortgage

---

8 According to unpublished research by the author, German savings banks in 2002 paid social dividends of approximately 700 million Euros, the majority of which were soft loan disbursements. The conflict of interest arises from direct public ownership that preempts disbursement of greater social dividends in favour of other uses, e. g. self-finance of growth.

9 See for example the critique in Sinn (1997), who finds German co-operative banks as likely to serve low-income households as are savings banks.

10 Quote from Daphnis (2006).

lenders, rather than promoting their own small loan portfolio, a mistake that Slovakia avoided.[11]

Investing in Mortgage Market Infrastructure

A high social return and improvement of access can be realised through public investment in mortgage market infrastructure, when private financial institutions become increasingly active in mortgage lending. Three factors are required to support private sector involvement:

- Use of communication networks: communication access points such as cell phones and other wireless systems, fixed IT access points and the essential corresponding deregulation efforts (e. g. acceptance of non-bank correspondents) facilitate an e-payments network that can significantly lower the costs of access to savings and to loans. Porteous[12] describes the example of Brazil.

  The public sector can support the creation of communication networks where they are unprofitable for the private sector, or enforce interregional (and intersocial) cross-subsidisation within the licensing process of private sector networks.

- Public information infrastructure: in combination with greater efforts for private sector data pooling (credit bureaus, etc.), public investment in information systems can greatly support low-income access. Examples are:

  - local/regional property market information (supply/demand) systems that stabilise expectations and reduce price volatility;
  - systematic and comprehensive consumer information from public surveys that lead to better assessments and benchmarking of affordability;
  - assistance in the development and verification of private sector scoring systems using loan-level credit risk data.

  The more detailed the publicly available information is, the more comfortable private lenders will be about market opportunities and risk levels in the low-income sector.[13]

- Consumer-lender relations infrastructure ("consumer empowerment"): improved accessibility and better performance of courts is an important long-term task in most emerging markets. So is better financial education for broad masses of the public.

---

[11] See Dübel (2003).

[12] See Porteous, D. 2006. "Banking and the Last Mile". Presentation at the World Bank Global Conference on Access to Finance, May 30–31, Washington, D. C.

[13] Efforts to improve the information infrastructure often result from increased regulatory pressure after a crisis. Since the 1997 crisis in Thailand, for instance, most lenders have improved their internal process and IT systems, and introduced new scoring tools for underwriting.

However, below the level of courts, as discussed before, a low-cost and fast complaint and redress system for small value claims is important. The public sector should encourage ombudsman structures that banking trade groups are often willing to sponsor. Banks may also support independent consumer groups as advisors through system-wide small taxes. Government bodies should accord a high priority to consumer protection.

Where such infrastructure is essentially in place, as in Mexico with the assistance of SHF, demand by private investors for risk-taking rises. While domestic banks are the workhorse of liquidity generation, finance companies, capital market investors and international investors may add technology and capital to promote their development. Some of them fail, such as GMAC (General Motors Acceptance Corporation), the symbol of 'create and trade' securitisation of subprime loans, that had to withdraw from Mexican (and European operations) after being rescued at home in the U. S. Others, such as Soros Foundation's joint venture with the Danish mortgage industry, are more resilient. History suggests that these new entrants will sooner rather than later connect to bottom-up institutions looking for capital and technology. This creates the potential for a division of labour, or partnership with government.

Conclusion

We have found the following main findings concerning the efficiency of the instruments of public support in low-income housing finance in emerging markets:

- First, direct lending by government and the agency model have, with few exceptions, historically performed poorly in emerging markets. This has partly been due to design flaws that include centralised lending, crowding-out or reliance on tax funds rather than bond markets. It is also partly due to governance issues that create grey areas between a loan and a grant. Only recently, a number of turnaround stories are sending encouraging signs. Permanent direct public lending should be considered primarily when the private sector is not willing to take risks in the relevant area, or when new products require support to be introduced. In this situation, an exit strategy is essential. However, the lending or guaranty capacity of public agencies should remain as a temporary backstop when private markets fail. These varying targets require a flexible setup of the agency, such as in the case of Mexico's SHF.

- Second, using regulation to direct credit to housing finance has proved to be risky, especially if simultaneously combined with loan product interventions, as in Brazil. Regulation may provide a useful incentive that gets innovation underway, but only if accompanied by clearly defined programme goals, time limits, and risk-based pricing. Macroeconomic and legal risk factors often explain the absence of lending. These should be addressed prior to large interventions and may in fact remove the problem that the large intervention was designed to solve.

- In contrast, incentive-based models encourage low-income lending, while fraught with risk, appear to have been more successful. Good performers have defined explicit 'social contracts' with lender groups that carry quid pro quos such as tax incentives against targeted loan delivery. In contrast, many social contracts are in practice only implicit and lack enforceability. The classic example is savings banks with their extremely heterogeneous mandates. Subsidising borrowers or certain types of properties that produce self-targeting is often more efficient than providing incentives to institutions, especially if these have already incurred the entry costs for loan distribution and servicing networks.
- Fourth, providing or assisting access to funding and risk management – especially to enable the supply of fixed-rate mortgages – seems the most promising form of institutional support that government can apply to upscale successful bottom-up institutions. In such business lines, scale effects often blur the distinction between private and public activity, justifying some level of public intervention, even the monopoly control of a private entity. Again, governance is key: for example, public bond guarantees should carry risk-based premia, and refinancing agencies should exit the market as private institutions enter. The Mexican case provides a promising example of flexibility in approach and sound implementation.
- Finally, public investment in mortgage finance infrastructure should no longer be marginalised in the policy debate because of its low political visibility and lack of immediate impact. Among the public investments promising the greatest social returns for low-income housing provision are: a) financial education, b) courts and more accessible redress systems, c) access to internet and thus e-finance, d) access to land registers, e) consumer credit risk databases and surveys, and f) property market information systems. These peripheral elements are especially important in a globalising financial services industry with an increasing risk appetite that materialises when basic infrastructure is in place.

References

Alberdi, B. and A. Dübel (2000) "Housing Finance in Brazil: Legacy of the SFH and the Road Ahead", Technical and Policy Note, Infrastructure, Finance and Private Sector Department, Latin America and the Caribbean Regional Office. The World Bank. Washington, D. C.

Beck, T. (2006) "Creating an Efficient Financial System: Challenges in a Global Economy." Paper for the G20 Seminar on Economic Growth in Pretoria, August 2005. The World Bank. Washington, D. C.

Caprio, G., Fiechter, J., Litan, R. and M. Pomerleano (2004) "The Future of State-owned Financial Institutions". World Bank/IMF/Brookings Emerging Market Series, Brookings Institution Press. Washington, D. C.

Daphnis, F. (2006) "Housing Microfinance: Current Issues, Opportunities and Challenges". Presentation at the World Bank Conference on Housing Finance in Emerging Markets, March 15–17, Washington, D. C.

Dübel, A. (2008) "Does Housing Finance Promote Economic and Social Development in Emerging Markets?" Study commissioned by the International Finance Corporation. Washington, D. C.

Dübel, A. (2003) "Financial, Fiscal and Housing Policy Aspects of Contract Savings for Housing (CSH) in Transition Countries – the Cases of Czech Republic and Slovakia". Study commissioned by the Financial Sector Development Department of the World Bank. Berlin.

Hassler, O. and B. Renaud. (2009) "State Housing Banks". In: Chiquier and Lea (eds) 'Housing Finance Policy in Emerging Markets'. The World Bank.

Hassler, O. (2006) "Going Up Market to Serve Low-income Groups". Presentation at the World Bank Conference on Housing Finance in Emerging Markets, March 15–17, Washington, D. C.

Lea, M. (2005) "Attracting Private Capital to Low-Income Housing Finance", Paper presented to Harvard Joint Center for Housing Studies International Housing Conference. Bellagio/Italy.

Peachey, S. and A. Roe (2006a) "Access to Finance – What Does it Mean and How Do Savings Banks Foster Access?" A Study for the World Savings Banks Institute. Brussels.

Porteous, D. (2006) "Banking and the Last Mile". Presentation at the World Bank Global Conference on Access to Finance, May 30–31, Washington, D. C.

CHAPTER 6

Wholesale Funding Instruments

Michael J. Lea

San Diego State University

Introduction

This chapter explores how lower-income housing in emerging markets can be funded through wholesale sources, specifically through the capital markets and lender-to-investor channels. Access to wholesale finance can expand the supply of funds available for housing and manage the associated risks of lending. While the financial crisis of 2008–09 led to a collapse in wholesale funding worldwide, the use of this instrument will rebound as the global economy recovers.

There are essentially four ways of raising funds for housing: (1) private equity, (2) private debt typically through wholesale funding, (3) deposits, and (4) government funded or directed credit.[1] These are all forms of capital mobilization looking for a return, be it social or economic. The best way to raise funds depends on the expected return, operational costs and the ability of risk management.

Equity investment plays a central role in funding private financial markets. Although equity is usually a small source of actual funding, it bears most of the risks. It is the cushion supporting both debt and deposit obligations of financial institutions. In wholesale finance, equity is the highest risk bearing class of security, a critical credit plays a central role in funding private financial markets. Private equity and hedge funds have been important sources of credit enhancement in subordinated securities and in specialized lending companies. As a result of the financial crisis, equity is likely to play a larger role in mobilizing both depository and securitized finance.

Deposits are the main source of funding for housing globally. The importance of deposits is based on the dominance of banks and the retail nature of mortgage lending. In many emerging markets, expansion of mortgage lending has occurred with increasing commercial bank involvement.[2]

---

1 See Diamond and Lea 1995 for a discussion. We will not deal with direct government funding here.

2 For example, in China mortgage debt-to-GDP rose from less than 1% in the mid-1990s to more than 11% in 2005, mainly in the form of bank lending. In India and Mexico, the entry of banks has increased competition and the volume of lending.

D. Köhn and J.D. von Pischke (eds.), *Housing Finance in Emerging Markets: Connecting Low-Income Groups to Markets*, DOI 10.1007/978-3-540-77857-8_6,

However, the use of deposits to fund housing has limitations. Deposits are usually short-term with maturities of up to one year, whereas longer-term financing is needed to fund housing. This maturity mismatch subjects the lender to liquidity and interest rate risk. Deposit taking banks in emerging markets may experience volatility in their deposit base, creating liquidity risk. Commercial banks often use variable interest rate loans to manage interest rate risk, shifting that risk to the borrower and consequently increasing credit risk. The question is whether the saver, borrower or intermediary is best positioned to deal with cash flow volatility and whether predictability is more desirable in nominal or real terms.

Although the interest cost of retail deposits is typically low, retail deposit taking requires maintaining branches to attract customers, which entails significant operating costs. Deposit-taking is largely the province of established institutions – creating a bank to provide mortgages is time consuming, expensive and subject to regulatory approval, creating a barrier to entry. Also, banks often avoid making loans to lower-income borrowers due to relatively high servicing costs.

Wholesale funding can be an alternative or a complement to retail deposit funding. Wholesale funding may be obtained in different ways. The most common form is the sale of mortgage-related securities to institutional investors such as pension funds, insurance companies and banks. The lender may obtain funds through an intermediary institution that mobilizes funds by issuing bonds. Or the lender may sell loans to another lender. Funding housing through wholesale sources has a number of desirable features. Raising debt in large amounts from institutional investors generally involves low operating costs if long-term investors are present. Liquidity and cash-flow risks can be managed better. While wholesale funding represents a smaller portion of housing finance than retail funding, improved risk management through wholesale funding can make more mortgage loans available.

Capital markets in many emerging economies may provide access to an attractive and potentially large source of long-term funding for housing. Pension and insurance reform has created significant and growing pools of funds. The entry of institutional investors can increase the availability of funds and skills to manage the complex cash flow risks involved in housing finance.[3]

Wholesale funding can also spur competition in housing finance. In many countries, financial sectors are mainly concentrated on banking. Non-bank lenders financed in the capital markets can introduce new products, develop market niches and decrease spreads.[4]

---

3 See for example Impodavio et al., 2003, who demonstrate that contractual savings development has a positive and significant impact on domestic capital market development. Interestingly, they find that the effect on bond market development is stronger in bank- as opposed to capital market-based systems.

4 Australia presents an interesting case study of the impact wholesale-funded lenders can have on the mortgage market. Specialized non-bank lenders (mortgage managers) funded through securitization entered the market in the early 1990s and quickly gained a 20% market share. Spreads were reduced from 400 to less than 200 basis points and the managers introduced new products to the market. See Gill, 2001.

Wholesale funding has also disadvantages. Its interest rates are usually higher than retail deposits, and processes and instruments can be complex with high transaction costs. As demonstrated in the financial crisis, wholesale funding can be highly unstable, both in availability and cost. Investor aversion to risk has led to the collapse of private wholesale finance in most markets. This has particularly impacted financial institutions that had no access to deposits, many of which are no longer in business. Despite this setback, wholesale finance remains useful for retail lenders to augment and diversify their funding.

The focus of this chapter is on owner-occupied housing, since rental housing finance through the capital markets is not common in emerging markets.[5] We examine the instruments, institutions, and challenges of using this funding channel in emerging markets.

Wholesale Funding: What Has Been Tried?

There are three major wholesale funding types: unsecuritized whole loan sale (the transfer of a loan to a new owner), mortgage bond issuance (including debt securities issued by liquidity facilities) and mortgage securitization (pass-through and pay-through securities).

Whole Loan Sale

The sale of whole loans can be an important way for primary lenders to raise funds and manage risk. Mortgages can be sold either individually or more commonly in pools to other lenders or investors. There are no data on direct whole loan sales in emerging markets. Savings and loan institutions in the US in the 1960s and 70s sold whole loans extensively before the development of the mortgage securities market. Whole loans have been sold to wholesale lenders in the UK and US through the correspondent-wholesaler model where small lenders originate and fund individual loans and sell them to large wholesale lenders that aggregate loans for sale in the secondary market. This aggregation facilitates economies of scale, better pricing and developing relationships between sellers and investors.

Lenders may be reluctant to sell loans (and customer contacts) to other lenders and due diligence on whole loan portfolios is costly, reflecting the lack of standardization and performance data. Recourse (loan repurchase) arrangements or loan participations can reduce the risk for the buyer and maintain an incentive for proper underwriting and servicing for the seller. In small markets with a limited

---

[5] In developed markets, substantial amounts of wholesale finance are used for rental housing. In the US, multi-family housing loans are financed through securitization and real estate investment trusts. Social rental housing loans have been securitized in a number of European countries. See *Housing Finance International,* June 2003.

number of buyers and sellers and a low potential of developing a liquid mortgage securities market, a whole loan purchase arrangement (e. g., between a bank lender and insurance company purchaser) may be a cost effective form of refinance.

The US has an active market for whole loan sales under the Community Reinvestment Act (CRA). The CRA requires depository lenders to provide loans in the communities in which they obtain funds. CRA loans are typically made to low- and moderate-income borrowers, often from communities with disproportionate concentrations of such borrowers. Lenders get credit for originating CRA loans but do not have to hold them in their portfolio.

There is an active secondary market between lenders short of their CRA requirements and lenders with an excess of such loans. The loans have good credit performance and are less sensitive to prepayment, making them attractive to investors. Although securitizations of CRA loans first occurred in 1997, the market consists largely of whole loan sales.[6] Law makers in several emerging markets, including Malaysia and South Africa, have issued mandatory lending requirements. If lenders were allowed to purchase loans to fulfill these lending requirements, it might lead to the development of a whole loan sale market.

Wholesale Funding Through the Capital Markets

Mortgage Securitization

Mortgage securities are backed by a specific pool of mortgages. They may be in the form of pass-through or pay-through bonds. A pass-through is a single security issued against a single collateral pool with cash flow matching between the loans and security. Pay-through securities are multiple securities issued against a single collateral pool. Pay-through securities modify cash flows between borrowers and investors to meet investors' requirements.

An example is the sale of mortgage strips, which are separate securities backed from either the principal or interest of a mortgage pool. Another example is collateralized mortgage obligations (CMOs) in which a number of securities are issued that repay principal sequentially. Most mortgage securities in developed and emerging markets (see Table 1) are pay-through structures. Issuers may be lenders or special purpose vehicles that purchase loans from multiple lenders and issue mortgage-backed securities.

---

6 Research by the Harvard Joint Center for Housing Studies found that CRA-regulated lenders originate a higher proportion of loans to lower-income people and communities than they would if CRA did not exist (Ford Foundation 2002). A 1999 survey of CRA lenders revealed that the loans were profitable but less so than conventional loans because of their higher origination and compliance costs (Meeker and Myer 1999). Canner and Bhutta (2008) conclude that CRA lending was not the cause of the sub-prime crisis.

Table 1. Geographic use of mortgage securities in emerging markets

Covered Bonds	Structured Finance			Conduits	Liquidity Facilities
Chile	*Argentina*	*China*	*Latvia*	*Argentina*	*Armenia*
Colombia	Brazil	Hong Kong	Morocco	Brazil	Egypt
Czech Republic	Colombia	India	Russia	Colombia	India
Hungary	Mexico	Indonesia	Saudi Arabia	Hong Kong	Jordan
Korea	Panama	Korea	South Africa	Korea	Malaysia
Poland	*Peru*	*Malaysia*		*Trinidad*	*Trinidad*
Slovak Republic	Trinidad	Philippines		Thailand	Ukraine
Ukraine		Taiwan			
		Thailand			

Source: Chiquier, Hassler and Lea 2004, updated by author

Mortgage (Covered) Bonds

Mortgage (covered) bonds are issuer obligations backed by a mortgage collateral pool. Investors have a priority claim against the collateral in the event of issuer bankruptcy. The issuer may be a specialized mortgage bank, as is the case in Denmark, Germany and Sweden; a commercial bank as in Chile, the Czech Republic or Spain; or a centralized issuer as in France or Switzerland. The collateral pool may consist of all of the qualified assets of the issuer, as is the case with the German Pfandbrief; a specified pool, as in the case of Dutch, UK and US structured covered bonds; or one bond loan as in Chile and Denmark (the individual bonds are aggregated into large series). Mortgage bonds are a significant source of finance in several transition countries, in particular the Czech Republic and Hungary.

Agency Bonds

Agencies specialized in mortgage finance at a secondary (i. e., not the loan origination) level issue agency bonds.[7] Issuers include liquidity facilities which refinance primary market lenders and the mortgage Government Sponsored Enterprises (GSEs) in the US.[8]

Their bonds are not specifically backed by mortgage loans, but the assets of the issuers are almost entirely mortgages or loans backed by mortgages. Liquidity fa-

---

7 Some housing banks (first tier lenders) issue unsecured debt (e. g., the Government Housing Bank of Thailand). Bond sales account for a small proportion of total funding for these entities, which primarily obtain funds through retail deposits.

8 GSE stands for Government Sponsored Enterprise, a special class of institutions in the US. The GSEs are government chartered, limited purpose corporations that are owned by either their members or the general public. They enjoy tax and regulatory privileges that translate into lower funding costs. The best known enterprises are Fannie Mae, Freddie Mac and the Federal Home Loan Banks.

cilities are second tier agencies that make loans that are collateralized by mortgage portfolios or that purchase loans on a recourse basis from lenders. Liquidity facilities are a significant source of finance in several emerging markets.

While mortgage-related securities have been introduced in a number of emerging markets, there are only a few successful wholesale funding channels. The most successful examples have been the Chilean mortgage bonds and the Cagamas (Malaysia) liquidity facility bonds, which were continuously issued since the mid-1980s. Mortgage securities finance a significant part of the mortgage market (40% in Chile and 20% in Malaysia).[9] Chilean mortgage bonds have been the dominant fixed income instrument in that market, enjoying widespread acceptance without government guarantees. Cagamas, a partially government owned liquidity facility, is the largest private debt security issuer in Malaysia. Principal barriers to more widespread use include a lack of required infrastructure, lack of issuer demand for wholesale finance and difficulties in gaining investor acceptance.

Prerequisites for Wholesale Funding

Wholesale funding requires that issuers need the funds, investors want the assets, governments provide the proper infrastructure, and lenders create good quality loans. The prerequisites are discussed in detail in Annex 1.

Legal and Regulatory Infrastructure

A wholesale funding channel requires relatively well-developed legal and regulatory infrastructure, especially for mortgage securities issuance and investment. There must be adequate facilities for mortgage lien registration and assignment at a reasonable cost.[10] A legal, tax and accounting framework is essential for securitization and secured bond issuance. Protection of investors against the bankruptcy of the originator or servicer is important. Incomplete or weak infrastructure has delayed or prevented capital market funding in a number of emerging and transition markets.

In addition, there must be issuer demand and investor appetite for wholesale finance. Issuers depend on wholesale finance, if they have no access to retail deposits or reasonably priced bank funds. Bank lenders may use wholesale finance if they face capital constraints, particularly regulatory capital, or liquidity constraints. Issuer demand is often overlooked in attempts to create secondary mort-

---

9 However, wholesale finance in both countries dropped significantly in recent years reflecting increased liquidity of banks.

10 For example, many states in India place punitive (up to 13%) stamp duties on lien registration. The ability to transfer liens also impacts liquidity facility lending. This tax results in liens not being registered and thus not attractive for wholesale finance. It also precludes securitization, because it is charged on transfer. Several states have lowered their stamp duties, facilitating recent MBS issues.

gage markets. This occurred after the 1997 crisis in Asia where new secondary market facilities in Korea and Thailand were unsuccessful in getting liquid banks to securitize loans.

Investor Requirements Are Important

Mortgage securities or whole loans must offer attractive risk adjusted returns (i. e., a spread over comparable duration government bonds). Investors must have proper authority and capacity to invest in mortgage assets. The latter requires a sizable balance sheet, adequate systems (e. g., to account for monthly amortizing assets) and management to understand the sometimes complex cash flows (in particular pass-through and pay-through securities). Liquidity is a key attribute for investors. The ability to sell securities at a relatively narrow bid/ask spread is important to investors as demonstrated in the crisis.

Good Quality Assets

The characteristics of the assets must be well understood so that investors (and rating agencies) can assess their likely performance. Standardization of documents and underwriting procedures can lower assessment costs and improve ratings. High quality servicing and historical performance data are essential. And professional standards of property appraisal are necessary for investors to determine the risk of loss. Rating agencies are key players in wholesale finance as investors depend on them to assess the credit quality of securities. In the context of the financial crisis which began in 2008, poor performance of rating agencies has been a major factor in the collapse of private wholesale finance.

Can Low-Income Housing Loans Also Be Funded in Wholesale Markets?

On the surface, there is no reason that mortgage loans to lower-income households cannot be funded in wholesale markets. However, the prerequisites for wholesale funding are frequently not met for low-income housing loans. Performance history is often not available. Without such history investors may assume a worst case scenario, increasing the cost of funding. This is exacerbated by the perception that low-income borrowers are more likely to default given their relatively low and often unstable incomes.

Investors may view the collateral backing of low-income housing loans as more problematic than that of backing higher income housing. Governments may be less willing to enforce liens to this clientele, the value of the collateral may be suspect or appraisal standards weak, or lenders may face onerous requirements for defaulting borrowers.

Low-income borrowers may not have established credit histories, making it more difficult to assess the likelihood of default. As such, the origination, underwriting and servicing is more costly and time consuming than for high-income borrowers. The higher costs and risks suggest that low-income housing loans require higher interest rates than loans to higher-income borrowers with established credit records. However, it is frequently difficult to obtain higher interest rates from low-income borrowers. There may be affordability constraints, and it may be politically unacceptable to determine loan rates based on risk or cost of service. If returns are insufficient for wholesale investors, this channel is unlikely to develop.

In the US, a significant portion of sub-prime loans (to credit impaired borrowers) went to lower-income households. Unfortunately poor underwriting, fraud and mispricing led to the demise of the market. In Mexico, several Sofoles successfully securitized their portfolios of lower- and middle-income housing loans prior to the crisis. However, the combination of rising default rates (largely due to the economic downturn), fraud and poor underwriting by two of the largest Sofoles has paralyzed the market.

Securitization: Structures and Credit Enhancement

Credit enhancements are essential to mitigate risks associated with wholesale funding. New issuers, particularly in emerging economies, have limited historical performance data, making it difficult to predict the probability of default. Untested legal procedures (e. g., foreclosure) or lack of default experience make it difficult to forecast loss severity. Originator or third party credit enhancement may reduce investors' credit risk.

All forms of wholesale funding involve credit enhancement. Whole loan sales may be participations in which the lender and investor share in any loss, or with recourse or seller repurchase requirements. Liquidity facility lending is on an over-collateralized or recourse purchase basis.

To attract a wider group of investors, securitization structures must include highly rated tranches or classes through risk subordination. The amount and type of credit enhancement will be dependent on the credit rating that is desired (AAA, AA, A, BBB, etc.) for each of the classes of the security. The estimated losses for each of the classes are the basis for the credit enhancement. Rating agencies forecast the required loss coverage amount as a product of the estimated probability of default and loss per default.

Credit enhancements are required to ensure that investors receive timely payment of principal and interest from the securities. This form of cash flow insurance differs from loan loss insurance, typically provided by mortgage insurers, which compensates the insured (typically the lender but possibly the investor) for ultimate loss due to a default. Credit enhancements and prioritizing cash flows make the securities resemble bonds (e. g., government, mortgage or corporate) in the certainty of their cash flows.

Credit enhancements can come from external or internal sources. External credit enhancement is provided by highly rated third parties. Internal credit enhancement comes from structuring and prioritizing the cash flows from the underlying mortgage pool. Prior to the crisis, many securities were enhanced through risk subordination. Since the onset of the crisis in 2008 virtually, no mortgage securities were sold without a government guarantee or issuer support.

External Credit Enhancement

Table 2 shows the types of guarantees offered for securitizations, the entities that offer them and some of their advantages and disadvantages. Techniques are described in Annex 2.

Issuer Guarantees

The simplest form of credit enhancement is a guarantee by the security issuer. However, this credit enhancement is effective only if the guarantor is highly rated. Examples of issuer guarantees are securities issued by the Government Sponsored Enterprises (GSEs) in the US (Fannie Mae, Freddie Mac and the Federal Home Loan Banks) and the Hong Kong Mortgage Corporation (HKMC). These corporations guarantee timely payment on the securities they issue. Their securities are highly rated, primarily due to government backing.[11] The GSEs have been essential in developing the deep and liquid mortgage securities market in the US.

Mortgage covered and agency bond issuers provide corporate guarantees. Covered bonds have additional credit enhancement in the form of a priority claim on the collateral in the event of bankruptcy of the issuer. The priority claim is established in covered bond legislation in most European countries, although structured covered bonds have been issued in the Netherlands, the UK and the US without benefit of legislation.[12] Covered bond issuance was disrupted in fall 2008 but resumed in spring 2009 after a decision by the European Central Bank to purchase up to €65 billion.[13] Spreads have declined significantly and the market has reopened to most issuers.

Agency bonds issued by liquidity facilities typically have no additional credit enhancement. However, they are regarded as very safe, reflecting the business practice of taking little or no mortgage credit risk and their government affiliation. Liquidity facilities purchase loans on recourse from primary lenders or make overcollateralized loans to lenders.

---

[11] The US GSEs were backed by the government. Investors believed the government would not allow default on their securities due to their special status and significance to the market. Thus their debt traded better than AAA but not as well as government securities with explicit full faith and credit backing. Ambiguity about the government backing led to rising debt spreads in 2008, resulting in the takeover of Fannie Mae and Freddie Mac by the government in September 2008. The HKMC is owned by the Hong Kong SAR government.

[12] For information refer to Stöcker, O., "Mortgage Bond Legislation in Europe", Association of German Mortgage Banks presentation, 2006.

[13] For information refer to Winkler, S. and A. Batchvarov, "Covered Bonds on a Rebound", Bank of America Merrill Lynch, Covered Bonds Research, June 5, 2009.

Government Agency Guarantees

An alternative to issuer guarantees is the guarantee of a third party government agency. Agency guarantees have been important sources of credit enhancement in Canada (through the Canada Mortgage and Housing Corporation) and the US (through Ginnie Mae and the Government National Mortgage Association as described in Annex 2). A major advantage of agency guarantees is that they facilitate issuance by any qualified lender, thus promoting competition. In the US, many Ginnie Mae supported lenders are small mortgage banks with limited capital and ability to access capital markets.

Government guarantee programs focused on affordable housing operate in Colombia and Mexico. In Colombia, the government deposit insurance agency, FOGAFIN (Fondo de Garantías de Instituciones Financieras), has provided 100% cash flow guarantees on social housing loans defined in terms of borrower income (2 minimum wages or less) and loan size, included in residential mortgage-backed securities.[14] FOGAFIN guaranteed the performance of loans in the pool of social housing loans. A second pool of non-social housing loans with internal credit enhancement was also created.[15] The guaranteed and non-guaranteed pools were merged into a single trust, and a waterfall structure prioritizing payments was developed.[16] FOGAFIN charged a premium based on estimated loss from default. The issuer pays either a one-time fee of 3.22% of the principal of the insured bonds or 0.81% of the capital balance as an annual fee.

The presence of guaranteed loans increased the scale and liquidity of the issues. However, according to the World Bank, the guarantees have not resulted in an overall increase in social housing lending, which is constrained by interest rate caps and judicial uncertainty about the structure and enforcement of the loans.

In Mexico, the Sociedad Hipotecaria Federal (SHF) provides several guarantee products to support the refinance of Sofoles (mortgage companies). SHF issues bonds and provides loans to Sofoles, provides partial default loss insurance on individual loans, enhances bank lines of credit to developers and provides partial guarantees of mortgage-backed securities. As a national development bank, SHF benefits from a credit guarantee of the Mexican government. The Sofoles have focused on the moderate to middle income households (6 to 15 times the minimum wage). Their ability to access the capital markets with SHF partial guarantees, and subsequently through internal and private external credit enhancement, provided an example of how wholesale markets can fund affordable housing. The government did not take all the risk, giving issuers an incentive to properly underwrite and service the loans.

---

[14] The Vivienda de Interés Social (Social Priority Housing) program.

[15] The initial transaction also included an IFC partial guarantee on the non-social portion of the senior bonds. See http://www.ifc.org/ifcext/treasury.nsf/AttachmentsByTitle/SF_Titularizadora/$FILE/Titularizadora.pdf.

[16] A waterfall structure prioritizing payments across different security classes. An example is provided below.

Table 2. External credit enhancement

Type	Description	Offered By	Advantages	Disadvantages
Issuer Guarantee	Issuer guarantees of timely payment of P&I (principal and interest)	Fannie Mae, Freddie Mac, Hong Kong Mortgage Corp., Federal Home Loan Banks, covered bond issuers	Simple, easy to understand, can be relatively cheap (~20 bp in US); stimulates competition by allowing access to a wide range of lenders; offered by government or quasi-government institutions with high ratings	Creates contingent liability of government; may be miss-priced (+/-); not off-balance sheet for corporate issuer
Government Agency Guarantees	Third party guarantee of timely payment of P&I from government agency	GNMA, CMHC, Colombia, KfW	Simple, easy to understand, can be relatively cheap (6 bp in US, 20 bp in Canada); stimulates competition by allowing access to a wide range of lenders	Explicit liability of the government; subject to agency risk (due to actions of lenders); may be miss-priced; should be properly capitalized and budgeted
Monoline Financial Guarantees	Provides guarantee of timely payment of P&I. Typically covers 100% of loss up to stipulated aggregate loss limit	Bond insurers (AMBAC, MBIA), Private mortgage insurers (PMI, Genworth, UGI)	Insurers rated AA or AAA – improves credit quality of securities. Provider may assist in structuring	Cost: 15–45 bp for AAA wrap (pre-crisis); bond insurers provide guarantees only in investment grade countries
Political Risk Insurance	Provides insurance against non-commercial risks such as currency transfer restrictions, certain types of expropriation	Multilateral Agencies (MIGA, IFC, ADB, IADB,AfDB), Bilateral (OPIC)	Applicable for emerging markets with unstable economies and/or legal systems. Allows issuance of securities for international investors	Cost: 8 bp/yr. for 1.5 yrs in the 2004 Baltic American transaction (the first Central-Eastern European securitization)
Multilateral and Bilateral Agency Guarantee	Provides guarantee of timely payment of P&I up to a specified percentage of the pool or tranche balance	World Bank (back-stopped by governments), IFC, EBRD, ADB, IADB, AfDB	AAA + guarantees, will assist in structuring and marketing	Some require govern-ment. counter-guarantee; cost – e. g., 25 bp for IFC partial guarantee, additional delays and cost for agency approvals
Liquidity Provider	Covers temporary shortfalls in cash flow due to disruption in servicing. Typically limited to a max % of the outstanding balance	Banks, IFC	Steps in before timely payment guarantor if shortfall not due to loss	Cost (10–20 bp commitment fee); Could be covered by reserve fund

SHF provides top loss mortgage insurance on individual loans that cover up to 35% of exposure. The insurance is priced from extensive data on default experience and is paid up front by the borrower. SHF signed contracts with two US private mortgage insurers to reinsure 70% of its risk.[17]

SHF provides guarantees to protect commercial banks from payment default on construction loans to Sofoles. The guarantee covers up to 85% of the lines of credit used for construction. The premium on the guarantee is negotiated individually with each Sofol. In case of default by the Sofol, SHF pays the commercial bank the unpaid balance within two days following the bank's claim.

SHF also provides partial guarantees on mortgage backed securities[18] with the issuer taking a first loss position through subordination or over-collateralization.[19]

Through 2009, SHF had provided RMBS guarantees on more than $4.9 billion.[20] In addition, several Sofols issued securities using internal or private external credit enhancement in 2007 and 2008.[21] Two other quasi-government agencies,[22] have issued over $5.2 billion in mortgage securities between 2004 and 2009. These agencies provide mortgages to lower income salaried workers.[23]

The financial crisis adversely affected the Sofol/SHF funding model. Problems in two large Sofoles undermined investor confidence in Sofol securities and forced SHF to repurchase a significant portion of the outstanding issues. Currently, no Sofol is able to issue a mortgage security and the remaining institutions are entirely dependent on SHF direct funding.

---

17 One of the US private mortgage insurers has withdrawn.

18 Bonos Respaldados por Hipotecas (BORHIs).

19 The GPO (Garantia de Pago Oportuno, or Timely Payment Guarantee) is a credit enhancement at the deal level of the structure. Sometimes referred to as a partial guarantee (PG), the GPO is similar to a credit line. If the trust does not have sufficient cash to make a given payment, the line of credit can be drawn to pay interest and principal. Once the line of credit is repaid, it can be drawn again if the need arises. The fee to the provider of the GPO is part of the expenses of the trust. See Credit Suisse 2006.

20 See Gavito, J., "Mortgage Market in Mexico: Projects, Strategies and Challenges Ahead", SociedadHipotecario Federal presentation for Mexican Housing Day, New York, March 2010.

21 Private external credit enhancement was provided by monoline insurance companies Ambac and MBIA.

22 Instituto del Fondo Nacional para la Vivienda de los Trabajadores (INFONAVIT) & Fondo de la Vivienda del Instituto de Seguridad y Servicios Sociales de los Trabajadores del Estado (FOVISSSTE).

23 INFONAVIT securities are not explicitly guaranteed by the government and utilize internal credit enhancement. INFONAVIT is the largest mortgage originator. It receives funds from a payroll tax on private sector workers. FOVISSSTE is a similar fund for public sector workers.

Multilateral and Bilateral Guarantees

A number of multilateral and bilateral agencies provide credit enhancement to catalyze the development of wholesale funding in emerging markets. They provide cash flow insurance, purchase subordinate securities, create liquidity facilities and provide political risk insurance.

The International Finance Corporation (IFC) offers the widest range of credit enhancement for securitization transactions among the multilaterals. IFC invests in domestic or cross-border securitizations and provides credit enhancement to transactions through funded or unfunded participations, mainly at the mezzanine (subordinated or second loss) level.[24] In addition, IFC provides liquidity support, currency and interest rate swaps, and warehouse line facilities to build up asset pools for securitization. Also, the IFC Guaranteed Offshore Liquidity Facility (GOLF) can be used for cross-border transactions to achieve higher credit ratings through mitigation of currency transfer and convertibility (T&C) risk.

The Overseas Private Investment Corporation (OPIC), a US bilateral agency, has provided guarantees on mortgage securities issued by emerging market lenders that are sold in the US. For example, in April 2005, OPIC provided a $7.5 million partial guarantee on securities issued by the Guatemala Mortgage Corporation, which gathered mortgage loans from four Guatemalan banks for the project. OPIC's guarantee enabled the sale of the notes in the US, which has a larger pool of long-term funding than the local investor market. This was the first mortgage securitization in Central America.

A typical product offered by these guarantors is a partial guarantee covering from 10% to 90% of the credit risk. A partial guarantee can provide liquidity or absorb a certain level of losses on an underlying pool of assets and reduce the probability of default on note payments. The guarantor may be senior, subordinated or pari passu with investors. The guarantee can cover principal and interest or principal only. The partial nature of the guarantee properly aligns incentives between the loan originator and guarantor, which share the default risk. According to Fitch Ratings [2009], there were more than 60 partial guarantee transactions in emerging markets through mid-2009.

KfW Bankengruppe (KfW banking group) provides credit enhancement on pools of mortgage and small and medium enterprise (SME) loans in Germany. KfW's domestic securitization programs are typically synthetic, involving no loan transfer, true sale or funding. Loan originators conclude credit default swap (CDS) contracts with KfW to transfer credit risk of a pool of loans, in which KfW may retain a small first loss position. KfW in turn negotiates a CDS with one or more highly rated banks. The transaction boosts the credit quality of the portfolio to sovereign level, reducing the capital risk weight for investors. The credit enhanced loans are included in jumbo Pfandbrief (German covered bond) issues. Obtaining the guarantee allows the mortgage bank to avoid the 60% loan-to-value (LTV)

---

[24] http://www.ifc.org/ifcext/treasury.nsf/Content/Securitization.

limit on the collateral portfolio backing the mortgage bond. The major advantages are in liquidity and regulatory capital relief. KfW has been involved in securitization transactions in markets, using mortgage collateral in Russia and Ukraine.

Monoline Financial Guarantees

Prior to the crisis, private mortgage and bond insurers (monolines) provided guarantees ("wraps") to improve the rating of certain tranches of securitization transactions. Financial guarantee insurance offers unconditional and irrevocable guaranties of principal and interest on mortgage-backed securities. Pool insurance provides supplemental coverage to holders of mortgage debt by providing loss protection on loans in aggregate. Pool policies require the guarantor to pay all credit-related losses, subject to an aggregate limit of claims paid. Monolines were active mainly in investment grade countries. Genworth, Ambac and United Guaranty Insurance (UGI) operated in Mexico, and Genworth started to offer insurance in India.[25] As a result of the crisis, the major monoline guarantors have been downgraded and have not been active in emerging markets.

Liquidity Provider

A liquidity provider makes payments in the event of a disruption to servicing. Disruptions can occur through financial difficulties of a servicer, of servicing transfers or a servicer system failure. Typically, transaction liquidity support is provided to domestic or international banks but is also available from multilateral financial institutions. A reserve fund is an alternative to a liquidity facility.

Internal Credit Enhancement

Prior to the crisis, an increasingly common channel in emerging markets was internal credit enhancements.

Various internal credit enhancement techniques are used in securitization transactions (Table 3 – for more detailed explanations see Annex 2). These techniques generally prioritize the payments made to various security holders and other interests (e. g., servicer, issuer) adding excess collateral to support the transaction.

Typically, a transaction includes sequential use of several credit enhancement structures applied in "a waterfall". An example waterfall structure with external credit enhancement is shown in Figure 2, taken from the 2004 Baltic American transaction (the first Central-Eastern European securitization) with the following elements:

---

[25] The US credit market turmoil that began in 2007 has led to large losses for both bond and mortgage insurers. In turn, this has led them to significantly curtail their international guarantee and pool insurance activity. In April 2008, S&P downgraded four mortgage insurers which will severely limit their ability to credit enhance securities. The ratings of the two most internationally active mortgage insurers, Genworth and UGI, along with the ratings of the two largest bond insurers (Ambac and MBIA) has so far remained unchanged.

Table 3. Internal credit enhancement

Type	Description	Advantages	Disadvantages
Excess Interest/Spread	Difference between interest rate on mortgages and interest rate on securities, net of servicing fees and other expenses, is reserved and paid to cover loss	Provides incentive for aggressive servicing as issuer can "earn out" the excess; no need for additional funding	Reduces income earned by issuer, particularly in early years of issue
Over-collateralization	Balance of loans is greater than balance of securities. Excess is used to absorb losses on collateral pool	Simple	Opportunity cost of foregone interest on collateral (typically around 2%); issuer needs funding source for collateral
Subordination	Rights of junior class subordinated to that of senior class of security holders. Junior class(es) are in first loss position and shield senior security holders from losses in collateral pool	More complex, need to find investors to buy subordi-nated tranches. Sometimes held by issuer (no capital relief) for a period (season-ing) over which performance can be assessed	Higher yield requirements of junior security investors, potentially large size of junior class if lack of loss experience history and/or volatile environ-ment (can range between 2–25%)
Reserve Fund/Cash Collateral Account	Funds (securities) deposited with trustee to be used if proceeds from pool are insufficient to make required bond payments	Simple, robust (cash or securities easy to value, very safe)	Opportunity cost on funds. Issuer needs funding source for collateral if pledged up front. May be built from excess spread
Early Amortization	If certain negative events occur, all payments from assets are applied to the more senior securities until they are paid. Turbo feature uses excess spread to pay down principal until target over-collateralization (O/C) level reached	Contractual; protects senior bond holders	Delays or eliminates payments to other security holders

- Losses are first incurred from a reserve funded through accumulation of excess interest;
- Second losses are funded through 2% over-collateralization (balance of assets in excess of securities);
- Third losses are provided by holders of subordinate (junior) notes equal to 5% of the initial balances;
- Additional credit enhancements from a liquidity provider covering temporary cash shortfalls and from MIGA political risk insurance.

The structure is designed to maximize investments in Class A securities tranche which has the lowest risk and are the easiest class to sell to investors.

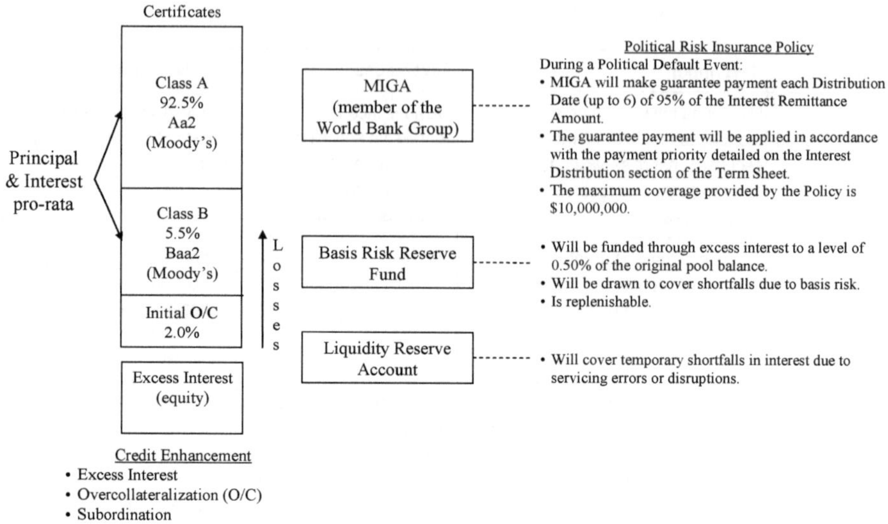

Fig. 1. Credit enhancement waterfall
Source: Schaub 2005

The waterfall structure is complex, which increases the cost and required size of the issue. Each transaction is likely to be different, making it difficult to achieve liquidity through repeated issuance of standardized securities. With the exceptions of Colombia and Mexico, the loans being sold are representative of the market and do not have a low-income focus.

There are many examples of structured finance in emerging markets. Mortgage structured finance transactions have occurred in countries as diverse as Colombia, China, Russia, Ukraine, Mexico, Morocco, Korea and South Africa. Latin American issuers have been the most prolific users of structured finance. In 2007 and 2008, Mexican Sofoles issued $681 million of structured securities. Su Casita, one of the largest Sofoles, issued the first cross-border mortgage-backed securities in 2005 with bonds issued in dollars swapped to pesos with mono-line wrap. The Colombian mortgage-securitization company Titularizadora Colombiana (TC) has continued to issue through the crisis, demonstrating that a well regarded issuer with strong domestic demand can continue to function in adverse market conditions. TC is a private company owned by domestic banks and the IFC. It issues securities in inflation-indexed units and pesos enhanced through senior subordination and over-collateralization. Banco Hipotecario (BH) a majority privately-owned bank in Argentina was the first Latin American MBS issuer to sell bonds in the US. They broke the sovereign ceiling with internal credit enhancement.

South Africa has seen a number of RMBS issues from both securitization companies (South Africa Home Loans) and major banks (ABSA, Standard Bank). Pension-backed housing loan MBS have been issued in South Africa by Absa

Bank, HomePlan Financial, and Standard Bank. Borrowers obtain loans for the purchase or improvement of housing without mortgaging the property. Instead, a portion of their pension is used as collateral. Typically, these loans go to lower income formal sector workers living in townships. Difficulties in foreclosure and repossession have led lenders to use pensions as alternative collateral for housing borrowers.

Liquidity Facilities

A liquidity facility is an institution that provides loans to lenders and funds itself through bond issuance. These institutions can reduce liquidity risk inherent in depository lending by allowing lenders to obtain funds using their housing loans as collateral, to tap alternative sources of funds through capital markets, and to create efficiencies in issuing bonds. Credit enhancement on liquidity facility debt comes from the capital of the issuer and from the low credit risk of facility assets which are loans purchased on a recourse basis or loans provided to primary lenders on an over-collateralized basis.

There are numerous examples of liquidity facilities. The Swiss Pfandbrief Bank and the US Federal Home Loan Banks are the oldest examples. In emerging markets, liquidity facilities have been created in Egypt, India, Jordan, Malaysia, South Africa and Trinidad.

The most successful example of affordable housing in emerging markets is Cagamas in Malaysia.[26] Cagamas Berhad was created in 1987 following a recession and liquidity crunch that restricted credit for housing, particularly for moderate-income households. The purpose of Cagamas was to provide more liquidity to mortgage lenders, reduce market risks, assist social housing finance, sustain the construction sector, and develop private fixed-income markets. Cagamas finances over 20% of the housing market and is the largest bond issuer after the government.

Cagamas purchases mortgage loans – the principal balance outstanding – from mortgage originators, with full recourse to the primary lenders, at a fixed or floating rate for three to seven years. This is in effect a secured financing with Cagamas having first recourse to the financial institutions when mortgage loans default. Cagamas issues debt securities to investors in the form of fixed or floating rate bonds, notes, or Cagamas Mudharabah (Islamic) Bonds.

Cagamas supports low-income housing by refinancing the loans. Banks are required to originate a fixed quota of loans for low-cost housing with a ceiling interest rate on loans for houses priced below MYR100,000 ($31,000). Cagamas bonds carry a low capital risk weight and are eligible as liquid instruments, which increases their demand and lowers Cagamas' cost of funds. As the market matured, interest subsidies were scaled back in 2004. Yields on Cagamas bonds rose by

---

[26] See Chiquier, L., O. Hassler, M. Lea, "Mortgage Securities in Emerging Markets", World Bank Financial Sector and Operations Working Paper, April 2004.

only 20–30 basis points after the discontinuation of its subsidies, without significantly affecting lending to lower-income groups.

Government plays a strong role in Cagamas – a prototype public-private partnership. The Malaysian Central Bank owns 20%. Cagamas loan and bond privileges were instrumental in its development, without which its refinancing activities would not have been perceived as sufficiently attractive for primary lenders. Spreads over government debt rose during the 2008/09 crisis, but have subsequently returned to levels.

The Jordan Mortgage Refinance Corporation (JRMC) is a liquidity facility that makes loans to banks and other mortgage lenders, 120% over-collateralized by their mortgage portfolios.[27] Since its creation in 1997, JRMC has been instrumental in increasing the stock of market-rate mortgage loans outstanding, the number of active mortgage lenders (from 1 to 11) and improving the terms of the loans. Banks now require smaller down payments from borrowers, as low as 10% compared to 50% prior to its creation. Maturities of housing loans have more than doubled and are now generally between 12 and 15 years, with some lenders offering up to 20 years.

The liquidity facility provides several significant advantages for wholesale finance in emerging markets:

- The first is that it makes liquidity and long term finance available for primary lenders who can use their mortgage portfolios as collateral for borrowing.
- Second is liquidity in the bond market. As a centralized, repeat bond issuer, the facility amortizes transaction costs over numerous issues and creates a secondary market in its debt, which it passes on to its customers.
- Third is an alignment of incentives. Credit risk remains with the originating lender, which has an incentive to originate and service loans properly. It also makes the facility bonds easier to sell because of their low credit risk.
- A fourth virtue is simplicity. Liquidity facilities issue corporate bullet bonds which are easy for investors to understand and price. The facility can assist lenders to reduce maturity mismatch through loans with different maturities.[28]
- Fifth, the model may be easy to adapt to low-income housing because borrowers (primary lenders) can mix loans of different quality. The facility can manage its risk by adjusting its over-collateralization requirements and/or pricing. Investors buying the corporate debt of the facility, backed by its capital and pledged collateral, or by purchased loans, bear little credit risk.

---

[27] Daher 2006; http://www.jmrc.com.jo.

[28] In the US, the Federal Home Loan Banks (FHLB, a liquidity facility), Fannie Mae and Freddie Mac also issue callable debt that allows better match funding of long-term fixed rate mortgages with a prepayment option.

There are limitations to this model. In particular, it provides no capital relief, as there is no credit risk transfer. In emerging markets it provides only a limited asset liability risk management benefit, as the facility is dependent on its ability to find investors. A fundamental question is whether liquidity facilities can be created without government involvement. All the cited examples continue to enjoy some government support, often through government minority shareholdings. There is one example of a private liquidity facility, the French Caisse de Refinancement de l'Habitat (CRH), which is owned by a number of its large bank users.[29] The government guaranteed its debt during its first three years.

Challenges in Wholesale Finance for Low Income Housing

The challenges in obtaining wholesale finance for low-income housing in emerging markets are to identify in (i) capable and interested investors and issuers, and (ii) a track record and standardized documentation procedures. But even if these conditions are largely in place, two factors complicate low-income housing. First, lengthening the term of the loan through access to longer maturity funding can provide significant affordability benefits in a low interest rate environment. But long-term investors are still few in many countries, leading some lenders to seek funding from international sources. Second is the high cost of structured finance.

Small Pool Size and High Transactions Costs

Structured finance involves significant transaction costs, which increases the overall cost of finance and may render transactions non-self-active. The typical issuer must pay legal fees, investment banking fees for structuring and distribution, rating agency fees and in domestic transactions various legal and regulatory fees such as security registration and issuance fees. For small transactions, these costs can represent as much as 2% of the amount issued. Thus, issuers have to create significantly larger pools to securitize, reducing the transactions' costs. Larger transactions are also typically more liquid, enhancing their attractiveness to investors.

Small pool size and infrequent issuance are likely to be more significant for smaller, specialized lenders in newly developing markets. Such lenders often do not have the ability to build large portfolios.

---

[29] The Federal Home Loan Banks (FHLBs) are owned by their members, banks, savings institutions and insurance companies. One disadvantage to the member ownership model is the possibility that the facility will not be open to all lenders. In the US, the mortgage banks cannot be members, and in France membership is restricted to banks and does not extend to non-depository lenders. The FHLBs have legislatively mandated affordable housing investment requirements. The French CRH has none.

As a rule of thumb, the transaction must be at least $100 million to offset the fixed costs of issuance. According to Su Casita, the minimum size requirements for Mexico were $50 million[30] for domestic issues and $100 million for international issues prior to the crisis. Costs for a domestic transaction were reportedly about 80–90 basis points[31] and for international transactions between 130–170 basis points.[32] Higher costs of international transactions reflect higher rating agency and legal fees, and investment banking costs.

There have been examples of smaller transactions in transition countries such as Latvia and Russia including the 2004 Baltic American sale of a $63 million portfolio of Latvian mortgages originated by the Baltic American Enterprise Fund (BalAEF). Originally funded by the US government to catalyze the development of a mortgage market, the portfolio was accumulated over a four-year period.

In addition to legal, structuring and rating agency fees, BalAEF had to support servicing, trustee, back-up servicing, liquidity reserve and premiums for political risk insurance. The CEO of BalAEF estimated that 12 employees put in 620 hours of overtime to get the deal closed, delivering about 3000 loans with all the correct documentation for the sale.[33] Despite these costs, the transaction was successfully placed in the US market.

Feasibility of Multi-lender Issues

High transaction costs and scale problems are diminished by multi-lender issues. The first two mortgage securities issued in Mexico were multi-lender transactions involving GMAC-RFC and Hipotecaria Su Casita. These transactions combined loans made to lower-income borrowers by Su Casita with loans to middle-income borrowers made by GMAC-RFC. The purpose was to obtain larger scale given the high transactions costs of issuance. The first transaction was $53 million and the second $104 million. Since then, both institutions have issued separately, achieving an efficient transaction size of their own.

An alternative to a multi-lender transaction is a conduit that purchases loans from multiple lenders and issues its own securities. TC in Colombia, HKMC, Fannie Mae and Freddie Mac as well as the Korean National Mortgage Corporation are conduits. Conduits have several advantages – the ability to amortize costs over a greater volume of issuance, to create liquidity and secondary markets in the securities, to diversify risk across lenders and possibly geographic areas and to enhance investor understanding of the securities. With the exception of TC, the examples cited above have some government backing – providing credit enhancement but also creating a contingent liability. However there were numerous private conduits set up in the US

30 All numeric references to Mexican currency are expressed in US dollars.

31 Definition of basis point: A basis point is 1/1000 percentage point.

32 Mark Zaltzman, Finance Director, Hipotecaria Su Casita, September 2006.

33 Schaub 2005.

prior to the crisis to accumulate loans and issue securities. A disadvantage of the structure in emerging markets is the cost and difficulty of creating it: primarily finding investors and obtaining legal status and regulatory approval. In addition, as they obtain scale and liquidity in their securities, a conduit can become a monopoly issuer. This situation can create systemic risks for the financial market and crowd out private sector issuers, as is the case in the US.[34]

Currency Risk and International Investment

Currency risk poses a major challenge to expanding the investor pool for wholesale funding of housing. International investors prefer to invest in major convertible currencies. The mismatch between domestic and international currencies creates currency risk that must be allocated in the transaction. The currency risk may reside with the mortgage borrower, the mortgage lender/security issuer or the ultimate investor.

In a number of countries including Hungary, Poland, Romania and Russia, significant amounts of mortgage loans are made in foreign currency. Such loans are in demand because their interest rates are lower than those in domestic currency. A mismatch normally occurs if borrower income is in the domestic currency, as is likely to be the case for most borrowers. With their limited income and resources they are ill-equipped to bear the risk of fluctuations in payments deriving from exchange rate movements. Loans in foreign currency thus bear increased risk of default in markets with volatile exchange rates. Concern about borrower ability to manage foreign exchange risk has led several central banks to curtail foreign exchange lending through higher reserve or capital requirements (e. g., Poland, Romania).

Alternatively, the lending institution or issuer could bear the exchange risk, making mortgage loans in domestic currency that are funded by loans or securities in foreign currency. The lender can price the risk by simulating the cost of the mismatch under different exchange rate scenarios. Alternatively, the lender could hedge the risk through a currency swap. However, in many emerging markets, currency swap markets are not very developed – in particular for longer maturity swaps necessary for long-term housing loan transactions. In larger emerging markets with stable currencies (e. g., Czech Republic, Mexico, South Africa), a longer-term swap may be available, but most markets have no swaps above three years and the cost of the swap may be prohibitive.[35]

---

[34] There are a number of examples (Brazil, Ghana, Thailand) where government-backed conduits for mortgage finance failed to take off. Typically the problem has been a lack of seller interest. Ghana, the Home Finance Corporation changed its business model from being a second tier funds provider to a primary lender, working with developers, because it could not interest banks in providing loans for housing.

[35] In Mexico, currency swaps for up to 10 years were available, however only with fixed amortization schedules which did not suit pass-through issues. Asset Securitization Report 2005.

A third alternative is for the international investor to take the exchange rate risk. Arguably, this is the appropriate locus of risk as major international investors are best equipped to monitor, price and manage risk. The Asian Development Bank and IFC have developed local currency borrowing and lending programs in a number of emerging markets. They issue debt in local currency and use the proceeds to on-lend (or purchase securities denominated in) the same currency. This allows making a loan to or purchase of a security denominated in domestic currency.

Some international private investors have been willing to invest in local currency transactions. With yields on emerging-market dollar debt near historic lows in 2006, investors put money into higher-yielding local-currency government bonds in Mexico, South Africa, Brazil and Turkey. Investor interest in local-currency bonds was clearly rising before the crisis. For instance, foreign investors held only 4% of Mexico's local currency debt at the start of 2004, according to J. P. Morgan. At the end of 2006, that figure had increased to 20%. Some investor interest in emerging market debt has remained during the financial crisis, albeit at much wider spreads than before the crisis (2008). But devaluation risk remains a concern along with the relative lack of liquidity.

Conclusion

This study has shown that capital markets offer a feasible approach for funding housing, in general and more specifically for medium- to lower-income households. A variety of instruments and institutions can help lenders access domestic and international capital markets for funding, including securitization, mortgage and agency bonds and whole loan sales. Funding may come directly to lenders or indirectly through conduits and liquidity facilities.

The best examples of funding housing through capital markets in emerging markets could be found in Malaysia and Mexico. Cagamas has been a highly successful liquidity facility in Malaysia – a portion of its activity has been directed to lower-income households. The liquidity facility model is a cost effective approach for lenders to enter domestic bond markets – however it appears that government backing is required to be successful. In Mexico, SHF has pioneered securitization of lower and moderate-income housing loans through its insurance and partial guarantee products. This market evolved to the point that larger Sofols accessed the capital markets without the assistance of SHF, using a combination of internal credit enhancement and international partial guarantees, before the crisis.

Wholesale funding of housing in emerging markets has been adversely effected by the financial crisis. Issuers with government backing, such as Cagamas in Malaysia, SHF in Mexico and the Korea Housing Finance Corporation have continued to be regular issuers. However, the Mexican Sofoles access to wholesale funding collapsed due to the failure of two of the largest issuers and rising default rates on the underlying collateral. Non-bank issuers in South Africa also lost market access.

Capital markets are unlikely to be the dominant funding source for affordable housing lenders. Even in developed markets, bank deposit funding is dominant except for Denmark and the US. Advocates of increased funding of low and moderate income housing should focus on improving the infrastructure for and attractiveness of such loans for domestic banks. This will improve the prospects for capital market funding through the improved quality of assets, longer performance histories and strengthened legal standing of mortgages. As lending conditions in emerging markets improve, we should expect to see more lenders going down market and a portion of these loans funded through securitization or other capital market instruments.

Development of mortgage capital markets can stimulate greater lending for lower-income borrowers by specialist lenders. In India and Mexico, specialist lenders have used securitization to serve this market. The viability and ultimate success of specialist lenders will depend on the creation of good quality assets and finding investors for the credit risk embedded in subordinate securities.

The financial crisis has shown the fragility of wholesale funding as a resource for non-bank lenders. Lenders without other sources of funding can quickly find themselves without liquidity as demonstrated in developed and emerging markets. The future of specialized lenders may depend on their ability to become banks or part of banking groups. For example, in Mexico new regulations require Sofoles that issue debt to obtain a limited banking license.[36]

It is unlikely that international capital markets become a sizable funding source for affordable housing in emerging markets. International issues are more costly and complex than domestic issues, and most emerging markets do not have long term swap markets to hedge currency risk. However, international capital markets can play an important role in developing domestic markets. The involvement of international financial institutions can spur development of the domestic capital markets by demonstrating the feasibility of transactions. These investors can provide partial credit enhancement, assist in structuring and enhancing the attractiveness of an issue by their reputation and high credit standing.

Although the financial crisis has set back the use of wholesale funding for housing finance in many countries, it is likely to re-emerge, when markets recover. The demand for housing finance by low and moderate income borrowers will grow as a result of improving demographics and economies.

References

Asset Securitization Report (2006) "Metrofinanciera 2005 Latin America Deal of the Year".

Chiquier, L., O. Hassler, M. Lea (2004) "Mortgage Securities in Emerging Markets", World Bank Financial Sector and Operations Working Paper.

[36] The basic difference from a full banking charter is a lower initial capital requirement.

Canner, G. and N. Bhutta (2008) "Staff Analysis of the Relationship between CRA and the Sub-prime Crisis", Board of Governors of the Federal Reserve System.

Congressional Budget Office (2001) "Federal Subsidies and the Housing GSEs".

Crabb, P. (2004) "Foreign Exchange Risk Management Practices of Microfinance Institutions", Journal of Microfinance.

Daher, I. (2006) "Jordan Mortgage Refinance Corporation", presentation at the Second World Bank Conference on Housing Finance, Washington DC.

Davidson, A., A. Sanders, L. Wolff, A. Ching (2005) "Securitisation: Structuring and Investment Analysis", Key Finance.

Diamond, D., M. Lea (2005) "Sustainable Financing For Housing: A Contribution To Habitat II", Fannie Mae Office of Policy Research Working Paper.

Developing World Markets, "Blue Orchid Microfinance Securities I", at www. dwmarkets.com.

Dowers, K. (2006) "IFC's Role in Securitisation Transactions", presentation at the Turkish Capital Markets Board Conference on Mortgage Finance.

Fernando, M. (2004) "Managing Foreign Exchange Risk: The Search for Innovation to Lower Costs to Poor People", Microvest.

Fitch Ratings (2005) "Partial-Credit Guarantees Help Improve Recovery Rates in Emerging Markets".

Fitch Ratings (2009), "Criteria for Partial Credit Guarantees in Emerging Markets".

Ford Foundation (2002) "The 25th Anniversary of the Community Reinvestment Act: Access to Capital in an Evolving Financial Services System," Study by The Joint Center for Housing Studies, Harvard University.

FM Watch (2001) "Shuttered Dreams: How Fannie Mae and Freddie Mac Misspend the GSE Housing Subsidy".

Gavito, J., "Mortgage Market in Mexico: Projects, Strategies and Challenges Ahead", Sociedad Hipotecario Federal presentation for Mexican Housing Day, New York, March 2010.

Gill T. (2001) "Australian Residential Mortgage Backed Securities – The PUMA Story", Housing Finance International.

Housing Finance International (2003) "Social Rental Housing in Europe", June 2003 issue.

HUD (2006) http://www.hud.gov/offices/hsg/gse/gse.cfm.

Impadivio, G., Musalem, A., and T. Tressel (2003) "Impact of Contractual Savings Institutions on Securities Markets", World Bank Working Paper 2948.

Kokularupan, N. (2006) "The Evolving Role of Secondary Market Institutions and Securitisation: Experience of Cagamas Berhad", presentation at the Second World Bank Conference on Housing Finance, Washington DC.

Lea, M. (2005) "Attracting Private Capital to Low Income Housing Markets", Housing Finance International, September 2005.

Mayer, Pratt, Rowe and Maw (2007) "Securitisation in Poland: Some Legal Issues", At A Glance.

Meddin, L. (2009) "What Happened? The Anatomy of a Global Credit Crunch", Euromoney Global Securitisation Review 2008/2009.

Meehan, J. (2004) "Tapping the Financial Markets for Microfinance", Grameen Foundation USA Working Paper.

Mecker, L. and M. Myers (1999) "Community Reinvestment Act Lending: Is It Profitable", Federal Reserve Bank of Kansas City.

Merrill Lynch (2008) "A Sluggish Start to 2008", Latin America Structured Finance Quarterly.

Moody's Investor Services (2006) "ROOF CEE 2006-1 Pre Sale Report".

Morgan Stanley (2006) "BOLD 2006-1 Blue Orchard Loans for Development, $[106]MM Equivalent Microfinance CLO".

Ng, S. (2008) "Delinquency Rate Growing More Slowly", Wall Street Journal, April 30, 2008.

OPIC Highlights (2007) "OPIC Supports Housing and Mortgage Finance".

OPIC News (2005) "OPIC Guarantees First Mortgage-Backed Security in Central America", 7, 3, April 2005.

Roubini Global Economics (RGE) Monitor 2006.

Schaub, W. (2006) "Heading for International Best Practices: Baltic Securitisation Analysis, Latvian Case Study", presentation at USAID Mortgage Conference, Bucharest, Romania, April 2006.

Stöcker, O. (2006) "Mortgage Bond Legislation in Europe", Association of German Mortgage Banks presentation.

Urban Institute (2006) "Feasibility Study of a Partial Credit Facility For Mortgage-Backed Securities In Romania".

S. Winkler and A. Batchvarov (2009), "Covered Bonds on a Rebound", Bank of America Merrill Lynch, Covered Bonds Research.

You, S.-D. (2003) "Establishing a New Government Sponsored Enterprise", Korean National Mortgage Corporation, Housing finance International, December 2003.

Zaltzman, M. D. (2006), "Leveraging Non-Traditional Lenders as an Origination Strategy for Reaching Underserved Borrowers", presentation at the International Housing Finance Program Wharton Business School, June 2006.

Annex 1: Prerequisites for Wholesale Funding

Issuer Need

Why should a housing lender seek wholesale funding? Generally speaking, wholesale funding enables lenders to expand and diversify their funding sources, relieve capital and/or liquidity constraints or better manage the risks of housing lending. While market-based wholesale finance is typically not cheaper than retail funding, it may lead to lower cost mortgage credit by expanding the supply of funds, improving competition and facilitating risk management.

One reason a lender may seek wholesale finance is if it is **capital constrained** (at least at the margin). In such circumstances, the all-in costs of wholesale funding (through asset sale) may be lower than retail funding, taking into account the high expense of equity capital. In this case, the capital savings afforded by securitization can more than make up for the higher cost of debt if the lender can get the assets off balance sheet for risk-based capital purposes. From a balance sheet and regulatory capital management perspective, however, the lower risk weight of residential mortgages may lead the lender to securitize other classes of assets (e. g., consumer loans with a 100% risk weight rather than mortgage loans with a 50% risk weight (or lower under Basel II). Non-depository lenders are more likely than banks in most countries to seek capital relief. Not surprisingly, these lenders – mortgage banks in the US, centralized lenders in the UK, mortgage managers in Australia, Sofols in Mexico, housing finance companies in India – have been the leaders in securitization.

Alternatively, the lender may be **liquidity constrained**. Taking into account a liquidity risk premium, wholesale funding may be cheaper than retail, particularly at the margin where the alternative to wholesale funding is raising additional funds through retail sources which may entail pricing up the stock of outstanding deposits. Lenders may also want to diversify their funding sources. Even if wholesale funding is currently more expensive than retail, a lender may wish to create a wholesale funding channel to better manage future liquidity and funding risk. The more liquid the lenders, however, the less likely they are going to ascribe a value to the liquidity premium of mortgages. Most banks in emerging markets are quite liquid.

The lender may have cash flow **risk management** needs. For example, it may wish to offer products with characteristics that are difficult to manage via traditional retail means, such as a medium- or long-term fixed rate mortgage which may be appropriate for lower-income households. On-balance sheet funding of such loans entails significant cash flow risk, and both interest rate risk if not match funded and prepayment risk if the borrower has that option. Lenders offering reviewable rate ARMs (adjustable rate mortgages – a common emerging market mortgage instrument) have less need to fund these through wholesale sources as they entail virtually no interest rate or prepayment risk. Countries with a greater proportion of funding coming from the wholesale markets (Denmark, Germany, US) have high proportions of mortgage loans with extended fixed interest periods.

In a relatively low rate environment, extending maturities can offer significant affordability benefits for borrowers. However, lenders in emerging markets are often particularly concerned about the maturity mismatch between long-term mortgages and short-term liabilities. Developing a wholesale funding channel to attract long term investors, if any exist, can reduce this risk. It can also potentially increase the supply of funds and the maturity of loans. That said, the concern about maturity mismatch may be overstated or mask other concerns of lenders (e. g., credit risk). Maturity risk is best judged from a portfolio perspective and may not be significant until mortgage assets constitute a significant portion of total assets.

An obstacle that mortgage lenders may confront when turning to wholesale finance is whether the pricing of the loans will support the costs of the transaction. Investors will compare the expected risk-adjusted returns from whole loans or mortgage securities to other investment alternatives. Depository lenders that price mortgage loans based on retail funding often find that there is insufficient yield to sell at par, particularly after transaction costs are taken into account.

Investor Requirements

A wholesale funding channel requires investors with an appetite and capacity for securities backed by mortgages. In certain circumstances the demand may come from other lenders. If there is a geographic mismatch, for example, some lenders may be asset rich and others liability rich (historically the case in the large US market). Or some lenders may not have the processing and distribution capabilities for housing lending and may prefer to purchase loans from other lenders rather than develop proprietary infrastructure for retail lending. Or, the demand may come from institutional investors such as insurance companies or pension funds. These investors have long-term liabilities and thus seek longer term assets to match their cash flow and investment targets. The task is to get these investors to fund housing through the purchase of mortgage securities.

When will investors be interested in mortgage-related securities? There are several prerequisites:

Mortgage securities must offer **attractive risk-adjusted returns**. In most cases, institutional investors will consider mortgage securities as an alternative to government bonds that provide a benchmark yield which typically represent a default-risk free, liquid investment alternative. Investors will seek a premium over government bond yields to reflect credit risk, liquidity risk and transaction costs of purchasing and managing the assets.[37] The premium required by investors may be

[37] Institutional investors typically prefer highly rated securities that can be created with credit enhancement. The credit risk in the underlying mortgage portfolio remains and

reduced if credit enhancement (either by third parties or through structuring, discussed below) is credible and if the market is somewhat liquid. Mortgage securities can be an alternative to corporate bonds, offering greater security due to their collateral backing.

Ultimately, the twin objectives of affordability and availability of funds may conflict. If institutional investors have an objective to maximize the risk-adjusted returns for their policy holders, they will invest only in mortgage securities, if these produce adequate returns. Yet, policymakers often believe that the interests of the poor are best served through below market rate loans. Requirements that force these investors to provide funds earning below market returns ultimately weaken retirement systems and reduce or preclude investment.[38]

Investors must have a **capacity** for mortgage-related securities. In markets in which governments excessively issue debt, the capacity of institutional investors to purchase mortgage securities may be limited or non-existent, because the government may crowd out other issuers. Capacity may also be related to the investors' liability mix. If investors have short duration liabilities, they will seek short duration assets as a match. Investors may prefer short duration assets in volatile environments to minimize the price risk in their portfolios. The characteristics of the loans and the investors' preferences may differ as well – e. g., lenders may create variable rate loans while investors may prefer fixed rate assets or vice versa.

Investors must be **able to invest** in mortgage-related securities. This is an infrastructure development issue. Investors must have the legislative and regulatory authority to invest in such assets, and the regulatory treatment must be well defined for capital adequacy, liquidity and asset allocation purposes, eligibility to technical reserves, etc. Investors' regulatory framework – for example through a minimum performance benchmark – may also force them to prefer secure, shorter-term and liquid securities.

Investors may require a liquidity backstop for securities, particularly in the early stages of market development. The Central Banks of Chile and Malaysia offered to repurchase mortgage related securities for a short time after their introduction. More recently, SHF in Mexico has repurchased a significant portion of the RMBS market pursuant to an agreement to be a liquidity provider for the market.

---

must be allocated in the transaction, either staying with the issuer or sold to specialist investors.

[38] The example of Korea is instructive. The Korean Mortgage Corporation (Komoco) was created in 1999 as a public-private partnership to develop a secondary mortgage market. As banks did not want to sell their mortgage loans they focused on securitizing below market rate loans originated by the National Housing Fund (previously required to be funded by pension plans). The government agreed to make up the difference in the cash flows required by investors and made by borrowers. After several transactions it decided that this approach was too expensive. KMC was subsequently reconstituted as the Korean National Mortgage Corporation (a government owned corporation) which provides guarantees on loans originated by the Fund. See You 2003.

Their purchases have strained their capital and are not sustainable. A more effective way to enhance liquidity is for Central Banks to allow highly rated mortgage securities to be eligible collateral for refinance transactions. The European Central Bank has done this for both AAA-rated covered bonds and RMBS.

Legal and Regulatory Infrastructure

The development of a wholesale funding channel is critically dependent on a country's legal and regulatory infrastructure. Adequate legal, tax and accounting frameworks are necessary for securitization and secured bond issuance. The accounting and tax treatment of mortgage securities for both issuers and investors must be clear and complete. Adequate disclosure of information about the collateral and the issuer is necessary to assess risk.

An important prerequisite for mortgage lending is proper facilities for **lien registration**. There must be an accurate and timely recording of the lender's interest in the collateral. Recording of liens must involve no more than a modest cost, particularly for existing housing, which is underdeveloped in most emerging economies.

The ability to **enforce liens** is also critical. Because investors can be last resort bearers of the credit risk attached to underlying mortgages, the enforceability of the lender's security interest is a major determinant of the attractiveness of mortgage-related securities, their pricing and required credit enhancement. If liens are not enforceable there is little to distinguish mortgage loans from unsecured debt – perhaps only a belief that the likelihood of default on an owner-occupied dwelling is less than that of a consumer debt. Lack of enforceability causes mortgage lending to be perceived as an unsafe activity in many developing countries, as in mature markets.

The ability to **transfer (assign) security interest** is necessary for securitization, which involves the transfer of the lender's beneficial interest to the investor. The legal system must recognize and record the transfer at only a modest cost.[39] In the case of mortgage bonds, the ability to transfer beneficial interest is important in the event of bankruptcy of the issuer.

Protection of investors **against bankruptcy** of the originator or servicer is an important feature in securitization. The credibility of the legal provisions ensuring bondholders that the collateral backing their assets would remain out of the reach of other creditors in case of insolvency proceedings is crucial. For securitization purposes, the concept of a special purpose vehicle or other construct that isolates the collateral pool from the issuer/servicer is essential to obtain "true sale" off-balance sheet accounting and capital treatment for the issuer. The concept of a bankruptcy-remote, special purpose vehicle (SPV) is critical for the development of securitization and is often lacking in developing country law. In many emerging

[39] In the event of default of a borrower, the facility may have to transfer or take possession of the loans.

markets, it has been necessary to pass specific laws on covered bonds (Egypt, Poland, Romania, Russia, Turkey and Ukraine) and securitization (Argentina, India, Poland Spain, South Korea and Thailand) to facilitate their issuance.[40]

Creating Good Quality Assets: Assessing the Probability of Default and Loss per Default

The creation of a wholesale funding channel starts with the creation of good quality assets. The characteristics of the assets must be well understood for investors to assess their likely performance – in particular the probability of and loss per default, but also the likely prepayment behavior of borrowers.

A starting point for creating good quality assets is standardization of documents and underwriting practices: The more standardized the products, documents and underwriting practices, the lower the transaction cost of due diligence and credit enhancement costs in the case of securitization. This constraint is less stringent for mortgage bonds, which shift the emphasis of standardization from the loans to the securities, but it is essential that mortgage bond legal frameworks define clear quality lending requirements. Standardization contributes to liquidity and thus lower yield premiums on mortgage securities. Underwriting practices must be well documented.

High quality servicing and collection is a necessary component for good quality assets. Investors in mortgage securities depend on external agents to collect and remit payments and deal with arrears. A secondary mortgage market is more likely to develop, and the relative cost of funds is likely to be lower, if investors have confidence in the ability of issuers to perform this function. Historical performance data from servicing systems is necessary to establish the cash flow characteristics of the pool and risk.

Professional standards of property appraisal are necessary for investors to determine the risk of loss. Investors must be confident in the value of the collateral underlying the lien. Appraisal standards may be based on concepts of mortgage able or open market value. In either case, it is necessary to develop a historical data base of transaction prices and characteristics for use in valuation.

Annex 2: Types of Credit Enhancement

There are two types of credit enhancement for wholesale funding: external and internal. External credit enhancement is provided from a highly rated third party that offers loss insurance (i. e. the insurer agrees to pay part or all of a loss arising

[40] The legislative process is often time consuming, costly and imperfect. For example, it took several years to pass legislation in Poland that made it possible to create SPVs. However, obstacles still remain with the result that off-shore transactions are more likely than on-shore. See Mayer, Brown, Rowe, September 2006.

from loan default) and cash flow insurance (i. e. the insurer agrees to make timely payment of principal and interest on the security). Internal credit enhancement is created by prioritizing and structuring the cash flows from a pool of loans.

Types of External Credit Enhancement

External credit enhancement can come from issuers that provide timely payment guarantees on the securities. Non-government issuers do not typically guarantee their own securities for several reasons. First, they typically do not have a high enough stand-alone rating. Second, providing a guarantee will negate true sale treatment for the security sale and thus capital relief. The guarantee would result in the loans being included in the balance sheet of the issuer and the securities being classified as debt for accounting and regulatory capital purposes.

The most notable issuer guarantees are provided by the US GSEs (Fannie Mae, Freddie Mac and the Federal Home Loan Banks) and the Hong Kong Mortgage Corporation. The advantages of issuer guarantees are their simplicity and their relatively low expense: the average guarantee fee charged by the GSEs is around 20 basis points. This structure can work well, if the objective is to foster acceptance of the securities of a centralized issuer in the market. Repeat issuers of standardized high quality securities can promote market acceptance of and liquidity in mortgage securities.

Each of these entities targets some of its purchases for affordable or low income housing. The GSEs have affordable housing obligations in the form of requirements for a majority of their purchases to be loans made to borrowers at or below the median income of an area or from designated low income housing submarkets.[41] However, the GSEs are not viewed as particularly effective in expanding the supply of credit to lower income households.[42]

Agency guarantees are provided by third party government agencies to credit enhance securities issued by lenders. These are cash flow guarantees promising

---

41 Specifically, 45% of their activity should be for low and moderate income households, defined as households with incomes below or equal to the area median, 17% for special needs households (mainly households with incomes of less than or equal to 60% of the area median) and 32% for underserved areas). The goals are not separate so one loan could count in one, two or all three categories.

42 Although HUD 2006 finds that the GSEs meet their goals, critics note that the vast majority of GSE purchases of affordable housing loans would have been made by lenders without their involvement. Several studies, notably the Congressional Budget Office 2001 and FM Watch 2001, find that only a fraction of the implicit subsidy of government support actually reaches borrowers. The development of the sub-prime market has probably been more instrumental in expanding the supply of credit to low income households. These borrowers are typically more risky than higher income borrowers and are a segment the GSEs have not engaged in order to protect their high ratings and earnings.

timely payment of principal and interest in the event of a disruption or default of the servicer or issuer. If issued by a government agency, such guarantees are full faith and credit of their governments and have a zero capital adequacy risk weight. The best known example of agency guarantees is the Ginnie Mae (Government National Mortgage Association) program. Ginnie Mae provides 100% cash flow insurance on pools of government loss insured (Federal Housing Administration – FHA and Veterans Administration – VA) mortgages. The first pass-through securities, issued in 1970, had Ginnie Mae guarantees. The Canada Mortgage and Housing Corporation (CHMC) has a similar program providing guarantees on securities issued by providers of government insured loans.[43]

Agency guarantees expose the guarantor to the risk of fraud or misrepresentation on the part of the originator (e. g., the quality of underwriting) and/or of the servicer (e. g., improper reporting of delinquency and prepayment). This risk can be substantial, if the guarantees are provided to thinly capitalized or lightly regulated issuers. Management of the risk is costly, requiring extensive quality control and servicing audits. While they have worked well in Canada and the US, their use is problematic in many emerging markets where the ability to monitor the risk and legal sanctions against fraud are weaker.

A major issue with both government-backed institution and third party agency guarantees is their continued existence long after their market development mission is accomplished. There are many critics of the GSEs in the US who point out that nearly all their activities are now undertaken by the private sector. Thus, the public policy benefit of implicitly backing these institutions is questionable. As their securities issuance and guarantees total more than $3 trillion, they expose the US government to a large contingent liability and the financial markets to systemic risk. It is notable that the SHF charter in Mexico requires the institution to stop issuing government–guaranteed debt by 2009 and stop providing government-backed guarantees by 2013. This was done out of concern that a government-backed institution could dominate the Mexican market in much the same way that the GSEs dominate the US market.

Multilateral development agencies including the World Bank Group (WBG), the Inter-American Development Bank (IADB) and the European Bank for Reconstruction and Development (EBRD) provide various forms of guarantees to enhance the credit on securitization transactions. The World Bank can offer partial credit and risk guarantees for pools of loans or individual projects. In most cases, the World Bank will require a government counter-guarantee. MIGA (Multilateral Investment Guarantee Agency) provides political risk insurance against specified acts. The insurance is provided to private sector investors and does not require a government counter-guarantee. The International Finance Corporation (IFC) –

---

[43] There are more than $600 billion in Ginnie Mae securities and $96 billion in CMHC securities outstanding. In both countries the government mortgage insurance programs they support are designed to facilitate homeownership by lower and moderate income households by lowering the down-payment requirement.

part of the World Bank – is a particularly active guarantor working with private sector issuers.

Bilateral guarantors include OPIC (Overseas Private Investment Corporation, US), TDA (US Trade Development Agency), and FMO (Dutch Overseas Investment Corporation). They provide similar forms of enhancement as multilateral guarantors. OPIC also provides political risk insurance. The principal advantages of the bilateral and multilateral guarantees are the reputation and expertise of the guarantor and the ability to limit the involvement to one or a few transactions, thus demonstrating feasibility without requiring a government to create a permanent institution or program. The disadvantages may be timeliness, sustainability and cost (relative to domestic government guarantees – however, both should be actuarially priced).

Multilateral and bilateral agencies typically provide partial guarantees. A partial credit guarantee represents a promise of full and timely debt service payment up to a predetermined amount. Typically, the sum that is paid out under the guarantee covers creditors irrespective of the cause of default. The guarantee amount may vary over the life of the transaction based on the borrower's expected cash flows and creditors' concerns regarding the stability of these cash flows. The partial nature of the guarantee properly aligns incentives between the loan originator and guarantor, which share the default risk.

Partial guarantees can be either in local currency (for domestic transactions) or foreign currency (for cross-border transactions). Partial guarantees benefit clients by bringing them improved market access, longer-term funding, a broader investor base, and embedded liquidity support. A borrower facing temporary liquidity problems may proactively draw upon the guarantee to prevent a default on creditors.

Private mortgage insurers and bond insurers (monolines) provide guarantees (sometimes referred to as wraps) to improve the rating on certain tranches of securitization transactions. Monoline guarantees are provided by private mortgage insurers (PMIs including Genworth, UGI, PMI, Radian) rated AA, and AAA bond insurers including AMBAC, MBIA and FGIC. The advantages of a monoline guarantee are the ability to improve the rating (including piercing the sovereign ceiling) and help in structuring. The limitations of this product are that they can be difficult to attract, expensive and often subject to investment grade ratings before the guarantee. Furthermore, if the monoline looses its AAA status, the bonds it guaranteed would be downgraded and it would not be able to continue providing guarantees.

Liquidity facilities are often part of securitization transactions. The timely payment of principal and interest depends on a qualified, financially sound servicer. Many securitization transactions benefit from access to a liquidity facility provided by a financial institution in the form of commitment to lend, a commitment to purchase assets or a letter of credit. Liquidity facilities are used in structures to cover potential time lags between inflows of revenue from the securitization's asset pool and its payment obligations under the ABS.

Types of Internal Credit Enhancement

Excess Interest/Spread: The difference between the coupon or interest rate paid by the borrowers and the coupon or interest rate paid to the certificate holders is deposited into an account that accumulates over time to cover any losses that occur during a specified period. Thus, if a loan defaults, the excess interest could be used to make payments to the certificate holders. Once a deal has reached its target level, any remaining excess spread is distributed to the residual holders. This form of credit enhancement provides an incentive for good servicing.

Over-collateralisation (OC): This involves transferring to the issuing vehicle receivables in amounts greater than those required to pay the securities if the proceeds of the receivables were received as anticipated. The amount of over-collateralization (usually 5% to 10%) is determined by the rating agencies and the underwriters/placement agents, and this in turn will depend upon the quality of the receivables, other credit enhancement that may be available, the risk of the structure (such as the possible bankruptcy of the originator/servicer), the nature and condition of the industry in which the receivables are generated, general economic conditions and, in the case of cross-border securitization, the sovereign risk. If all goes well, it is repurchased at the end of the transaction as the receivables are returned as part of the residual interest. This form of credit enhancement is present in virtually all securitization transactions.

Senior/Subordinated Structure: In this form of credit enhancement, subordinated or secondary classes of securities, which are lower rated (and bear higher interest rates) are sold to other investors or held by the originator. In the event of payment problems, the higher rated (senior) securities receive payments prior to the lower rated (subordinated) securities. It is not uncommon for there to be a number of classes of securities that are each subordinated to the more highly rated, resulting in a complex "waterfall" of payments of principal and interest. In the common structure, senior and subordinated classes of notes would be paid, in order of priority, prior to any equity securities or to any residual interest to the issuer. This form of credit enhancement is routine.

Cash Collateral Account/Reserve Fund: In this form of credit enhancement, the originator deposits funds in an account with a trustee to be used if proceeds from receivables are not sufficient to make required bond payments. The amount may be adjustable depending upon events.

Early Amortisation: If certain negative events occur, all payments from underlying assets are applied to the more senior securities until they are paid. This type of credit enhancement is very common. Another version, a "turbo", is used to reach and maintain the target level of over-collateralization. In general, "turbo" refers to the use of the excess spread (the difference between the interest paid on the underlying mortgages and that paid out on the MBS) to pay down bond principal.

CHAPTER 7

Primary Mortgage Market Development in Emerging Markets – Is the Central and Eastern Europe Experience Replicable in Sub-Saharan Africa?

Friedemann Roy

Senior Housing Finance Specialist, World Bank*

Abstract

The provision of more and better housing remains a long-standing policy problem in the transition from central planning to market economies in the early 1990s in Central and Eastern Europe (CEE) and Central Asia. Broad financial sector reform and favourable economic development supported the introduction of mortgage products, the development of keen competition and the emergence of various instruments or models to fund the increasing demand for home purchases. The region responded to this challenge through different financing mechanisms such as the covered mortgage bond, contractual savings schemes or the securitisation of mortgages.

With this experience in mind, this chapter explores whether models, techniques and mechanisms of housing finance developed in CEE offer lessons and useful adaptations for emerging markets, such as in Africa. This chapter was originally prepared before the outbreak of the global financial crisis (the crisis). Although most of the findings of this paper refer to the period before the crisis, they have been reviewed to consider their relevance in light of the effects of the crisis. Whereas most markets in CEE collapsed due to high exposure to foreign currency mortgages and loose lending standards, markets in Sub-Saharan Africa (SSA) have remained relatively stable (with the exception of South Africa) reflecting insulated smaller and simpler markets which had only weak links to international capital markets.

---

* The findings, interpretations, statements and conclusions expressed herein are those of the author alone and do not necessarily reflect the views of the World Bank and its affiliated organisations, or those of the Executive Directors of the World Bank.

D. Köhn and J.D. von Pischke (eds.), *Housing Finance in Emerging Markets: Connecting Low-Income Groups to Markets*, DOI 10.1007/978-3-540-77857-8_7,

Introduction[1]

Before the outbreak of the crisis, economic growth in CEE had been high for a number of years and outpaced Western Europe. The region was hit particularly hard during the crisis. GDP growth declined from 6.8% in 2007 to –6.1% in 2009. Mortgage markets in CEE collapsed to less than half of the pre-crisis mortgage loan origination level fuelled by a combination of loose standards, poor regulation of intermediaries and products, excessive reliance on refinancing in foreign currency and foreign banks.

Despite the crisis, the region experienced a remarkable transformation from a system of centrally allocated credit to market-oriented systems.[2] The rising incomes of households have become one of the main drivers of banking markets and many banks have expanded into mortgage lending. Therefore, it remains worth discussing how far the models, financing mechanisms and instruments are replicable in other regions or countries. Which measures have been successful and why? What are the lessons? Which conditions are required in other countries to replicate the successes of lending models established in CEE?

This chapter analyses the lessons for home purchase finance for other regions. It focuses on the primary market, where loans are initiated by commercial banks, savings and loan associations, credit unions or mortgage companies. The borrowers are usually expected to keep their property as security for the debt. Whether the loan can be issued, depends on the applicant's debt service capability.[3]

The chapter begins by discussing the criteria which are considered essential for the development of primary mortgage markets. It then explores mortgage markets in CEE, based on key macroeconomic indicators, the housing sector and the development stage of mortgage lending as well as the different funding instruments and mechanisms of mortgage loans. Market developments in SSA are presented.

With an average growth rate of 5–6% between 2003 and 2008, SSA was heading for stability and prosperity. Most of SSA weathered the crisis and has returned to economic growth albeit at a lower than pre-crisis level. Countries with strong linkages to international markets such as Nigeria and South Africa experienced a stronger contraction.

Most of the recent surge relates to a recovery of primary commodity markets, SSA's most important drivers of exports and economic growth, while political conditions in most countries remain fragile (e. g., disruptions in Kenya after the elections of a new government in 2008). Despite these unstable conditions, lenders have entered SSA markets more aggressively, thereby also focusing on retail customers. At present, most mortgage markets (except South Africa) are in very early

1 I would like to thank Mr. Raymond Struyk for his valuable comments and remarks.

2 See K. Kosareva/R. Struyk, "Emerging Long term Housing Finance in Russia," in Housing Finance International, March edition, 1996, pages 20–30.

3 See www.mortgagefit.com/primary-market.html, "What does the Primary Mortgage Market offer you?" 30 July 2008.

stages of development. As governments seek solutions to accelerate mortgage market development consideration of the CEE experience may be useful.

The penultimate section compares CEE markets with those of SSA and offers a host of measures to foster primary mortage market development. The final section provides a summary and future outlook.

Assessing Progress in Primary Market Development

Which criteria are necessary to create sustainable primary mortgage markets? We can differentiate between two categories: the first refers to the enabling environment and the second to those factors which initiate primary market development. An important measurement in this context is access to mortgage loans at reasonable cost (i. e. low interest rates, long terms, etc.), which is crucial in determining the eligibility of low- and middle-income groups. Long term sustainability requires the integration of the primary market into the capital markets to ensure continous funding. This aspect could represent a third category, i. e. elements necessary to secure capital market funding, in particular through secondary markets, which is not addressed here and only referred to where it is deemed appropriate.[4] Market development in CEE and SAA is assessed here against the criteria listed in table 1.[5]

The third category, funding mortgage loans through capital markets, often refers to covered mortgage bonds[6] or mortgage backed securities (MBS) as the most common instruments. Their availability depends on a number of prerequisites such as:

- **Legal and tax framework.** Securitisation must be supported by basic security laws, clear and reasonable off-balance sheet valuation guidelines for securitised assets and the guarantee of the bankruptcy remoteness of the special purpose vehicles (SPV) among others.
- **Large asset volumes.** Lenders must have sufficiently large pools of standardised mortgages for securitisation to achieve economies of scale to justify advantages of securitisation over alternative funding sources.[7]

---

4 See the chapter by Michael Lea for a discussion of secondary market development.

5 If not otherwise specified, CEE includes the Czech Republic, Estonia, Hungary, Latvia, Lithuania, Poland and Slovakia. Southeast Europe includes Albania, Bosnia and Herzegovina, Bulgaria, Croatia, Macedonia, Romania, Serbia and Slovenia.

6 A covered mortgage bond is a debt instrument that is secured against a dynamic pool of specially identified and eligible mortgages.

7 Advantages include diversification, cheaper funding, access to long term funds, balance sheet management, and economies of scale. Particularly, initial securitisations may be costly reflecting the lack of lender experience in the valuation of assets, legal procedures and in dealing with rating agencies.

- **Lender preparedness.** The originator's organisation must be prepared for securitisation, especially departments in charge of underwriting, servicing, information management[8] and treasury.
- **Investor demand.** Various factors influence investor demand for MBS. These include the performance of the mortgage loan pools, liquidity in the market, and availability of a benchmark or yield curve. Typically, investors compare the return on an MBS issue to that of government bonds which they view as the quasi risk-free alternative investment to the MBS issue. To compensate for the higher risk of an MBS issue, they expect an attractive risk-adjusted return.

Table 1. Criteria to assess primary market development in emerging markets

First category: creating the enabling environment	
1. Macroeconomic stability	An important prerequisite for housing finance development. Often linked to the inflation rate as the most important determinant of interest rates.[9]
2. Appropriate laws and regulations and functioning enforcement	A workable system of land registry and basic banking laws for foreclosure and other procedures.
3. Proper institutional framework	Important elements include a working and reliable credit bureau and clearly defined appraisal standards for property evaluations.
4. Financial development (banking sector reform and banking law reforms)	Characterised by financial depth measured as the ratio of outstanding bank credit to GDP [10] and the ratio of broad money (M2) to GDP.[11]
5. Effective housing policy to support mortgage market development	This criterion covers the legal and regulatory framework and government intervention to influence the supply of mortgage finance.[12]

[8] The IT architecture of the lender is important and must be capable of producing historical performance data and tracking future performance of mortgage loan portfolios (assets). In addition, the IT system must be able to support the administration of a securitisation programme by segregating assets, collections and payments.

[9] Other indicators include unemployment, government debt, or the current account deficit.

[10] See J. Hegedüs/R. Struyk, "Housing Finance – New and Old Models in Central Europe, Russia, and Kazakhstan", Open Society Institute, Budapest 2005, page 17. The emergence of housing finance is closely related to financial sector reform, bank privatisation and abolition of state monopoly institutions. Foreign banks were essential in providing capital and know how to the poorly capitalised and managed banks which they acquired.

[11] Broad money is defined as M1 (money in public circulation comprising banknotes, coins and immediately available deposits) plus savings and small time deposits, overnight repos at commercial banks, and non-institutional money market accounts (M2). See P. Honohan/T. Beck, "Making Finance Work for Africa", The World Bank, Washington DC, 2007, page 27.

Table 1 (continued)

Second category: initiating the primary market	
1. Adherence to minimum quality standards	Primary market quality depends primarily on the quality and consistency of underwriting standards and servicings.[13]
2. Provision of insurance services	Lenders typically require property and life insurance.[14]
3. Level of product innovations	Which products or specific product features do lenders offer to attract customers, e. g. indexed loan products and mortgage insurance/guarantee schemes? Which strategies do they pursue to widen their customer base, especially to low and middle income groups?
4. Access to long term funds	Which funding alternatives are available for lenders (terms, cost, and sustainability)? These include deposits, credit lines from other banks, international financial institutions, bonds, and others.

Market Developments in Central and Eastern Europe

How has the CEE managed to provide better housing and access to housing finance for their citizens after the fall of the Berlin Wall? The transition process in the 1990s posed a double challenge to CEE: on the one hand, there was a need to establish massive reforms to build market economies. On the other, citizens had to shift their perspective and embrace the realities of market economies. The conflict of the legacy of central planning policies and the introduction of new market oriented policies and instruments had a large impact on housing finance systems. Table 2 shows key economic indicators of the region including the considerable drop in GDP growth as a result of the crisis.

Table 2. Key economic indicators of countries in the region (2006–2010)

	2006	2007	2008	2009*	2010*
GDP growth (percentage change)	6.6	6.8	4.3	-6.1	3.3
Consumer prices (annual average, percentage change)	7.2	7.8	12	8.5	6.3

Source: IMF

---

12 Ideally, housing policy should not lead to market distortions. Interventions could be appropriate to initiate market development but should be subject to exit to enable market based solutions.

13 When investors are asked to place their trust in the loans backing securities, the minimum standards become critical. (See EBRD, Mortgage Loan Minimum Standards Manual, April 2004, page V).

14 In a later stage of development, life insurance is often replaced by mortgage payment protection insurance to guarantee repayment in the event of loss of job or income.

After the political changes in 1989/1990, the CEE economies went into a deep recession. The GDPs in the region fell by 30%-50%. Despite significant difference in strategy ranging from "shock therapy" to soft reforms, widespread privatisation of enterprises and price liberalisation led to a new economic and political system with a strong representation of large employer and investor interests. The associated recession lasted until the end of the 1990s for the CEE, and because of the Balkan conflict it lasted about five additional years in Southeast Europe. The onset of the ongoing global financial crisis came before Southeast Europe had fully recovered from the recession induced by the transition and the war. The recovery of the Baltic States from the ongoing crisis started earlier than in the Southeast Europe countries, but the adverse impact on the economy was deeper.[15]

The Transition to Modern Mortgage Markets in Central and Eastern Europe

Creating the Enabling Environment

The characteristic features of the "East European Housing Model" inherited from the planned economies included housing estates, poorly-maintained public housing, and rationed "elite" houses for the nomenklatura.[16]

In the transition process housing finance development was tied to economic stabilisation. The new EU member countries in Central Europe as well as Croatia spearheaded the reform process in the early 1990s followed by the Balkans and Russia about ten years thereafter. The early presence of foreign banks in new EU candidate countries had a great impact on the financial market development.

In the early years of transition, all countries experienced surging inflation, plummeting GDP growth, and falling real household incomes. The combination of reduced purchasing power and higher interest rates led to a fall in demand for long term loans. Concurrently, new housing construction fell to around half of the pre-transition levels (see Fig. 1). The collapse of government housing construction decreasing affordability reduced housing demand, as housing price increases exceeded that of household incomes.

All countries worked to establish appropriate legal and regulatory frameworks and enforcement systems. Hungary and Slovakia inherited a functioning land registry and basic banking laws supporting foreclosure and focused efforts on improving these laws and regulations. In the absence of such laws Russia and Albania needed to enact new laws. In Serbia, property legislation was based on two title

[15] See J. Hegedüs, "Emerging new housing regimes and the global economic crisis in CEE countries – case of Hungary", Symposium on Housing Markets and the Global Financial Crisis, Hong Kong, December 9-11, 2009, page 3.

[16] See J. Hegedüs/R. Struyk, "Divergences and Convergences in Restructuring Housing Finance in Transition Countries," in Housing Finance, New and Old Models in Central Europe, Russia and Kazakhstan, edited by J. Hegedüs and R. Struyk, LGI Books 2005, page 8.

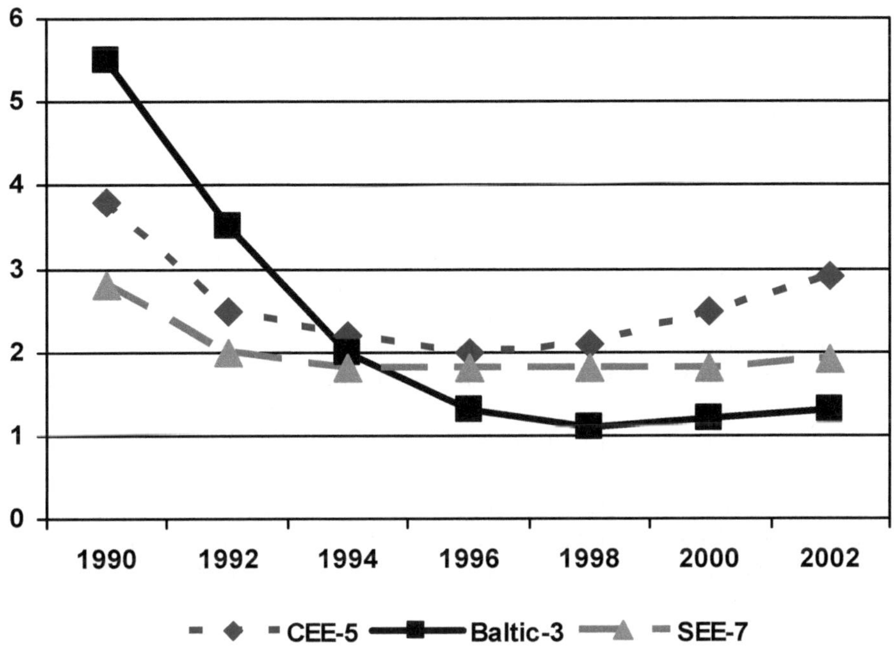

Fig. 1. New construction 1990–2002 – weighted average of homes per 1,000 inhabitants[17]
Source: Hegedüs/Struyk (2005)

systems and required harmonisation. In northern Serbia, there is a variant of the Austrian system, while in the south the Turkish Tapijeh system is dominant. This dual legislation, as well as inefficient enforcement, made the registration of mortgages difficult for banks, causing additional risks for registration and foreclosures.

The prospect of EU membership and the rising number of foreign financial institutions investing in the region had a major impact in shaping the new legal and regulatory framework.

Although all countries pursued market-oriented reforms, the housing sector benefited from massive government intervention. While the privatisation of the state-owned housing stock allowed for private homeownership, most households did not borrow against pledging the value of their homes to buy better and larger units, reflecting the continued preference of pre-transition tenure security through lifetime rental contracts and very low rental prices.

Other government interventions included considerable subsidy programmes to promote new construction ranging from direct subsidies, such as interest bonuses, construction subsidies, to tax-related incentives such as deduction of home purchase

[17] CEE countries comprise the Czech Republic, Poland Slovakia, Hungary, and Slovenia. SEE countries encompass Bulgaria, Serbia, Albania, Croatia, Bosnia and Herzegovina, Macedonia, and Romania. The Baltic States include Estonia, Latvia and Lithuania.

cost and mortgage interest payments from taxable income or VAT exemptions on construction material.

Initiating the Primary Market

The state dominated housing finance system collapsed in 1990 and it took about 10–15 years to establish a market based system. Since 2000, housing finance has become an important element of the banks' retail banking activities in CEE reflected by the substantial increase of outstanding mortgage loans to GDP from about 2% (2001) to 15% (2007). In Estonia, Latvia, and to a lesser extent in Lithuania, mortgage finance was influenced by a speculative demand fuelled by house price inflation. In the Czech Republic, Hungary, Poland, Slovakia, and Slovenia, the growth was fast but more balanced, while in Romania and Bulgaria housing finance markets have begun developing only in 2004.[18]

During the first years of CEE transition, innovative loan products, such as indexed loans and mortgage insurance/guarantee schemes, were introduced to address risks in the highly inflationary environment. However, these products failed under continued unstable macroeconomic conditions and unclear incentives for lenders. At that time, lenders were more interested in corporate finance than in retail banking, which they associated with higher risks. Households' decreasing real incomes were another obstacle to banks entering this market.

The determining factors for the growth of mortgage markets were decreasing inflation and interest rates as well as rising household incomes. Subsidy schemes also played an important role in boosting demand. For example, subsidies in Hungary reduced mortgage interest rates by up to 300 basis points.

In the Balkans, lenders entered retail banking around 2002 and offered mortgage loan products a few years later. Mortgage loans were typically denominated in EUR or in local currency indexed to the EUR. In Serbia, the establishment of a credit bureau in 2004 provided a major incentive for lenders to expand into mortgage lending.

Commercial banks with foreign ownership were the main providers of mortgages. Austrian banks like Erste Bank and the Raiffeisen Group, and Italian banks such as Unicredit and Banca Intesa, built strong networks through which they offered mortgage loans. Specialised lenders were also present: Bausparkassen started operations in the Czech Republic, Slovakia, Hungary, Croatia and Romania. Specialised mortgage banks were established in Poland and Hungary. Their presence was linked to the adoption of specialised legislation in the form of acts regulating the activities of Bausparkassen or acts governing the issuance of covered mortgage bonds. The attraction of the Bausparkassen products was largely dependent on the size of a savings bonus granted by the respective government.

[18] J. Hegedüs, "Emerging new housing regimes and the global economic crisis in CEE countries – case of Hungary, Symposium on Housing Markets and the Global Financial Crisis, Hong Kong, December 9-11, 2009, page 12.

The former monopolistic market position of the state-owned savings banks faltered during the privatisation process and rising competition from new market entrants, often foreign bank acquisitions of domestic banks. However, the state-owned institutions in Russia succeeded in maintaining leading roles in their markets. For example, Sberbank still holds 35% of banking system deposits and 30% of banking system loans in Russia.[19]

Funding Instruments and Mechanisms

A primary market requires a variety of funding instruments to match different financing activities of lenders consistent with their asset-liability management strategies. Similar to the EU 15, the CEE countries have introduced a host of funding instruments and generally countries which have welcomed foreign ownership have developed most rapidly. Funding options mainly depend on the progress of transition. The following stages can be defined:

1. **Primarily deposit-based lending.** Lenders in Albania, Bosnia and Herzegovina, Croatia, Macedonia and Serbia use deposits to finance their mortgage loans. Since savings terms are typically not longer than one year, lenders are exposed to interest rate and liquidity risk. Longer-term credit lines from international financial institutions (such as EBRD or KfW) or a parent credit institution can help mitigate these risks.
2. **Establishment of capital markets.** In Bulgaria, Slovenia and the Baltic States, the covered mortgage bond was introduced as a funding instrument. In Romania, the legal framework for secondary mortgage markets was implemented in 2006.[20] However, deposits and international credit lines still play an important role in financing mortgages. In Poland, the restrictive design of the Act on Mortgage Banks hampered the development of the covered mortgage bond system.
3. **Transition to market-based lending.** In the Czech Republic, Hungary and Slovakia, lenders can select various funding options. The introduction of a regulatory and institutional framework supporting funding of debt through the capital market, and the covered mortgage bond as a funding instrument of mortgage debt, have spurred market development in these countries. Table 3 highlights the importance of the covered mortgage bond in funding mortgage loans. In the Czech Republic and Hungary, its importance ex-

[19] See E. Moser/T. Nestmann, „Russia's financial sector", Deutsche Bank Research, August 20, 2007, page 12.

[20] See A. Sacalschi/O. Stöcker, "Neues Gesetz über Covered Bonds in Rumänien", in Immobilien und Finanzierung 15-2006. The Covered Bond law that the Romanian Government enacted merges elements of the traditional German legislation on covered mortgage bonds with MBS features.

ceeds that of EU countries. In Russia, the share of mortgage backed securitisation to mortgage lending amounted to 3.76% as of early 2007. The great demand for mortgages denominated in foreign currency has an impact on the banks' funding. In Hungary, for example, the share of outstanding covered mortgage bonds in relation to total residential lending decreased from 98% in 2005 to 58% in 2006, since increased lending in foreign currency allowed the banks to issue fewer bonds in the Hungarian stock market.

Table 3. Outstanding covered bonds to total residential loans outstanding in % (2006)

Czech Republic	Hungary	Poland	Latvia	Lithuania	EU 15 average
68.8	58.0	2.0	1.4	1.4	16.2

Sources: EMF Hypostat 2005 (Nov. 2007)

With the enactment of covered mortgage bond laws, CEE commenced to tap capital markets to fund mortgage loans. Although the German law on Pfandbriefe served as a general model, variations appeared. For example, Polish and Hungarian covered bond laws retain the specialty principle, i. e. only specialised mortgage banks are entitled to issue covered mortgage bonds. Latvian and Slovakian legislation requires a licence to issue covered mortgage bonds while the Czech Republic and Lithuania do not require a licence.[21]

Meanwhile lenders in most CEE countries have securitised their mortgage loan portfolios at a modest scale.[22] Several reasons explain lenders' reluctance: first, covered mortgage bonds have provided the necessary funds. Second, most banks have been financed by their parents. Third, regulatory hurdles remain. Legislation in most countries permits securitisation, at least as a cross-border transaction including the transfer of national assets to a special purpose vehicle governed by international law.[23] However, most of the relevant laws require time-consuming re-registration of the mortgage and related assets. Another obstacle is the lack of le-

---

21 See T. Lassen, "Specialisation of Covered Bond Issuers in Europe", in: Housing Finance International, December 2005.

22 CEE countries contrast to the Russian MBS market prior to the crisis. From 2006 to the second half of 2007, the volume of Russian MBS issuances almost doubled (from USD 377 million to USD 703 million). The securitisations denominated in Rubles increased as well. The reason for the predominant share of USD denominated MBS is that most mortgages are in USD. In addition, USD apparently attracted foreign investors, while national investors lacked experience with MBS. (see J. Wookey, "Securitisation is no longer a dirty word", Euromoney, Volume 38, Number 461, September 2007, page 344).

23 See Mayer, Brown, Rowe & Maw LLP, "At a glance", information leaflets on securitisation in various countries in central and south east Europe, September 2006.

gal precedent. In Southeast Europe the enabling environment is still weak. For example, in Serbia half of the housing stock is not registered, and the different title systems within the country are a further obstacle. Finally, lacking data due to the short history makes it difficult to predict more reliable loan default levels.[24]

The Situation of Mortgage Markets in Central and Eastern Europe

Most countries still face a backlog in housing construction. In Poland, for example, the housing deficit is estimated at 1.5 million apartments. Lack of supply is one reason for relatively high house prices, which have risen faster than average incomes, producing housing price-to-income ratios that undermine affordability. Especially in urban areas, houses have become unaffordable for an average income household.[25] For example, in Moscow in 2004, an average house costs USD 68,000 a multiple of 25 times the average annual household income of USD 2,700.

Another reason for house price hikes has been the increasing availability of mortgage loans which has driven up demand for houses. For example in Serbia, the volume of mortgage loans grew by 244% in 2005. Despite this remarkable rise in mortgage supply, most people cannot afford to buy a house. The price for a 55 square metre apartment was about EUR 69,000, while the average annual salary was about EUR 3,816. In Bulgaria, the ratio of mortgage lending to GDP rose by 1.4% (2004) to 2.1% (2005) while house prices surged by 47% and 36.5% during the same years.[26] Fig. 2 illustrates the trend in Bulgaria.

Since 1997, the supply of mortgages steadily increased, fuelling demand for housing. House prices surged between 2003 and 2004 by 71%. As a result, housing affordability declined.

Without an increasing housing supply, the increased offer of mortgage financing is likely to exacerbate the affordability problem. This supply gap reflects that (i) cities do not provide enough land for residential housing, (ii) the number of qualified developers is fairly limited and (iii) access to finance for developers is restricted. Resolving this dilemma is difficult. On the one hand, developers do not build more houses unless finance is available. On the other, private persons are not able to buy houses without mortgages. Concerted efforts of policy makers, municipalities, lenders and developers may help to mitigate these effects.

Mortgage debt outstanding in CEE countries accounts for about 5% of GDP in 2005 compared with 47.5% in the Euro zone. Figure 3 indicates the positive association of percapita income and mortgage market development in the CEE and the EU.

---

24 This is also a reason why mortgage default insurance has not yet taken up in CEE.

25 Data are from J. Hegedüs/R. Struyk, "Housing Finance – New and Old Models in Central Europe, Russia, and Kazakhstan", Open Society Institute, Budapest 2005.

26 See EMF Hypostat 2005, "A review of Europe's Mortgage and Housing Markets", November 2006, pages 129 and 138.

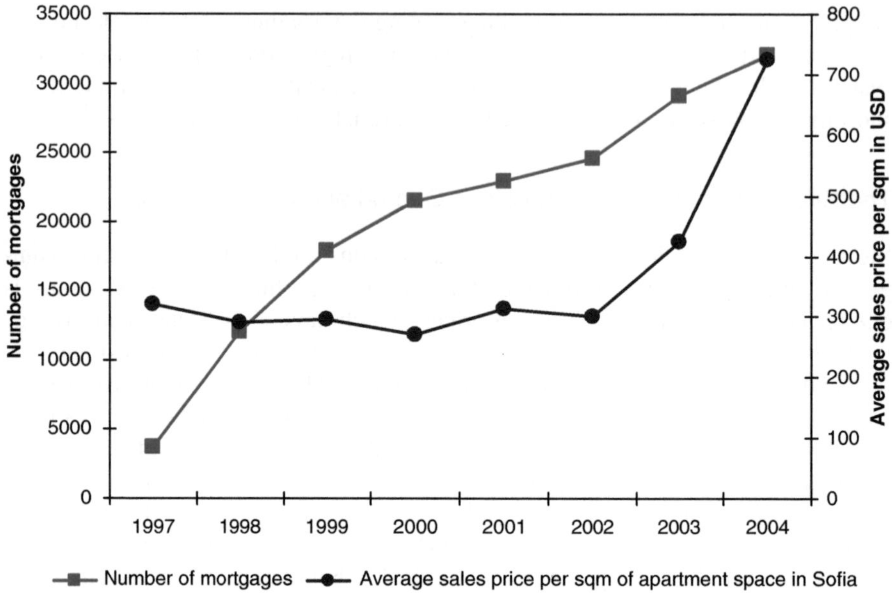

Fig. 2. Correlation between supply of mortgages and house prices in Bulgaria (1997–2004)

The market penetration levels in Southeastern Europe in comparison with Central Europe reflect the later start in transition because of the Balkan war and a lack of (i) clear property rights, (ii) clear systems of title deeds and (iii) effective institutions for the valuation of non-financial assets. Further growth of mortgage markets depends on a higher outreach of lenders especially to rural areas. An indicator of penetration is the number of households with a bank account, which lenders view as a platform for servicing mortgage repayments. In Hungary and Poland, the share of bank accounts/bank relationships to households amounts to about 70%, whereas in Bulgaria and Romania, it accounts for 33% and 35% respectively (EU: 98%).

The most common mortgage product in CEE is a loan for purchase or construction. In Southeastern Europe, home improvement loans have also become popular, although they are slowly being replaced by cash loans due to the latter's simpler procedures.

Table 4 provides an overview of mortgage loan conditions in selected countries. Conditions in Germany provide a benchmark. The majority of banks in these countries are subsidiaries of foreign banks, underwriting and servicing standards were in line with those practised in Western Europe. Due to fierce competition, many banks softened their lending standards, leaving borrowers with low safety margins in case their financial situation worsened.

The house price increase coupled with the introduction of new loan products led to an extreme increase in outstanding loans in the Baltic States, especially Latvia and Estonia, where the loan to GDP ratio surpassed 30%.

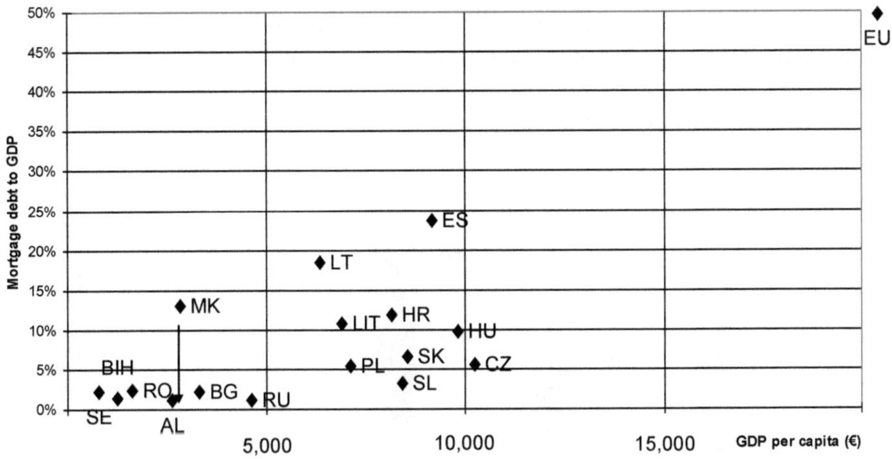

Fig. 3. CEE and EU mortgage debt to GDP and GDP per capita in 2005

Sources: BMI, Emerging Markets Monitor, Vol. 13, Issue 9 (Sept. 2006), EMF Hypostat 2005 (Nov. 2006), Central Banks of respective countries

Table 4. Mortgage loan conditions in selected countries (2007)

	Estonia	Poland	Croatia	Slovakia	Russia	Germany
Average interest rate (in %)	3.3–3.9 (in EEK)	4.95–6.7 (in PLN)	5–5.71 (in EUR or CHF)	5.09 (fixed for 1 year) – 5.59 (fixed for 15 years)	15 (in RUR) 9.5–12.5 (in USD)	4.55–5.42 (60% LTV ratio)
Loan term in years	Up to 30	5–35	15–20	1–30	7–20	25–30

In the Baltics as well as in most CEE countries, borrowers were attracted by loans denominated in foreign currency. Borrowers believed that they could reduce their payment burden since the interest rate on a foreign exchange loan was lower in nominal terms. However, most of them did not take into consideration the exchange rate risk since their salaries were paid in domestic currency. In Hungary, for example, a CHF denominated loan bore an interest rate of 5.75% p. a., whereas in HUF it would have cost a borrower about 14%.[27]

[27] Central banks are concerned about the volume of foreign currency loans. To combat lending in foreign currency, the National Bank of Poland introduced new requirements for these types of loans. The main rationale behind this policy is to promote safer mortgage lending.

Since funding cost in foreign currency was relatively lower for the banks than in local curreny and helped to attract customers, lending in foreign currency became an attractive lending model in most of CEE. In the Czech Republic and in Slovakia, lenders did not offer mortgage loans denominated in foreign currency.

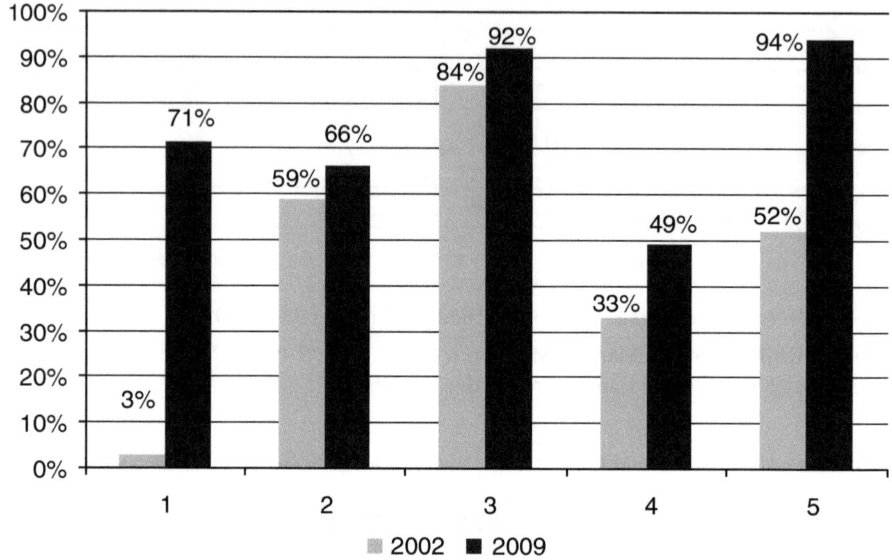

Fig. 4. Mortgage loans in foreign currency to total mortgage loans in selected CEE countries
Sources: Central Banks (data for Bulgaria and Romania, January 2007).

The growth in the mortgage market in the 2000–2007 period coincided with a rapid credit expansion in the financial sector, large capital inflows often from foreign banks, and spiralling house price inflation. The growth came to an abrupt halt with the onset of the crisis, which triggered massive devaluation, market liquidity shortages and interest rate increases.[28]

The crisis highlighted the vulnerability of foreign currency based lending. Depreciating local currencies, rising unemployment and stagnating incomes led to the default of many borrowers. In Hungary, for example, non-performing loan ratios amounted to 8% of the total mortgage loan portfolio (as per March 2010).

[28] See H.-J. Duebel/S. Walley, "Regulation of Foreign Currency Mortgage Loans – the case of transition countries in Central and Eastern Europe", Washington DC, May 2010, page 10.

What Has Driven Product Development and Better Access to Mortgage Credit?

What can we learn from the experience of CEE? From a common point of origin, a great variety of products, funding instruments and mechanisms emerged. Some countries like the Czech Republic or Romania adopted the Bausparkassen system, while most countries in the region adopted the covered mortgage bond system reflecting the diversity that exists in Western European countries.

There are no simple explanations as to why a country chooses a particular model. Arbitrariness and the advice and marketing of specific instruments by aid agencies and financial institutions may have played an important role.[29] However, the following factors were important in establishing mortgage markets in CEE:

- **Rising incomes and falling interest rates.** Favourable macroeconomic conditions have fuelled demand for housing. Households have experienced increasing incomes, sometimes exceeding productivity rises, as in Latvia.[30] Coupled with lower interest rates, many can afford to take out a loan. On the negative side, the improved availability of loans has driven house price inflation.
- **Improved regulatory and institutional frameworks have** been pivotal in better access to housing finance. The availability of titles, the registration of mortgages and the right to enforce a lien in case the borrower defaults enabled large scale mortgage financing. Other important factors were the existence of a credit bureau and a transparent valuation regime. Central and Eastern European countries now possess regulatory and institutional frameworks which are comparable with those of Western European countries. Southeast European countries are catching up. In this context, Bulgaria and Romania showed more progress than the other Balkan countries. In all countries, central banks appeared to have strongly supported reforms.
- **Better access to funding**. As outlined above, the introduction of funding mechanisms, mainly the covered mortgage bond, has assisted in creating the framework for banks to tap long term funding in Southeast Europe. The funds provided by the headquarters of western banks to their subsidiaries in the region were another important organizations funding channel. However, the high dependency on funding from parents (mainly in foreign currency) crowded out domestic funding sources and increased the vulnerability of the private households to flucutations in the national currency in relation to for-

[29] J. Hegedüs/R. Struyk, "Divergences and Convergences in Restructuring Housing Finance in Transition Countries", in Housing Finance, New and Old Models in Central Europe, Russia and Kazakhstan, edited by J. Hegedüs and R. Struyk, LGI Books, 2005, page 33.

[30] See Financial Times, "Baltic Boom states face hard landing", July 5, 2006. In Latvia, wage growth has exceeded productivity increases by 20% per year.

eign currencies (especially CHF and EUR). Lenders obtained easier acess to liquidity at the cost of higher credit risk.

- **Competition**. Enhanced competition among lenders drove the introduction of new products and the expansion of banking services to lower and middle income groups. For example, interest rates on new mortgage loans in Slovakia fell from 10% in 2000 to 6.3% in 2006. In Estonia, the decrease was from 12.3% in 1997 to 4.4% in 2006.[31] However, competition fuelled a loosening of the underwriting standards and riskier products.

Another decisive factor has been the government's role in shaping the housing market, which sometimes led to ambiguous results. In Hungary, for example, mortgage loan subsidies have been fuelling the rising demand for mortgage loans. However, they imposed a mounting fiscal burden.[32]

Mortgage Market Developments in Sub-Saharan Africa

SSA countries have a longer history of independence and transition than CEE countries, starting with Ghana in 1957 and terminating in South Africa with the abolition of the apartheid regime in 1994. Today the region comprises 48 countries with a total of about 740 million people.[33] Despite the longer transition period, SSA countries have only recently experienced economic stability and growth.

This section describes mortgage markets in SSA highlighting risks and challenges for further development as well as interregional comparisons, the enabling environment and the progress of primary market development.[34]

How Do Sub-Saharan African Markets Differ from Central and Eastern Europe?

Before the outbreak of the global financial crisis in 2008, SSA countries experienced nearly a decade of economic growth. Growth rates averaged 5–6% since 2005. Inflation rates fell to single-digit levels. These positive developments were fostered by strong economic policies; a favourable external environment, especially

31 EMF Hypostat 2006, European Mortgage Federation, a review of Europe's mortgage and housing markets, Brussels, November 2007, page 138.

32 See also R. Rózsavölgyi/V. Kovács, "Housing Subsdies in Hungary: Curse or Blessing", Ecfin Country Focus, Volume 2, Issue 18, 10 November 2005. For further information on the government's role, see R. Struyk, "Home Purchase Affordability and Mortgage Finance", in Housing Finance, New and Old Models in Central Europe, Russia and Kazakhstan, edited by J. Hegedüs and R. Struyk, LGI Books 2005.

33 The population of Central and South-Eastern Europe is 135 million and in Russia 142 million.

34 Unless otherwise specified, South Africa and Zimbabwe are not included here.

Table 5. Key economic indicators of SSA (2006–2010)

	2005	2006	2007	2008	2009*	2010*
GDP growth (percent change)	6.2	6.4	6.9	5.5	1.1	4.1
Consumer prices (annual average, percent change)	8.9	7.3	7.1	11.6	10.5	7.2

Source: IMF African Department database, * = IMF estimates

rising commodity prices; debt relief and aid from the international community. Table 5 shows key macroeconomic indicators of the region.

The global financial crisis has had a considerable adverse impact on the continent since the last quarter of 2008, reversing the previous positive growth trend. According to the IMF, growth has fallen from 5.5% in 2008 to 1.1% in 2009 and is expected to recover to 4.1% in 2010. Inflation is expected to fall below double digit levels in 2010. Because of their stronger linkages to international markets, South Africa, Nigeria, Ghana and Kenya have been affected more severely than other SSA countries.

The global financial crisis affected SSA mainly through the real sector as well as through a decline of capital flows that affected the financial sector. Traditional export markets deteriorated, commodity prices declined and the volume of remittances decreased. Deutsche Bank Research estimates capital inflows at half of the 2007 level of about USD 32 billion.

However, SSA has generally avoided the major macroeconomic instabilities that followed previous crises. Foreign exchange reserves remain close to their historic highs, which should leave room for economic stimulus packages. Typically, lenders in most countries were not allowed to invest in toxic assets. Thus, the need to mark down has not impacted their performance. However, non-performing loans after a period of rapid credit growth and a contraction of business activities could lead to rising credit risk for lenders.

With the exception of South Africa, national mortgage markets have not come under severe strain. Mortgage housing loan portfolios are still quite small and the volume of mortgage lending to GDP accounts for 1–2% in most SSA countries (South Africa: 34%). Additionally, loan-to-value ratios (LTVs) are quite low (typically around 50%) and banks have granted mortgages mainly to upper middle and higher income groups. Lending has been done mainly in domestic currency and thus avoided foreign currency risks witnessed in CEE. Although short-term deposits have been the main funding instrument, liquidity risk has been manageable due to small mortgage portfolios. Specialised lenders (mainly state-owned housing banks) have been marginally affected due to strong financial support from their government sponsors.[35]

[35] See IMF, Regional Economic Outlook (2009), Sub-Saharan Africa, Washington DC. Deutsche Bank Research (2009), African frontier capital markets: More than a flash in the pan. Frankfurt.

A fragmented and inadequate legal and regulatory framework has prevented financial sectors in SSA from contributing more significantly to economic growth. Financial sectors are typically shallow relative to the size of the economies, with a narrow range of institutions and limited access to basic financial services – in particular for low and middle-income groups.

A key characteristic of SSA financial sectors is limited access to services. Only a disproportionately small fraction of the populations across the region is served by formal financial institutions. For example, the number of branches per 100,000 people is about 2.8 whereas in the CEE and SEE it reaches nearly 8. SSA also has one of the lowest levels of formal deposit account usage: only 390 people in 1,000 have a deposit account with a formal institution.[36] More recent data suggest that not more than 20% of African adults have an account at a formal or semi-formal financial institution.[37]

The Situation of Mortgage Markets in Sub-Saharan Africa

This section provides a review of the situation of mortgage lending. Particular focus is placed on barriers, risks and constraints to housing finance mechanisms and instruments.

Creating the Enabling Environment

Despite governments' concerted efforts to improve regulatory and institutional frameworks, most countries lack efficient property registries, functioning credit bureaus or clear foreclosure rights. Often, lenders cannot trace ownership rights, since a change of ownership is not registered. In Nigeria, banks require a title search to assess the legal situation of property offered as collateral. This procedure is regularly followed by title perfection to ensure the registration of the mortgage. The cost for these measures can amount to as much as 20% of the loan amount.

Land is often managed by tribal custom.[38] Different forms of law are a further reason of underdeveloped formal land systems,[39] resulting in the coexistence of overlapping systems (traditional, state and private).

---

[36] See T. Beck/A. Demirgüç-Kunt/M. S. M. Peria, "Reaching out: Access to and Use of Banking Services across Countries", World Bank mimeo, Washington DC, 2007.

[37] See P. Honohan/T. Beck, op. cit.

[38] In this situation, decisions on land use are made according to the customs of the tribe. Such decisions are rarely recorded in writing, creating no evidential basis for the use of rights.

[39] The United Kingdom brought common law to Kenya, Malawi, Tanzania, Uganda, Zambia and Zimbabwe. Southern countries such as Botswana, Lesotho, Swaziland, South Africa and Namibia were governed by Roman-Dutch law. Countries in West Africa (such as Côte d'Ivoire, Cameroon and Benin) were given Napoleonic law. In Angola and Mozambique, Portuguese law applies. See R. Groves, "Challenges Facing the Provision of Affordable Housing in African Cities", in Housing Finance International, XVII, June Issue, 2004, pages 26–31.

Recent research on creditor rights in SSA countries confirms that countries with stronger creditor rights and information sharing have deeper financial systems. Consequently, financial institutions are more willing to provide credit if contracts can be enforced by forcing repayment or seizing collateral in case of default.[40]

SSA cities have some of the fastest rates of urbanisation in the world. According to UN Habitat, the region will have an urban majority by 2030, with more people living in towns and cities than in the total population of Europe (about 492 million). Rapid urbanisation has created considerable growth in informal housing. Projections suggest that by 2030 about 72% of urban residents will live in informal settlements.[41] Projections reveal that not only the urban poor will live in these areas, and that low and middle-income groups will often be unable to obtain affordable housing. Several factors have led to this development:

- Limited and/or weak land and housing policy responses. In Ghana, for example, the numerous government programmes aimed at developing lower income housing failed to provide affordable units for these income groups.[42]
- Lack of an adequate supply of formal land zoning. In Zambia, for example, the capacities of local governments to zone new land, administer it well, and improve infrastructure networks are restricted.[43]
- Cost of construction material. Especially land-locked countries like Rwanda or Burkina Faso suffer from high construction material cost which is due to the lack of an adequate transport infrastructure. Coupled with that is an underdeveloped building material industry that struggles to produce good quality.
- Limited availability of home purchase finance overall, and sharply limited funding that is affordable only by higher income households.

The various systems of land ownership and administration are a major impediment to the efficient planning and functioning of land and housing markets. As a consequence, the majority of the urban population (in particular new migrants from rural areas) ends up in informal settlements. The lack of title prevents them from obtaining formal housing finance.

---

40 See L. Schumacher, "Creditor Rights in Sub-Saharan Africa", IMF, Regional Economic Outlook: Sub-Saharan Africa, Washington DC, 2008, page 22.

41 See Financial Times, Special Report on African Infrastructure, "A pressing concern", 21 November 2006.

42 See S. Merrill/M. Tomlinson, "Housing Finance, Microfinance, and Informal Settlement Upgrading: An Assessment of Ghana", Paper prepared for the African Union of Housing Finance and USAID, The Urban Institute, Washington DC, June 2006, page 18.

43 See D. Gardener, "Access to Housing Finance in Africa: Exploring the Issues in Zambia", FinMark Trust, May 2007, page 6.

Initiating Primary Mortgage Markets in the Region

Figure 5 shows the mortgage lending to GDP ratios of major SSA countries. The low ratios in housing finance reflect the small scale of the national banking sectors. Notable exceptions are the markets in South Africa (34%) and Namibia (20%). Figure 5 also shows the ratio for Europe as a comparison.

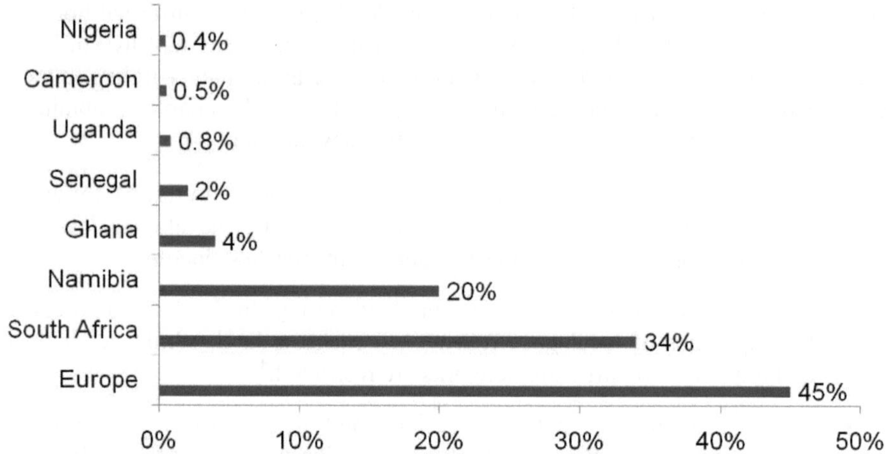

Fig. 5. Mortgage lending to GDP (2009)

Source: World Bank, various national statistical databases and authorities

Some lenders make loans for housing purposes that are issued as personal loans. Very seldom do lenders maintain separate statistics for these housing loans.[44] If mortgage loans are available, the borrowers are from higher income groups or are business owners.

Table 6 provides an overview of housing finance product features in selected markets in SSA. Typically, loans are offered in local currency and are secured by a mortgage and/or personal guarantees.

In most countries, housing microfinance products are offered by microfinance institutions, cooperatives or non-governmental organisations (NGOs). Loan amounts vary from USD 400 to USD 5,000 with tenors from 1 to 5 years. Interest rates are usually in the range of 20% and higher. The loans finance home improvement or the incremental house building process.

The Nigerian housing finance market is at an early stage of development. Fewer than 10,000 mortgages have been sold to date. But banks see great potential

44 See P. Honohan/T. Beck, op. cit., page 56. For comparison, housing finance amounts to between 15 and 21 percent of GDP in Chile, Malaysia, and Thailand.

Table 6. Housing Finance Product Features in Sub-Sahara Africa

	South Africa	Nigeria	Ghana	Senegal	Mali	Burkina Faso	Ethiopia	Uganda	Kenya	Rwanda	Zambia	Malawi	Mozam-bique
Average size of loan (in USD)	Minimum 10,000			50,000	30,000	10,000	15,000-20,000	35,000-60,000	up to 100,000	30,000	10,000-12,000	up to 35,500	
Term (in years)	20–30	up to 20	15	15–20	4–15	8–10	up to 10	up to 20	7–20	5–10	up to 10	up to 20	12–25
Interest rate	11% (prime rate)	16–20%	13.50% (Loans in USD) 28–30% (Loans in Ghanaian New Cedi)	9.5–11%	10–14%	10.5–12%	9.75% – 10.75% (term > 10 years)	16–18%	12.5–15.5%	15–16%	25–28%	19–24%	16–22.5%
LTV ratio	80–100%		up to 75%	50–80%	50–70%	up to 75%	up to 80%	up to 70%				80%	up to 70%
Typical Payment-to-income Ratio		35% (Loan amount depends on salary)	35% (Loan amount depends on salary)										

Source: FinMarkTrust, Worldbank, AfD, Roland Igbinoba Foundation for Housing and Urban Development

in this market. The housing shortage is estimated at about 12 million dwellings.[45] Prerequisites for an expanded range of mortgage products include lenders' access to longer term funds at favourable rates and an improvement of the enabling environment. In addition, banks stress the importance of keeping marketing messages for mortgage products simple and straightforward.[46]

In Uganda, the government estimates the housing shortfall at 377,000 units per annum until 2015. The average cost for a dwelling amounts to about USD 15,000. Currently, two banks offer mortgage loans. Their total mortgage portfolio is estimated at about USD 65 million. Their lending activities are mainly concentrated in the capital. A third lender, Stanbic, a South African subsidiary of Standard Bank, has recently entered the mortgage market.[47]

Risks in Mortgage Lending in SSA Markets

In SSA countries, lenders face the following risks which prevent their expansion into housing finance:

Credit Risk. High perceived credit default risk results in low intermediation. Typically, SSA lenders allocate more of their resources to liquid assets or to the purchase of government bonds.

- Inadequate legal systems for collateralised lending, land ownership and titling conditions. In Kenya, for example, laws and rules that govern land administration are complex, since there are a number of land tenure categories: customary/trust land, private leasehold/freehold land and government land as well as informal de facto tenure. In informal settlements, de facto tenure is the most common form of ownership. The lack of clear titles makes it very difficult to obtain a loan from a bank.[48] Coupled with this is poor legal protection of secured lending and weak enforcement of collateral. In Ghana, between 1998 and 2002, for example, 2,341 foreclosure cases were brought to court, but only 73 were resolved during this period.[49]
- Lack of credit bureaus. Where they exist, their coverage and the extent of information registered is very narrow. This is due to the informality of residence and the lack of stable reference points.[50]

---

45 See F. Roy, "Application of (Contractual) Savings Schemes for Housing in Africa", presentation given at 2nd African Microfinance Conference in Cape Town, 30 August 2005.

46 See N. Kochan, "Retail jump-start", in The Banker special supplement on Nigeria, April 2007, page 26.

47 See USAID, "Investigation into proposed Uganda Housing Securitisation", Afcap Consulting, April 2007.

48 See C. Williams, "Setting the Context: Kenya", in Housing Finance International, September 2005 edition, page 23.

49 See IFC Report, op. cit., page 14.

50 P. Honohan/T. Beck, op. cit., page 80.

- Poor real estate valuation standards. Uganda, for example, does not have any appraisal standards to determine the value of property to be offered as a security. In Tanzania, Nigeria and elsewhere, progress on this front is underway.
- Demographic patterns. Many lenders believe that they face uncontrolled financial loss as a result of loan default is rising as a consequence of the increase in the number of people infected by HIV/AIDS.[51]

Asset Liabilty Mismatch. The lack of long term local currency funding impedes the financing of long term mortgages. The financial systems are still greatly dominated by banks. Short term deposits are the main funding instruments for housing finance which exposes lenders to interest and liquidity risks. Capital markets do not play a significant role. Though growing rapidly, the domestic debt market in South Africa accounted for about 20% of GDP at the end of 2008 (emerging markets: 39%, developed countries: 139%). Sovereign debt is the most important debt instrument. Except in South Africa, there have been no issuances of MBS.

Interest Rate Risk. The mismatch in terms between assets and liabilities typically exposes lenders to considerable interest rate risk. The large spreads between the cost of funds and mortgage lending rates may reflect this situation. A recent study[52] found that high interest margins in SSA reflect weak property rights, weak creditor rights' enforcement, compromised courts, and insufficient insolvency frameworks.

Prepayment Risk. Since most SSA mortgage markets except South Africa are embryonic, few statistics on prepayment patterns are obtainable. However, with rising market development, prepayments are likely to rise. Due to significant liquidiy and interest rate risk, a high number of prepayments is a risk mitigating factor in the current environment.

Bank Practices Constraining Development of Housing Finance

As the result of risk adverse behaviour of banks, potential borrowers face the following obstacles in obtaining a housing loan:

- Weak affordability. Low levels of income and lack of steady income make large parts of the population "unbankable" in the eyes of banks. Often banks impose high minimum balance requirements or charge high fees for account maintenance to bar low and middle-income groups from using formal financial services.

---

51 See E. Matenge-Sebesho, "Managing the AIDS Risk in Housing Finance", Presentation given at the African Union for Housing Finance Conference, 6–7 September 2006, Kigali, Rwanda.

52 A. Demirgüç-Kunt/L. Laeven/R. Levine, op. cit., pages 593–622.

- Proof of identity. Documentation requirements constitute another obstacle to opening a bank account. For example, about 35% of adults in Namibia have no proof of their physical address, barring them from accessing banking services.
- Inappropriate product features. Bank products do not address the specific concerns of low and middle income groups. For example, term savings products in South Africa often do not permit withdrawals in case of emergency.
- Low branch and ATM penetration both in geography and demographics. Africa has the lowest road density in the world. Getting to a branch could easily consume an entire day. Uganda has one bank branch per 130,000 inhabitants; most are located in urban areas, despite the fact that 90% of the population live in rural areas.[53]

Funding Mortgage Loans

A well-functioning primary mortgage market requires adequate funding. This includes savings mobilisation and simple mortgage-backed debt instruments. Other areas requiring action include standardisation of the mortgage lending process, institutional and legal frameworks conducive to lending and appropriate risk management techniques.[54]

An absence of capital and financial markets, the lack of depth and liquidity where such markets exist, and the absence of debt management and issuance strategies are common features in SSA. This contrasts sharply to CEE countries. Some countries like Kenya or Nigeria are developing broader capital markets to offer investors a wider range of investments in different types of debt and equity.

The most commonly traded debt instruments are government securities. About 30 SSA countries issue or have issued treasury bills. Bond markets consist of only a handful of small issues and there are no meaningful secondary markets. Table 5 provides an overview of the capital market structure in selected SSA countries. A developed capital market comprises treasury bill and treasury bond markets, a corporate bond market as well as an equity market.

The most important buyers are domestic institutional investors, mostly state-owned pension funds, but also insurance companies and banks. Their main objective is to match the maturities of their liabilities with those of their longer-term assets. It appears that these investors pursue buy-and-hold strategies that are often a hurdle to the development of liquid markets. Debt instruments like the covered mortgage bond do not exist in SSA.[55]

---

[53] USAID, "Investigation into proposed Uganda Housing Securitisation", Afcap Consulting, April 2007, page 14.

[54] See O. Hassler, "Developing Housing Finance: Building blocks, challenges and policy options", World Bank for BNA Housing Finance Workshop, Luanda, November 2005.

[55] See IMF, "Regional Economic Outlook: Sub-Saharan Africa", Washington DC, April 2008, page 54.

Table 7. Capital market structures in selected SSA countries

Treasury bill and treasury bond markets, corporate bond and equity markets	Treasury bill and treasury bond markets, corporate bond or equity markets	Treasury bill and treasury bond markets	Treasury bill markets	No markets
Ghana, Kenya, Tanzania, Nigeria, Uganda, Zambia	Burkina Faso, Rwanda, Mozambique	Senegal	Madagascar, Ethopia, Malawi	Cameroon, Mali, Niger, Burundi

Source: IMF, Lukonga

More attention to the development of local debt markets would help to create the volumes necessary to offer long term funds to finance the issuance of mortgage loans. Several actions are required. For example, regulators should adopt stricter rules for asset-liability management to reduce maturity mismatch and differentiating risk-based capital standards by loan types.[56]

Savings play only a limited role in financing. Typically, maturities do not exceed one year, which restricts their use for long term mortgages. Another feature is the low savings mobilisation by citizens.

Comparisons Between CEE and SSA Markets

How do developments in CEE markets compare with those in SSA? Which potential solutions can be recommended for primary market development in SSA countries?

Is the CEE Experience Replicable in SSA?

Table 8 compares CEE with SSA mortgage markets. Since SSA generally lags behind CEE markets, the table assesses overall development in SSA countries and provides examples of countries that have already experienced progress toward accomplishment of these criteria, and also lists countries which have fulfilled a particular criterion or are very close to it. The countries with comparatively strong performance are close to the level of CEE countries.

In general, further reforms are required to reach the level of CEE countries. For example, some lenders in Ghana introduced modern lending standards within their organisations and developed new products to meet the rising demand for mortgage

[56] For mortgages, the risk weight is typically 50%.

loans. Because of small volumes, these efforts have not yet had much impact on overall market development.

During transformation in the CEE countries, a number of new product variants for financing housing and funding instruments and techniques were implemented to cope with rising demand. The biggest difference compared with SSA markets is the reliance on foreign currency funding in the CEE markets, although this is now decreasing. Models from Western European countries provided examples. The CEE markets increasingly resemble those of many Western European countries. Therefore, they are discussed here in more detail.

Savings Mobilisation. An instrument widely discussed in many countries is the German/Austrian Bausparkassen system. This system manages contractual savings schemes for housing (CSSH). CSSH offer a dedicated loan-linked form of saving. A phase of contractual savings, usually remunerated at below market interest rates, is tied to the promise of a housing loan at a rate fixed below the market level at the end of the saving period. CSSH systems require special regulation and supervision. Closed systems funding CSSH loans rely exclusively on savings collected by the CSSH institution. This creates exposure to liquidity risk or the risk that banks will have insufficient funds to meet future loan demands. Therefore, liquidity management crucially depends on whether products are individually viable and whether the performance of the scheme generates loans. The latter implies ensuring a sufficient ratio of loan allocations within the pool. The management of these pools is therefore a concern for regulators charged with protecting savers.

Another feature of the CSSH system is entitlement to a savings bonus which is paid by the government. The rationale for this subsidy is to provide an incentive to save and to channel these funds into construction activities.

Specialised institutions manage the German/Austrian Bausparkassen system. Open systems where the inflow of savings is insufficient to meet loan commitments are common in France and Slovenia. CSSH systems similar to the German/Austrian Bauspar system appeared in the Czech Republic (1993), Slovakia (1992), Hungary (1996), Croatia (1997) and Romania (2004). CSSH institutions are regulated by a CSSH act and supervised by the central bank. Customers are also entitled to a savings bonus.

Longer-term savings products have not been tested yet in most SSA countries. Therefore, their introduction may be exposed to scepticism from lenders and consumers alike. The final outcome largely depends on the individual scheme and the regulatory structure of the CSSH product. Lenders may use this product to expand or deepen their customer base.[57]

The main advantage of this scheme is that its savings period creates a credit history. The downside is its dependence on privileges. This makes its adoption controversial because of savings subsidies, specialised institutions and specialised

---

[57] Surveys in Germany have shown that bauspar customers have purchased at least two other bank products in comparison with non-bauspar clients.

Table 8. Comparisons between CEE and SSA markets[58]

	Criterion	Central and Eastern Europe	Southeast Europe	Sub-Saharan Africa[59]		
				Overall status	Typical country	Comparatively high performer
First category: creating the enabling environment	1. Macroeconomic stability	2[60]	2	1	Zambia	Rwanda, Botswana
	2. Conducive legal framework with a functioning enforcement system	2	1	Not yet present or very slowly emerging		
	3. Proper institutional framework	3	2	Not yet present or very slowly emerging		
	4. Financial development (banking sector reform and banking law reforms)	3	2	1	Uganda	Nigeria, Kenya
Second category: initiating the primary market	1. Adherence to minimum quality standards	2–3	1–2	1	Ghana	Kenya
	2. Provision of insurance services	3	1	Underdeveloped		
	3. Level of product innovations	3	2	1	Kenya	Ghana
	4. Access to long term funds	3	2–3	1	Ghana	Namibia

Legend: level of achievement from low (1) to strong (3). Blank cells indicate lack of comparables.

58 This comparison does not include Russia.

59 Excluding South Africa and Zimbabwe.

60 The GFC caused a significant drop in GDP growth. The economic recovery has been slow.

regulation.[61] An important issue is whether consumer confidence in these banks will be sufficient to encourage clients to sign multi-year savings contracts.

Experience in Germany and in transition countries has shown that CSSH schemes have helped improve low- and middle-income groups' access to credit because they are able to save for creditworthiness. Therefore, CSSH may be regarded as a tool to reach groups that have had little or no access to credit.

CSSH enhances long term funding because customers are expected to save for at least 2–3 years in order to receive a loan with at least a similar term. CSSH in Slovakia, for example, offers households almost automatic access to long term credit with typical loan durations of 10–20 years.[62]The case for CSSH is strongest outside the standard mortgage market. CSSH offers generally small volume loans, which are often not collateralised by mortgages and are therefore costly to securitise.[63] Even as financial systems develop, viable alternatives may never appear. In this context, CSSH may offer households an alternative to informal lending or costly consumer loans.

Refinancing Through Covered Mortgage Bonds. A covered mortgage bond is a debt instrument which is secured against a dynamic pool of specifically identified and eligible mortgages. The fundamental concept of this security is its reliance on the collateral (mortgage) as the primary source of credit quality, which significantly reduces the risk to the bondholder. Mortgage bonds are issued by a bank and usually remain on its balance sheet (on-balance sheet financing). The credit quality of the bonds is assured through conservative underwriting standards and strict regulation of loans and lending institutions, as well as strict valuation rules.

Typically, covered mortgage bonds have a fixed coupon and a bullet payment at maturity and are collateralised by underlying mortgage loans. There is no implicit or explicit government guarantee of covered mortgage bonds; their market acceptability depends completely on the quality of the underlying loan pool and the legal structure ensuring the security of the bonds, even in the case of loan defaults or bankruptcy of the issuer.

Similar to CSSH systems, specific laws govern the issuance of covered mortgage bonds to ensure the safety of the debt instrument and to establish a benchmark or brand for investors. Regulation requires that each issuance must meet the following criteria:

---

[61] For a broad discussion on CSSH see F. Roy, "Contractual Savings Schemes for Housing (CSSH) – an assessment of past experiences and current developments", paper prepared for World Bank/IFC conference "Housing Finance in Emerging Markets", Washington DC, 15–17 March 2006.

[62] For a detailed analysis on the Slovakian CSSH market, see A. Dübel, "Financial, fiscal and housing policy aspects of Contract Savings for Housing (CSH) in Transition Countries – the Cases of Czech Republic and Slovakia", study commissioned by the Financial Sector Development Department of the World Bank. Washington D. C. 2003.

[63] In the Czech Republic and Slovakia between two-thirds and four-fifths of loans are not collateralised and are given against a personal guarantee.

1. Principle of coverage. Covered mortgage bonds (principal and interest) are covered at all times by loans (principal and interest) at least equal to the nominal value of all outstanding issues and yielding at least an equal interest return. Mortgages in the cover pool must be high-quality assets secured by real estate.

2. Conservative lending limits. Only loans up to a certain loan to value ratio can be included in the cover pool. In Germany, for example, the maximum LTV ratio is 60%. Valuation rules for mortgaged real estate are strictly regulated.

3. Comprehensive regulation. The German legislation on covered mortgage bonds requires a trustee nominated by the German supervisory authority and oversees the characteristics of the mortgage collateral. The central bank regularly monitors the coverage of mortgage bonds. Mortgages included in the cover pool may be changed (as loans are paid off, for example), but any substitutions must meet the same requirements.

4. Protection of investors. In the event of bankruptcy of the lender, the bondholders have priority to access to the cover pool. Under this preferential right, in the case of a mortgage bank's insolvency, creditors of the German covered mortgage bond ("Pfandbriefe") do not participate in the insolvency proceedings. Instead, their claims are satisfied on schedule in accordance with the terms of the respective issue out of the cover assets, provided these are sound. If the claims in terms of coupon payments and redemptions cannot be satisfied on time, because the assets in the cover pool are inadequate, separate insolvency proceedings would be opened with respect to the affected pool.

These strict criteria have earned covered mortgage bonds a reputation as solid and safe investments. As a result, their spreads deviated only slightly from government bonds before the GFC (global financial crisis). During the GFC, covered mortgage bonds showed a certain level of resilience.

For example, the German covered mortgage bond (Pfandbriefe) has become a high-grade investment product, while they also pay a yield premium comparable with German government bonds. As high-grade credit, the Pfandbriefe compete with agency issues, e. g., from issuers like KfW or other AAA tranches of securitisations. Given their outstanding credit quality and liquidity, Pfandbriefe have increasingly drawn the attention of international institutional investors.

The attractiveness of covered mortgage bonds depends on strict and clear regulation and investors' appetite for mortgage-related securities. By requiring specific standards, it creates the confidence that potential investors look for. The legislation on covered mortgage bonds should also be in line with primary market prerequisites as listed in Table 1. If the covered mortgage bonds offer attractive risk-adjusted returns, demand may appear. In most SSA countries, government bonds are the only long term and lower risk asset class. If well structured and designed, demand may be channelled into covered mortgage bonds. In most CEE countries, the adoption of covered mortgage bond laws coupled with the emergence of debt markets provides an important incentive for this asset class.

Furthermore, lenders may buy covered mortgage bonds only if their funding is more advantageous than retail (typically deposit) funding, i. e., covered mortgage bonds help overcome liquidity and long term capital constraints as well as improving cash flow risk management. Most lenders in SSA countries that offer mortgage loans rely on short term deposits as a funding instrument. To manage liquidty risk, lenders typically maintain the right to adjust the interest rate (according to the loan contract), though loans appear to bear a fixed interest rate. In order to benefit from risk-adjusted and longer-term funding through covered mortgage bonds, lenders in SSA countries would require the skills necessary to manage their issuance. In addition, issuances would require careful preparation and proper marketing.

Liquidity Facilities to Support Secondary Market Development. A liquidity facility is an entity that purchases mortgage loans from banks or other lending institutions and issues securities to investors backed by the mortgage debt. For example, a sales-of-assets liquidity facility (SALF) indicates that the bank sells its assets (i. e., mortgage loans) to the liquidity facility, which then issues the mortgage bonds. A common model for structuring the bond issues is the portfolio model. In this case, bonds are essentially corporate bonds, the value of which is broadly based on the mortgages owned by the facility. The advantage of this structure is that it permits the facility to issue a range of bond types, particularly maturities, on the basis of its mortgages. This can be very useful in managing prepayment risks.

In the CEE countries, liquidity facilities were established in Russia and Kazakhstan.[64] With the help of KfW, a variant was set up in Armenia: KfW funds were channelled to the Central Bank of Armenia (CBA). Refinancing mortgage loans is subject to criteria such as participating financial institutions' status, loans in Armenian currency, a minimum term of 10 years, etc. The adherence to minimum quality standards as a further prerequisite for financing from the programme ensures the establishment of standardised mortgage loan portfolios. Since 12 out of 27 financial institutions are participating in the facility, the facility's financing standards have had an important impact on market development.[65]

Liquidity facilities can be viewed as an instrument to improve market liquidity, bank risk and capital management as well as a way to promote secondary market development.[66] How would liquidity facilities fulfil this role? To lower credit risk,

---

64 For more information on the Kazakh model, see F. Roy/A. Mananbaev/M. Yuldasev, "Mortgage Lending and Risk Management in Kazakhstan", in Housing Finance, New and Old Models in Central Europe, Russia and Kazakhstan, edited by J. Hegedüs and R. Struyk, LGI Books, 2005.

65 For more details, see K. Gevorgyan/S. Hirche, "Promoting Housing Finance Market Development in Armenia", in Housing Finance International, December Edition, 2006.

66 See M. Lea/L. Chiquier, "Providing Long term Financing for Housing: The Role of Secondary Markets", prepared for Office of Development Studies, Bureau for Development Policy, UNDP, published in Retailing Money: Private Finance for Human Development,

the facility should purchase loans with full recourse to lenders. In addition, it should only purchase loans that meet certain standards (loan documentation, LTV ratio, payment to income ratio, etc.). To do otherwise would give banks insufficient incentives to provide high quality underwriting and servicing. The facility could address liquidity through bond issues with differing maturities that would be priced to correspond with investors' views on prepayment risk. Indeed, this strategy could produce a lower average interest rate on the bonds. A major advantage of the facility compared with an individual lender is that its bond issuances would be larger, thereby giving it greater flexibility in structuring them.

The appeal of a secondary mortgage market is strong and its advantages to households and lenders alike are clear. In many ways, it appears to solve both housing finance and financial intermediation problems at the same time.

As already outlined regarding the possible introduction of covered mortgage bonds, the implementation of a secondary mortgage market is dependent on (a) demonstrable investor demand for mortgage-related securities in SSA countries, (b) possible price advantages over retail (typically deposit) funding, (c) clear and strict legislation, and (d) guidelines and supervision for secondary market operators. An additional prerequisite is a fully functioning and competitive primary mortgage market. This includes actuarially sound and increasingly automated mortgage underwriting, credit enhancements, mortgage insurance and a well-developed investment banking sector.

State-Owned Housing Institutions. A state-sponsored entity typically intervenes directly in the primary market. In CEE countries these institutions are specialised in housing, but often they are not a real bank. Some countries such as Serbia or Slovakia have established housing finance institutions to support mortgage lending. In Serbia, the National Mortgage Insurance Corporation offers mortgage insurance to lenders.[67] The involvement of the state in the mortgage loan market has been controversial. Shortcomings such as potential for market distortion, particularly through subsidised interest rates, often outweigh the advantages, such as access to long term funds.[68]

In many SSA countries, state-sponsored institutions were established to promote market development, including housing finance. In Nigeria, for example, the government established the Federal Mortgage Bank of Nigeria (FMBN) in 1956 to promote better legal conditions in mortgage lending, e. g., titling process and ac-

---

and R. Struyk (ed.), Homeownership and Housing Finance Policy in the Former Soviet Bloc, The Urban Institute, Washington DC, 2000.

67 See T. Elliot/A. Jovic/J. Pupovac, "A Rising Star: The National Mortgage Insurance Corporation of Serbia", in Housing Finance International, December Edition, 2006.

68 For a detailed discussion, see D. Diamond, "State Housing Banks: Handle Carefully!" presentation given at World Bank/IFC conference "Housing Finance in Emerging Markets", Washington DC, 15–17 March 2006.

cess to long term funds, including development of a secondary market.[69] This goal has not been achieved. Thus, experiences from CEE and SSA countries indicate that this approach has not led to more efficient housing finance markets.[70]

Potential Solutions for SSA Mortgage Markets

Would these models described above work in Africa? Their implementation requires the emergence of an enabling environment as outlined in Table 1, i. e., macroeconomic stability, a functioning title and enforcement system, clearly defined appraisal standards and among others, a credit bureau. There must also be a demand for finance. These criteria are often lacking in SSA countries or are at an early stage of development. Challenges would include increasing outreach so that more people have access to mortgage loans and to support overall market development, including the supply of affordable housing. Given the specific constraints and conditions in SSA, the following approaches appear feasible. They could be set up at two levels. The first deals with support for the demand for housing finance. The second focuses on the supply of funds and risk management.

Level 1: Increase Outreach

One characteristic of SSA retail bank markets is the number of "unbanked" people – possibly more than 80% of the adult population, typically belonging to lower and middle income groups.[71] This group will usually use informal institutions to save or borrow money. Microfinance may be helpful to increase outreach and support lending to this group:

Microfinance. Microfinance institutions (MFIs) may be suitable delivery channels for housing finance in SSA. First, MFIs serve customers who are typically not served by formal financial institutions. Second, classic mortgage finance is out of reach for most low and middle income earners, since they do not possess a formal land title that could be offered as a security. They often lack a verifiable regular income and the cost of title or lien registration is often prohibitive given the small loan sizes. Small loans appear more suitable to assist incremental construction.[72]

Some MFIs which have looked for ways to diversify their portfolios have originated loans dedicated to housing purposes (housing microfinance – HMF).

---

[69] FMBN was established as the Nigerian Building Society in 1956. It was reorganised in 2002 as a result of housing reforms. The institution was transformed into a funding vehicle for wholesale mortgage lending to support secondary mortgage and capital market operations.

[70] For a general discussion, see G. Caprio et al., "The Future of State-Owned Financial Institutions", Brookings Institution Press, Washington DC, 2004 and in particular J. A. Hanson, "The Transformation of State-Owned Banks" in the same publication.

[71] Even in South Africa, by far the most developed banking market in SSA, 52% of the adult population (14 million people) are unbanked. Source: FinScope 2004, www.finmark.org.za.

[72] See M. R. Tomlinson, "A Literature Review on Housing Finance Development in Sub-Saharan Africa", FinMark Trust, May 2007, page 20.

Loan underwriting is subject to MFI lending methodologies but terms are longer. Table 9 shows the differences between a classic mortgage loan, an MFI loan and a housing microfinance loan.

Though microfinance is firmly embedded in SSA, HMF is a relatively new area of intervention. HFC Bank of Ghana offers an HMF product that would provide loans of up to USD 2,000, and the Ghana Cooperative Credit Union Association funds loans for incremental housing.[73]

The general structure of microfinance loans has risk management advantages. The amounts are comparatively low and the maximum term is typically 2–4 years. The expected loss from a single loan is small and does not constitute a high burden to provision heavily; the relatively short duration facilitates liquidity management and management of interest rate risk, since the lender is able to rely on its local currency deposit base.

A number of constraints limit the outreach of HMF products: first, MFIs often lack the long term funds to issue longer term loans. Second, HMF products are as costly as traditional MFI products. Since HMF lending methodology is more or

Table 9. Comparison among conventional mortgage finance products, microenterprise finance and housing microfinance products

	Mortgage Financing in SSA	Microenterprise Finance	Housing Microfinance (HMF)
Borrower	Middle and upper income households	Low income entrepreneurs	Low income households
Originator	Commercial banks, specialised lenders	MFIs of different types	MFIs of different types
Use of loan funds	Purchase, construction, renovation/modernisation	Working capital, equipment and stock	Home improvement, incremental housing development
Amount[74]	Typically from USD 5,000 – USD 10,000 and higher	Typically small amounts from USD 50	Typically < USD 3,000
Underwriting	Assessment of household income, property value	Assessment of (future) cash flows	Assessment of (future) cash flows and savings history
Maturities	5–10 years	1–2 years	3–4 years (or less)
Collateral	Mortgage	Personal guarantees, movable assets	Personal guarantees, movable assets

Source: Ferguson (2004)

73 See S. Merrill/M. Tomlinson, op. cit., page 34.

74 Ferguson refers in his article to examples of loan amounts for microenterprise finance and housing microfinance in Latin America. These countries have the most developed housing microfinance markets. HMF products are not common in CEE countries. See B. Ferguson, "Scaling up Housing Microfinance: A Guide to Practice", in Housing Finance International, September 2004, page 5.

less identical to conventional microfinance, most lenders do not face major difficulties in introducing HMF products.

As in Central and Southeastern Europe, the loan density (loans per thousand households) is greater in urban and peri-urban settings given the cost associated with remoteness and low density. Borrowing costs could be substantial for remote borrowers. The challenge for MFIs is to achieve scale and reach remote areas without losing control of costs while maintaining creditworthiness.[75]

Mobile Banking. Africa has the fastest growing mobile telephone market in the world. In 2005 the continent's subscriber base increased by 66% to 135 million users.[76] Mobile banking technology can overcome some of the constraints in SSA markets, reaching customers in unbanked and rural areas without branches and other traditional banking channels such as fixed line telephones and the internet. In addition, it is simple to use[77] and offers security to the customer. Further advantages are lower fees and easier access to other banking products. For example, WIZZIT's transaction banking services in South Africa are on average one-third cheaper than a comparable account offered by one of South Africa's biggest four banks.[78] In Kenya, Vodafone, together with Safaricom (a local network provider), Commercial Bank of Africa and Faulu, has jointly developed the M-PESA mobile banking system which allows customers to borrow money, check accounts and transfer money using their mobile phones. For housing loans, this technology holds great promise for loan servicing.

However, a number of constraints or risks may hamper an expansion of this distribution channel:[79]

- Set-up costs could be substantial due to licences, technical infrastructure, and marketing costs.
- Cell phone antennae must be available across the whole country so that the customer can send and receive text messages in remote areas.

---

75 See P. Honohan/T. Beck, op. cit., page 141.

76 See S. Timewell/W. Atkins, "Mobiles begin calling shots on banking and payments", in The Banker, February 2007, page 79.

77 Everyone who knows how to send an SMS can transfer money. After sending his message to a financial service provider, he will receive a text message in which he is asked to provide a personal identification number (PIN) to confirm the transaction. Once this is done, the transaction is processed.

78 WIZZIT is a mobile banking service that targets the low income, unbanked market. It operates as a division of the South African Bank of Athens. For more information, please see www.wizzit.co.za.

79 See F. Roy, "Innovation, outreach, access – Spreading out banking services through cell phone technology in rural and urban Africa", paper prepared for 3rd Africa Microfinance Conference in Kampala, 20–23 August 2007.

- Selling a transaction account to a customer may not appear difficult. However, the sale of savings accounts or HMF products would require a dedicated and well-trained sales staff. Through a text message, the customer can initiate a transfer to her/his savings or loan account. These accounts are usually sub-accounts of the main transaction account. In markets where financial literacy and confidence in financial institutions is low, strong sales efforts may be necessary until a customer links a transaction account with a savings account.
- If conditions or product features are not transparent, customers will reject them, possibly creating damaging spill-over effects into other products in the market.

Remittance-Based Products. The volume of workers' remittances and compensation of employees received by SSA in 2008 reached around USD 21 billion.[80] In some countries they have reached amounts above 5% of GDP. Table 10 gives an overview of remittance inflows to selected SSA countries.

Housing loan products that take remittances into consideration could increase outreach. They could represent a downpayment or be used for the monthly loan instalments. Their use is, however, subject to a number of constraints:

- Creditworthiness assessment. The lender has no assurance that remittances will continue. Alternatively, the lender may take this risk into consideration when calculating the repayment capacity of the borrower.[81]
- Volality of remittance flows. The GFC caused lower remittance flows from Europe and the US to SSA countries as overseas Africans lost employment or faced salary cuts. Lower remittance payments exacerbated the effects of the GFC on low income households in SSA countries which depend on remittance to cover their living expenses and mortgage repayments.
- High transaction costs. The current costs of transferring money to SSA countries discourage remittances. Transfer charges between developed countries and SSA countries appear higher than to other regions.[82]
- Monetary policies and regulations. Exchange controls, bureaucratic transaction procedures, and limited rural branch networks contribute to a preference for informal methods of transferring funds.

---

80 This figure is taken from the World Development Indicators database of the World Bank.

81 This practice is applied in Armenia. The discount applied is 40% of the original remittance amount.

82 See R. Hernández-Coss/E. Chinyere/M. Josefsson, "The UK-Nigeria Remittance Corridor", World Bank and UK Department for International Development, Washington DC, 2006.

Table 10. Remittance inflows in selected SSA countries (2008)

Recipient country	Amount of workers' remittances and compensation of employees received (current US$ Million)	Workers' remittances and compensation of employees received (% of GDP)
Uganda	723.5	5.05
Nigeria	9,980	4.82
Senegal	1,288	9.70
Lesotho	438.6	27.04
Sudan	3,100.5	5.54

Source: World Development Indicators and Global Development Finance

Level 2: Improve Risk Management and Access to Long Term Funds

A lender offering variable rate mortgages seeks funds that match its re-pricing pattern of funding. Refinancing long term fixed rated loans with debt instruments of shorter maturities creates exposure to liquidity and interest rate risk. Access to long term funds with fixed interest rates would help lenders to manage liquidity and interest rate risk.

Promote Savings. The focus should be on longer saving terms that allow fixing interest rates for longer periods so that lenders can better manage the interest and liquidity mismatch. Contractual savings schemes could be a major force in providing long term capital.[83] However, any CSSH variants should take into consideration the specifics of SSA countries before recommending a direct replication of the CSSH models applied in CEE countries. Instead of creating specialised institutions, the focus should be on existing sales channels such as traditional banks, postal banks and microfinance institutions. Incentives to save should be embedded in the product structure and not dependent on state sponsored schemes to avoid crowding out existing savings products.

Establishment of Liquidity Facilities. The rationale behind this funding instrument is that participating lenders receive funds only if the loans comply with the refinancing criteria of the facility. It facilitates asset-liability management for participating lenders, because the facility manager offers financing of different maturities and interest rates. Participating lenders could be banks, microfinance institutions or specialised mortgage banks. Refinancing criteria would typically include adherence to well defined minimum quality standards,[84] minimum loan terms and loans in local currency.

---

83 See P. Honohan/T. Beck, op. cit., page 48.

84 Major international financial institutions (such as EBRD, IFC or KfW) have guidelines that define the necessary content of such standards.

Since the liquidity facility can operate in an environment that does not meet all requirements for a functioning secondary market (e. g., rating agencies), it appears to be a suitable model to develop the primary market, while simultaneously paving the way for a secondary market. Typically, the manager of the liquidity facility will perform a secondary underwriting to the loans presented, which is quite similar to procedures in developed countries (like the US).[85] Their implementation may involve the central bank or the government as a shareholder, or participation of international financial institutions to assist set up and ensure market acceptance.[86] Additionally, the participation of private lenders is required to ensure widespread acceptance within the national market. To avoid market distortions in the long run, a clearly defined exit strategy of the government and the central bank should be in place.

Ideally, such initiatives are linked to an improvement of the enabling environment so that a framework for further development is in place (see Table 1). These measures would reduce risks and increase competition in mortgage lending, lowering interest rates and lengthening terms, thus increasing overall housing affordability. To date, the concept of liquidity facilities has not been tested in SSA countries other than South Africa. As a result of the GFC, some countries have shown an increased interest in this model and are working on feasible ways to develop their national mortgage markets.

Conclusion

The collapse of the former Soviet Union and the shift from a planned economy to market oriented structures was a complete rupture with the past for Central and Southeast Europe. Mortgage market development was fuelled by the prospect of EU membership, which has generated strong leverage to implement the necessary, painful reforms. This facilitated the entry of international banks (mostly Italian and Austrian) coupled with new markets with similar roots and culture. International banks brought know-how and forced local lenders to adapt. For example, there is no difference between branch design in most CEE countries and Western European countries today. However, the considerable volume of funding in foreign currency proved the high vulnerability to currency fluctuations beyond the control of national regulators. In addition, the high share of foreign ownership made these countries vulnerable to strategic decisions of their parent organisations over which CEE governments have only limited influence.

---

85 In contrast to the manager of the liquidity facility who checks every loan, institutions like Fannie Mae will look at the overall portfolios presented. However, the general mechanism remains the same.

86 In Kazakhstan, the National Bank of Kazakhstan (NBK) was the only shareholder of the liquidity facility (Kazakhstan Mortgage Company).

Despite the turmoil at the close of the communist era, legislative conditions, albeit flawed, were in much better shape at the onset of the transformation process compared with the conditions of SSA countries upon their independence.

When the former colonisers left SSA, they left behind many structures that require adaptation to international standards and practices.[87] The political turmoil, wars and conflicts that have followed after decolonisation have failed to attract many international banks to invest in the region, with some exceptions concentrated on corporate and investment banking. In addition, old colonial ties played an important role in investment decisions. For example, French banks were predominantly active in the former French colonies. This is now changing. With rising household incomes, retail markets are drawing the attention of international banks. For example, South African and British banks have become very active throughout the region, especially in English speaking countries, purchasing or establishing new banks in some countries, such as Tanzania, Kenya, Uganda and Zambia. Their loan products and standards may become models for the region.

Whereas CEE countries mainly looked to Western Europe and the US, it appears that SSA countries have not yet studied CEE lending models. This may be due to a lack of cultural and historical ties. Typically, international banks that heavily invested in CEE countries have not yet expanded into SSA markets. Geographical distance and cultural considerations may have influenced this hesitation.

The development of mortgage markets in the CEE countries offers a number of lessons for SSA countries. Without a proper legislative and institutional environment, mortgage markets will not thrive. Importantly, if such an environment is established, lenders can rely on the land registry to trace ownership and register mortgages as well as the ability to foreclose in case a borrower defaults.

Strong involvement of foreign lenders can help transform mortgage markets and spur reforms. It seems that some governments lack strategies to attract more foreign banks.

There are many similarities in market development between the two regions: mortgage lending is concentrated in bigger cities or urban areas, incremental increases of loan terms are offered, more sophisticated products are available and the creation of long term funding instruments is crucial. However, there are also a number of differences:

1. SSA countries are experiencing considerable growth in urban areas and a significant increase of informal settlements. Urban growth in CEE countries is also fuelled by migration, but informal settlements are the exception.

2. The likely importance of microfinance in SSA markets as a distribution channel for home purchase loan products stands in marked contrast to Europe. In this context, housing microfinance is considered a tool with

[87] See E. Wiedemann, “Zwiespältiges Erbe”, Spiegel Special Geschichte, “Afrika – das unkämpfte Paradies”, Nr. 2, 2007, page 34–46.

unique characteristics for overcoming the barriers to credit access for low and middle income groups. Coupled with mobile banking technology (in particular cell-phones), outreach to rural and remote areas is achievable.

3. Little competition for housing loans exists in SAA, while it is strong in CEE countries. This results in less innovation and lower efficiency among SAA lenders.

A flourishing primary mortgage market depends on access to long term funding. CEE countries offer a number of interesting models and examples. The establishment of liquidity facilities could add a great deal of value to primary market development. They would stimulate the inclusion of many financial institutions such as banks, microfinance institutions and others. The funding structure would assist in setting standards and providing incentives to pursue reforms to obtain long term funds. The lessons from models in Armenia, Russia or Kazakhstan would be a good starting point for the introduction of similar models in Sub-Saharan Africa.

Secondary facilities require significant loan volumes to intermediate efficiently. It is possible for a secondary facility to foster development of the primary market, but premature ventures can set back development.

References

Beck, T., A. Demirgüç-Kunt and M. S. M. Peria (2007) "Reaching out: Access to and Use of Banking Services across Countries", World Bank mimeo, Washington DC.

BMI (2006) Emerging Markets Monitor 13(9).

Caprio, G. et al. (2004) "The Future of State-Owned Financial Institutions", Brookings Institution Press, Washington DC.

Demirgüç-Kunt, A., L. Laeven and R. Levine (2004) "Regulations, Market Structure, Institutions, and the Cost of Financial Intermediation", Journal of Money, Credit, and Banking 36(3).

Deutsche Bank Research (2009) African frontier capital markets: More than a flash in the pan. Frankfurt.

Diamond, D. (2006) "State Housing Banks: Handle Carefully!", presentation given at World Bank/IFC conference "Housing Finance in Emerging Markets", Washington DC, 15–17 March 2006.

Dübel, A. (2003) "Financial, fiscal and housing policy aspects of Contract Savings for Housing (CSH) in Transition Countries – the Cases of Czech Republic and Slovakia", study commissioned by the Financial Sector Development Department of the World Bank. Washington DC.

Duebel, H.-J. and S. Walley (2010) "Regulation of Foreign Currency Mortgage Loans – the case of transition countries in Central and Eastern Europe, Washington DC, p. 10.

EBRD (2004) Mortgage Loan Minimum Standards Manual.

EMF Hypostat 2005 (2006), „A review of Europe's Mortgage and Housing Markets", European Mortgage Federation.

EMF Hypostat 2006 (2007) "A review of Europe's mortgage and housing markets", European Mortgage Federation, Brussels.

Ferguson, B. (2004) "Scaling up Housing Microfinance: A Guide to Practice", in Housing Finance International, September 2004.

Financial Times (2006) "Baltic Boom states face hard landing", July 5, 2006.

Financial Times (2006) Special Report on African Infrastructure, "A pressing concern", 21 November 2006.

Gardener, D. (2007) "Access to Housing Finance in Africa: Exploring the Issues in Zambia", FinMark Trust, May 2007.

Gevorgyan, K. and S. Hirche (2006) "Promoting Housing Finance Market Development in Armenia", in: Housing Finance International, December Issue 2006.

Groves, R. (2004) "Challenges Facing the Provision of Affordable Housing in African Cities", in: Housing Finance International, June Issue 2004.

Hanson, J. A. (2004) "The Transformation of State-Owned Banks", in G. Caprio et al., The Future of State-Owned Financial Institutions, Brookings Institution Press, Washington DC, pp. 13–51.

Hassler, O. (2005) "Developing Housing Finance: Building blocks, challenges & policy options", World Bank for BNA Housing Finance Workshop, Luanda, November 2005.

Hegedüs, J. and R. Struyk (2005) "Divergences and Convergences in Restructuring Housing Finance in Transition Countries", in: Housing Finance, New and Old Models in Central Europe, Russia and Kazakhstan, edited by J. Hegedüs and R. Struyk, LGI Books.

Hegedüs, J. (2009) "Emerging new housing regimes and the global economic crisis in CEE countries – case of Hungary", Symposium on Housing Markets and the Global Financial Crisis, Hong Kong, December 9–11, 2009, p. 3.

Hegedüs, J. and R. Struyk (2005) "Housing Finance – New and Old Models in Central Europe, Russia, and Kazakhstan", Open Society Institute, Budapest.

Hernández-Coss, R., E. Chinyere and M. Josefsson (2006) "The UK-Nigeria Remittance Corridor", World Bank and UK Department for International Development, Washington DC.

Honohan, P. and T. Beck (2007), "Making Finance Work for Africa", The World Bank, Washington DC.

IFC (2005) "Housing Finance in Ghana: Market Study", conducted by Tel Aviv Strategic Consultants, Boulders Advisors & Lawfields Consulting, June 2005.

IMF (2008) "Regional Economic Outlook: Sub-Saharan Africa", Washington DC.

IMF (2009) "Regional Economic Outlook: Sub-Saharan Africa", Washington DC.

Kochan, N. (2007), "Retail jump-start", The Banker special supplement on Nigeria, April 2007.

Kosareva, K. and R. Struyk (1996) "Emerging Long Term Housing Finance in Russia", in Housing Finance International, March edition, pp. 20–30.

Lassen, T. (2005) "Specialisation of Covered Bond Issuers in Europe", in: Housing Finance International, December 2005.

Lea, M. and L. Chiquier (2000) "Providing Long Term Financing for Housing: The Role of Secondary Markets", prepared for Office of Development Studies, Bureau for Development Policy, UNDP, published in Retailing Money: Private Finance for Human Development, and R. Struyk (ed.), Homeownership and Housing Finance Policy in the Former Soviet Bloc, The Urban Institute, Washington DC.

Matenge-Sebesho E. (2006), "Managing the AIDS Risk in Housing Finance", Presentation given at the African Union for Housing Finance Conference, 6–7 September 2006, Kigali, Rwanda.

Mayer, Brown, Rowe and Maw LLP (2006) "At a glance", information leaflets on securitisation in various countries in central and south-east Europe, September 2006.

Merrill, S. and M. Tomlinson (2006) "Housing Finance, Microfinance, and Informal Settlement Upgrading: An Assessment of Ghana", Paper prepared for African Union of Housing Finance and USAID, The Urban Institute, Washington DC, June 2006.

Moser, E. and T. Nestmann (2007) "Russia's financial sector", Deutsche Bank Research, August 20, 2007.

Roy, F. (2005) "Application of (Contractual) Savings Schemes for Housing in Africa", presentation given at 2nd African Microfinance Conference in Cape Town, 30 August 2005.

Roy, F. (2006) "Contractual Savings Schemes for Housing (CSSH) – an assessment of past experiences and current developments", paper prepared for World Bank/ IFC conference on Housing Finance in Emerging Markets, Washington DC, 15–17 March 2006.

Roy, F. (2007) "Innovation, outreach, access – Spreading out banking services through cell phone technology in rural and urban Africa", paper prepared for 3rd Africa Microfinance Conference in Kampala, 20–23 August 2007.

Roy, F., A. Mananbaev and M. Yuldasev (2005) "Mortgage Lending and Risk Management in Kazakhstan", in Housing Finance, New and Old Models in Central Europe, Russia and Kazakhstan, edited by J. Hegedüs and R. Struyk, LGI Books.

Rózsavölgyi, R. and V. Kovács (2005) "Housing Subsidies in Hungary: Curse or Blessing", Ecfin Country Focus 2(18).

Sacalschi, A. and O. Stöcker (2006) "Neues Gesetz über Covered Bonds in Rumänien", in: Immobilien und Finanzierung 15-2006.

Schumacher, L. (2008) "Creditor Rights in Sub-Saharan Africa", IMF, Regional Economic Outlook: Sub-Saharan Africa, Washington DC, April 2008.

Struyk, R. (ed.) (2000) "Homeownership and Housing Finance Policy in the Former Soviet Bloc", The Urban Institute, Washington DC.

Struyk, R. (2005) "Home Purchase Affordability and Mortgage Finance", in Housing Finance, New and Old Models in Central Europe, Russia and Kazakhstan, edited by J. Hegedüs and R. Struyk, LGI Books.

Timewell, S. and W. Atkins (2007) "Mobiles begin calling shots on banking and payments", in: The Banker, February 2007.

Tomlinson, M. R. (2007) "A Literature Review on Housing Finance Development in Sub-Saharan Africa", FinMark Trust, May 2007.

Wiedemann, E. (2007) "Zwiespältiges Erbe", Spiegel Special Geschichte, "Afrika – das unkämpfte Paradies", Nr. 2, 2007, pp. 34–46.

Williams, C. (2005) "Setting the Context: Kenya", in Housing Finance International, September 2005 edition.

Wookey, J. (2007) "Securitisation is no longer a dirty word", Euromoney 38(461).

USAID (2007) "Investigation into proposed Uganda Housing Securitisation", Afcap Consulting, April 2007.

www.mortgagefit.com/primary-market.html, "What does the Primary Mortgage Market offer you?" 30 July 2008.

CHAPTER 8

Housing Finance from Post-conflict Intervention to Market Development in the Balkans*

Nico van der Windt[1], Rolf Dauskardt[2], Martin Heimes[3], and Jana Hoessel[4]

[1] Institute for Housing and Urban Development Studies
[2] Urban Development Studies (HIS) and now Rebel Group Advisory
[3] Frankfurt School of Finance and Management
[4] Frankfurt School of Finance and Management and CFA

Introduction

The war in the Balkans during the 1990s had a devastating impact on the population and on their livelihood, including housing. The cases of Bosnia and Herzegovina (BiH)[1] and Kosovo provide vivid illustrations.

At the signing of the Peace Agreements in 1995,[2] an estimated 1.2 million people, 28% of Bosnia's total population, fled abroad.[3] An additional million people fled their homes during the war in search of safety and better opportunities.

During the war, a large proportion of homes were completely or partially destroyed. A 1991 census reported that about 1.2 million housing units were affected. The Bosnian authorities estimated that 35% of BiH's housing units were completely destroyed. 18% of the units damaged lost more than 70% of their post-war values, while 20% suffered losses of 20% or less.[4]

---

* The authors of this chapter would like to thank Sylvia Wisniwski, Jasminka Muslic and Njomeza Shehu for their valuable comments and Heike Fiedler for providing data.

1 Throughout this document Bosnia and Herzegovina are referred to as Bosnia.

2 Also known as the Dayton Accords: formally the General Framework Agreement for Peace (GFAP) signed in Paris in December 1995 to end the war in Bosnia and Herzegovina.

3 This estimate is based on a 1991 Bosnia and Herzegovina census. In the absence of more recent and reliable statistics, it is difficult to compare the results of the EFSE Impact Study 2006, described in the fourth section of this chapter, with trends in income and expenditures.

4 Bosnia and Herzegovina. Ministry for Human Rights and Refugees, Department for Housing Policy and Analytical Planning. "Housing and Urban Profile of Bosnia and Herzegovina: An Outline of Devastations, Recovery and Development Perspectives,"

D. Köhn and J.D. von Pischke (eds.), *Housing Finance in Emerging Markets: Connecting Low-Income Groups to Markets*, DOI 10.1007/978-3-540-77857-8_8,

Due to the return of 1 million refugees from 1996 to 2005, the need for reconstruction increased dramatically. Post-war reconstruction aid helped to reduce the housing gap. More than 260,000 new housing units were constructed in the decade following the peace accord. Bosnian authorities estimated the cost of further reconstruction at about EUR 1.3 billion.[5]

Post-war Kosovo shows a similar picture. The International Management Group (IMG) estimated in 1999 that 120,000 housing units, or almost half the total stock of 250,000 units, were destroyed or damaged. About 40% of the affected units reported property damage exceeding 60% of cost, while 34% suffered damages of up to 20%.[6]

About one quarter of Kosovo's 2.1 million population suffered losses exceeding 40% of their unit's cost. The war exacerbated an already difficult housing situation. Construction stagnated in the 1990s and the quality of housing remained poor, especially in rural areas. IMG estimated housing repair and reconstruction costs of EUR 1.1 billion in 1999.

Since 1998 a multi-donor post-conflict reconstruction intitiative has actively supported housing finance in the Balkans, including Bosnia and Kosovo. Under that umbrella more than 45,000 loans amounting to EUR 280 million were issued through 2005. Roughly one third of these loans were used for home improvement and reconstruction. With the establishment of the European Fund for Southeast Europe (EFSE), this portfolio was transferred to EFSE.[7]

In 2006, EFSE's Development Facility commissioned a study to evaluate the development performance of its housing loan portfolio. The study[8] was conducted by the Institute for Housing and Urban Development Studies (IHS), which is based in the Netherlands. It examined the impact of loans to 12 of the 15 partner lending institutions (PLIs) that received funds for housing in BiH and Kosovo through September 2006.

---

pages 5-6. Available online at http://www.mhrr.gov.ba/PDF/Housing&Urban%20Profile%20of%20Bosnia.pdf.

5 Ibid. See also Minister Mirsad Kebo, BIH Ministry for Human Rights and Refugees, presentation (without title), 12 January 2006, Sarajevo. Available online at http://www.mhrr.gov.ba/PDF/Presentation%20by%20Minister%20Mirsad%20Kebo.pdf.

6 International Management Group (IMG) on behalf of the European Commission. "Emergency Assessment of Damaged Housing and Local/Village Infrastructure." July 1999. Available online at http://www.img-int.org/Central/Public08/Documents.aspx and European Agency for Reconstruction. "Kosovo 2000," summary of action programme. Available online at http://www.ear.eu.int/kosovo/main/kos-annual_programme_2000_part1_housing.htm.

7 The European Fund for Southeast Europe (EFSE) is a structured finance vehicle designed to refinance financial intermediaries in the region in order to assist micro and SME end-borrowers and households for housing loans.

8 Dauskardt, R. and van der Windt, N., "Building sustainable housing finance systems: Impacts of the European Fund for Southeast Europe," EFSE Housing Impact Study 2006, IHS. 2007. Available at www.efse.lu/publications/papers.hmtl.

This chapter illustrates the co-ordinated multi-donor effort supporting post-war reconstruction and development in Southeast Europe. It describes the international policy response supporting reconstruction of housing in Bosnia and Kosovo, followed by an overview of coordinated efforts by bilateral and multilateral funders, and subsequently the transformation of multi-donor support into EFSE. This vehicle supports sustainable financial and private sector development in Eastern Europe. Key results of the housing loan impact study from 2003 to mid-2006 are highlighted.

International Post-conflict Policy Response in Housing Construction and Rehabilitation

Rapid support was required to address the immediate challenges of the damaged housing stock. Given the lack of local government resources, or even the lack of effective government structures, support came mainly from international donors, especially for Kosovo and BiH. Programmes were initiated by a large number of donors, ranging from large international agencies[9] to smaller international NGOs.

Co-ordination of housing support remained a challenge after the immediate post-war period. Programmes focused on different target groups. In both Kosovo and BiH special UN missions played a co-ordinating role.[10]

Bosnia and Kosovo illustrate the importance of international donor support in a post-conflict situation. Between 1998 and 2005, 260,000 housing units were reconstructed in Bosnia, 65% of which were funded by donors.[11]

In Kosovo, international support focussed on the rehabilitation of damaged housing and on the reconstruction of housing units. Between the end of the war in mid-1999 and early 2000, about 12,000 housing units were repaired, funded by EUR 54 million in grants from more than 10 donors.[12]

---

[9] In Kosovo the European Agency for Reconstruction (EAR), a special EU agency for reconstruction, took a leading role. In Bosnia the EU and the US played a comparable role.

[10] UNMIK (United Nations Interim Administration Mission in Kosovo) and in BiH the Reconstruction and Return Task Forces (RRTF). A multi-agency task force led by the Office of the High Representative (OHR) and the United Nations High Commissioner for Refugees (UNHCR).

[11] At end-March 1997, RRTF estimated disbursements of about USD 1 billion of external assistance for reconstruction in BIH. Regional Legal Assistance Programme: A Study on Access to Pertaining Rights and (Re)integration of Displaced Persons in Croatia, Bosnia and Herzegovina and Serbia in 2006. p. 4. Available online at: http://www.osce.org/item/26660.html.

[12] European Agency for Reconstruction. "Kosovo 2001 Action programme part II." September 2000. Available online at http://www.ear.europa.eu/kosovo/main/kos-annual_programme_2001_part2_housing.htm.

Donor support programmes had similar characteristics. Initially provided as grants, the programmes primarily offered compensation targeted at returnees, while reconstruction resources were provided by donors or their implementing agencies. In Bosina, lump-sum compensation to home owners became common only in 2001.

Donor grants were provided in cash or in kind. In many cases, only a part of a house, for example the roof and some rooms, were reconstructed, while other parts of the building remained uninhabitable. However, owners of stand-alone houses often found new construction of units to be preferable to reconstruction. Also, many displaced persons were reluctant to return to communities where they were ethnic minorities, while others resettled in new communities and saw donor assistance as a way to finance their resettlement. As a result, owners often used the grants they received for investments in new stand-alone housing outside cities or villages. Much of this new construction remained semi-finished due to limited grant funding.

Despite massive donor support, demand for home improvement remained very high in the region, reflecting poor pre-war housing conditions and subsequent deterioration with the rapid change from predominantly public to private home ownership, which requires capital for renovation.

In addition to their own funds, private owners received support for housing investments from relatives and friends abroad. However, the magnitude of war damage created an enormous financing gap.

From Post-conflict Policy Response to Sustainable Housing Finance

Following the first wave of post-conflict reconstruction programmes, international funding dropped. In Kosovo, EU funds for housing rehabilitation dried up quickly, while initiatives continued for a longer period in Bosnia.

Together with post-conflict support, donors provided funds for broad financial sector reform and economic liberalisation. Local financial sectors in the Balkans were weakened by the withdrawal of Serbian banks. The financial sector in Kosovo, for example, had to be rebuilt from scratch. One international bank, ProCredit, initiated local operations and several other banks followed.

International agencies such as KfW, the EU and the German Government supported the development of domestic financial sectors, including housing finance in the Balkans. These initiatives provided a foundation for housing finance markets.

KfW's support for home owners worked through apex funding structures using domestic financial institutions.[13] The KfW programme was more selective than some others. It used the PLIs' assessment of the prospective borrower's ability to repay as the main eligibility criterium. The approach was supported through tech-

[13] Partner lending institution (PLI) is the term used throughout this chapter.

nical assistance to PLIs to build their capability to assess repayment capacity, for example through loan cash flow analysis.

KfW's support was provided under challenging and risky conditions. Local banks in Bosnia were relatively weak and those in Kosovo were rather unexperienced and unstable. Many banks were characterised by poor governance, lack of basic management capacity, weak risk management and internal controls, and a lack of retail and housing finance experience.

Between 1998 and 2004, KfW managed four European multi-donor funds for Bosnia and Herzegovina, Montenegro, and Serbia, which were amalgamated into the European Fund for Southeast Europe (EFSE) in December 2005. These revolving funds provided long-term refinancing through PLIs to housing borrowers and micro and small enterprises (MSE). Funding was provided by the European Union and the governments of Germany, Austria, and Switzerland.[14]

Under this umbrella, two housing loan programmes were implemented in Bosnia and Herzegovina and in Kosovo respectively. The programme in Bosnia included the construction of new housing units, while the one in Kosovo targeted renovation and improvement.

The programme in Bosnia started in 1998 with a contribution of EUR 25 million from the European Commission (EC).[15] It provided housing finance to households through six PLIs: Gospodarska Banka, ProCredit, Raiffeisen, UniCredit Zagrebacka, UPI Banka and Volksbank. The PLIs bore the full credit risk of the borrowers. Loan pricing gradually moved from an administrated rate of 3% p. a. to a market based rate at Euribor flat and finally to Euribor plus 200 bps. These refinancing rates were applied throughout a fixed period without differentiating pricing of the PLI risk. Maturities ranged from 7 to 10 years and the PLIs pledged the related housing loan portfolio as security.

The programme in Kosovo started four years later in 2002 with EUR 6.4 million. It provided housing finance through four PLIs: BpB, Kasabank, Raiffeisen and Finca, a microfinance institution (MFI). The smaller size of the programme reflected the limited experience and low absorptive capacity of PLIs founded between 2000 and 2002. It offered refinancing on market-based conditionts linked to Euribor plus 100 bps. Loan tenors were limited to 5 years, reflecting the focus on home improvement and reconstruction.

To ensure a focus on households as a target group and effective use of funds, both programmes imposed conditions on PLIs: loans were provided only to households, and PLIs were required to have a minimum of 80% of disbursed funds outstanding at all times in order to leave a margin for incoming repayments not immediately re-cycled into new loans. As PLIs built their business from scratch, and because they had no other source of long-term funding, this measure ensured the intended use of the funds.

[14] The latter two provided assistance for MSE lending in some countries only.

[15] The programme started as HCLP (Housing Construction Loan Programme). "Construction" was eliminated later to accommodate a broader definition.

The programmes applied further limits by purpose and a maximum loan amount of EUR 25,000, except in Kosovo where the average loan size should not exceed EUR 4,000 in order to target lower-to-middle income households.

The KfW housing finance programmes supported a move from the explicit targeting of grant programmes, favouring for example returnees, to a focus on access to creditworthy households that previously had no access to finance. In addition, international technical assistance (TA) customised lending processes for micro and small enterprise (MSE) lending to housing finance. MSE lending emphasises the cash flow analysis of the borrower.

Sustainable Housing Refinance: Establishing a Vehicle to Support Financial Market Development

With the establishment of EFSE in December 2005, the multi-donor revolving loan funds were transferred into an organisational structure for refinancing housing, MSE and agricultural lending while leveraging private funds through risk subordination.[16] With the completion of post-war reconstruction, EFSE focused on supporting financial market development for middle income households, raising the maximum loan size to EUR 100,000. As a result, EFSE became a general supplier of housing finance, broadening its scope. With increasing market sophistication, EFSE moved towards commercial pricing in its refinancing. EFSE also provided business to new PLIs in housing finance. In Bosnia, links with two MFIs were initiated, EKI and Sunrise; in Kosovo, a partnership with the New Bank of Kosovo was formed.

The Housing Finance Impact Study (2003–2006)

To evaluate the impact of the housing loan refinancing of the European Funds/EFSE housing loan portfolio, EFSE commissioned an impact study in 2006 covering the period from 2003 to mid-2006. The impact study covered BiH and Kosovo, which accounted for 70% of the housing loan portfolio at mid-2006. Extensive household surveys, interviews and analyses were undertaken. Data included the housing loan portfolios managed under the multi-donor funds from 2003 to 2005 and from December 2005 to mid-2006 by EFSE.

The study was a challenging task because of the lack of reliable baseline data, the complexity of measuring indirect effects of housing improvements, and broader additionality impacts of the funds. These challenges were partly addressed through extensive household surveys that included control groups which had not received support or which had obtained other forms of support. To determine

[16] For a detailed description of EFSE see Matthäus-Maier, von Pischke; Microfinance Investment Funds, Springer Frankfurt (2008), chapter 11 and www.efse.lu.

changing living conditions of households, the survey also used retrospective questions to construct historical data. Additionally, the study included a financial sector review, a housing finance product survey, and detailed interviews with PLIs and with local financial institutions that had not obtained such support.

Beneficiary Characteristics and Programme Impacts

The average beneficiary of a housing loan was male, married, in his early 40s with a household of 3.3 adults and 1.6 children. Beneficiaries in the sample had higher education, employment and income levels relative to the total populations of BiH and Kosovo. Among beneficiary households, more than half (54%) had a member with a tertiary degree, while only 20% and 13% of the citizens of BiH and Kosovo respectively had such education. Ninety-five percent of loan recipients were employed in full-time jobs, of which about 80% worked as emplyees and 20% were self-employed. In 2006, the reported average net monthly beneficiary household income was EUR 670.

PLIs targeted potential clients within income brackets ranging from no requirements in BiH to greater than EUR 256 per month. ProCredit did not specify a minimum monthly income, but required that a client be able to meet the minimum instalment of EUR 51 per month. In Kosovo, floors ranged from EUR 150 per month in Kasabank[17] to EUR 700 per month in BpB.

The study confirmed that PLIs were effective in reaching lower-income households. Approximately 25% of beneficiaries had household incomes below EUR 300 and almost 50% had household incomes below EUR 500.[18] The study also confirmed that microfinance institutions effectively supported lower income households (1/3 below EUR 300 per month) compared to commercial banks (1/3 below EUR 400 per month).

PLIs select beneficiaries based on their creditworthiness. The study evaluated the development outcome of the beneficiaries based on the following criteria: actual use of the housing loan; proportion of the housing loan to the overall investment; and alterntive choices of the benficiary if the loan were not granted.

The survey indicated an average loan size of EUR 6,569 per beneficiary, equivalent to about 40% of average total housing investment among the sample households. Beneficiaries financed the balance from savings (60%); borrowings from friends or relatives (30%); and additional loans from other sources (16%). Had they not received the loan, most (44%) of the sample beneficiaries would have sought other sources of financing and about a third would not have made

---

17 Kasabank was merged with New Bank of Kosovo and was renamed NLB Pristhina in 2008.

18 Because of problems in establishing household income in Bosnia and Kosovo, beneficiary household income could not be directly compared with national averages. In Bosnia, for example, the study relied on wage estimates to estimate household income, without being able to calculate other income including transfers from abroad, which were substantial.

the investment. Only 6% of beneficiaries indicated that they would have undertaken the housing investment without the loan. This result supports the strong additionality of the housing finance interventions.

The majority of loans were used to improve homes, as indicated in Table 1.

Table 1. Use of housing loans by country and PLI

	Total		Country		PLI		
			BiH	Kosovo	MFIs	Small Banks	Large Banks
	N	%	%	%	%	%	%
Expanding	64	18.3	18.3	18.3	20.4	21.2	10.9
Improving	255	73.2	57.1	89.2	85.5	82.0	43.5
Buying	53	15.3	24.9	5.7	4.6	8.6	39.3
Building	31	8.9	12.3	5.4	5.4	6.4	17.3

Note: as multiple uses are possible, percentage totals exceed 100%.

Source: EFSE Impact Study 2006, IHS

The use of home improvement loans is shown in Table 2 below, reflecting the predominant use for bathroom and kitchen improvements, which typically require larger investments. These purposes were financed by banks rather than MFIs.

Beneficiary satisfaction was assessed by its perception of the loan impact on wellbeing in four dimensions: physical capital – the state of the housing unit; human capital – education and experience; social capital – social position; and financial capital – the value of the housing unit.

Beneficiary households reported significant improvements in their housing and living conditions from 2003 to mid-2006, which the majority attributed to the loan. While positive impacts on human and social capital were reported, such as improvements in the warmth of homes in winter and increased contact with neighbours, these were less significant than physical impacts. Beneficiaries reported very significant improvements in the physical condition and in the perceived market value of their homes. Although beneficiaries did not consider their housing condition in 2003 as "very poor", the reported conditions were significantly below those of the control group. This indicates effective targeting of clients by PLIs.

Over the survey period, beneficiaries reported overall improvements ranging from an average 2.9 in 2003 to an average of 4 in 2006 based on a scale of 1–5, with 1 being very bad and 5 very good. An overwhelming majority of 92% attributed this to the loan. Not surprisingly, beneficiaries reported a perceived increase in the market value of their homes over the study period from an average of EUR 73,820 in 2003 to an average of EUR 86,673 in 2006. Seventy-five percent of the beneficiaries attributed this to the loan.

Table 2. Improvements made with housing loans

Item	Total		Nation/Entity		PLI		
			BiH	Kosovo	MFIs	Small Banks	Large Banks
	N	%	%	%	%	%	%
Kitchen	126	49.6	48.3	50.4	36.9	52.3	71.4
Bathroom	146	57.2	66.2	51.5	47.0	58.2	78.6
Living room	94	37.0	40.8	34.5	24.0	39.2	60.7
Bedrooms	76	29.8	28.7	30.5	20.4	33.9	39.3
Garages	16	6.2	7.7	5.3	2.4	10.0	3.6
Stables	2	0.8	0.8	0.7	0.9	0.9	0.0
Business/office space	20	8.0	5.8	9.4	10.8	7.3	3.6
Heating/insulation	44	17.3	21.4	14.7	17.1	13.9	28.5
Water heating/water pipes	28	11.0	18.8	6.1	11.3	9.8	14.3
Wiring/electrical goods	33	13.1	12.2	13.7	14.7	11.5	14.3
General physical condition (e.g. roof, walls, painting)	101	39.7	59.0	27.4	32.3	41.0	53.5
Inside improvements (kitchen, bathroom, living room, bedrooms, offices)	462	182	190	176	139	191	254
Outside improvements (garages, stables)	18	7	8	6	3	11	4
Utilities and infrastructure (heating, water, electrical goods)	105	41	52	34	43	35	57

Note: As multiple uses are possible the percentages total to more than 100%.

Source: EFSE Impact Study 2006, IHS

Finally, benefiaries did not perceive improvements in income, although significant reductions in utility bills were reported. Most beneficiaries noted reductions in bills concerning heating, water and electricity that were greater than those reported by the control group (18% versus 7%), and half of respondents attributed this to the improvements financed by the loan. Similar results were reported for maintenance costs, where beneficiaries reported a 22% drop versus 9% for the control group. About half the respondents attributed this to the loan.

The results indicate that household savings declined over the period, and almost two-thirds of the respondents attributed this to the debt service on the housing loan. This was further explored by asking beneficiaries to assess the effect of the loan payment on their overall household finances. On a scale of 1 ('huge burden') to 5 ('no impact on my expenditures'), the average value was 3.2. Fewer than half of the beneficiaries felt that loan repayments had seriously affected their household finances. This indicates that households were able to service the debt. 93% of the beneficiaries reported that they would recommend anyone in a similar situation to apply for a housing loan, confirming a high level of satisfaction.

Table 3. Changes in household expenditure, 2003 to 2006

	Decrease	Same	Increase	Change due to loan
	%	%	%	%
Heating, water, electricity	17.9	48.3	33.8	26.3
Maintenance	22.0	46.9	31.1	36.3
Food, education, leisure	14.5	51.0	34.5	25.8
Saving	29.1	45.1	25.7	41.1

Source: EFSE Impact Study 2006, IHS

Two Borrower Profiles

Camil R., a 42-year-old mechanical engineer, moved his family of four from Travnik to Vogosca in 2004. After his wife lost her job, it was increasingly difficult to make ends meet in the family house in Travnik. Camil had been offered a well-paid position at a Volkswagen factory in Vogosca, and its proximity to Sarajevo provided better educational and employment opportunities for his wife and daughters.

Camil and his wife rented the house in Travnik and used the rental income to repay a loan on a home bought in Vogosca. Camil and his wife purchased a war-damaged apartment, which was less expensive than buying a new one. To finance the renovation, they applied for a loan from Unicredit Zagrebacka Bank because it offered the most favourable terms. The loan was approved rapidly, and Camil was pleasantly surprised by the simple and straightforward loan application process. The EUR 15,000 loan covered the costs of buying and renovating the apartment. Camil and his family are very satisfied with the renovation and the location of their new home, which is within walking distance from a playground and local amenities. Camil's wife found a job and soon after began to work in Sarajevo.

Ymer H. applied for a housing loan from the Bank for Private Business to repair his war damaged apartment suffering from leaking pipes and poorly-insulated flooring. Because of the damage, Ymer's apartment in Kordra e Diellit could not be comfortably used with his family of five. Ymer found it cumbersome to obtain a guarantor for the small EUR 4,000 loan. However, the application procedure was clear and supplemented by adequate information. The loan was used to repair the damaged heating pipes and walls plus a new floor for the apartment. Ymer and his family are very satisfied with the results. Living conditions are now much more comfortable and the space is now fully available. Ymer was able to repay the loan instalments on time. He plans to apply for a second loan to renovate the kitchen and bathroom. He hopes to obtain a larger amount on better terms.

Programme Impact on Lending Institutions and Markets

The study divided impacts on PLIs into seven categories: market development; status and industry competitiveness; operational performance and capacity needs; financial products; portfolio structure; portfolio quality; and financing and capitalisation. The study reported significant results in: market development – the extent to which programme financing enabled PLIs to enter new markets or expand in existing products; financial products – the widening of products offered by a PLI as a consequence of programme financing; and portfolio structure – the importance of housing finance in the PLIs' portfolios that resulted from programme financing.

PLIs benefited strongly from the programme's impact on market development. With the exception of EKI in BiH, which initiated a housing finance programme with the support of an international agency in 1998, PLIs reported that they would not have entered this market segment without the programme support.

All PLIs reported that access to long-term financing was their principal motivation for joining the programme. PLIs also reported interest in entering the housing loan market and broadening their product mix as a motivation for PLI-banks, especially foreign-owned banks in Bosnia that embarked on cross-selling strategies to introduce new products to their existing clients. Initially, PLIs faced little competition in housing finance. While some PLI banks were successfully beginning to downscale into the microfinance market, there was limited competition among PLI banks and MFIs in mid-2006, partly reflecting the MFIs' pronounced rural focus.

All PLIs introduced housing loans as new products, with the exception of one MFI that revised an existing product into a housing loan product. While all PLIs were satisfied with the product development support provided by the programme, PLIs that received technical assistance developed housing products and business models more rapidly than those which did not.

Between 1998 and 2006 PLIs marketed their products as 'housing loans' or 'home loans,' with the exception of Finca Kosovo's 'housing improvement loan.' Loan purposes ranged from renovation and improvement (Finca Kosovo), to purchase and construction (UniCredit BiH).

Banks generally relied on borrowers' employment as security, while MFIs focused primarily on client cash flows.

Loan sizes ranged from EUR 500 to EUR 25,000 in Kosovo, and from EUR 150 to just over EUR 75,000 in BiH. Maturities ranged from 1 to 5 years in Kosovo, and from 1 month to 15 years in BiH. Loans generally had no grace period, reflecting small loan amounts and PLIs' determination to establish a rigorous repayment culture from the start.

Interest rates varied substantially. MFIs charged higher interest rates than banks, reflecting the high proportion of non-salary earning clients in MFI portfolios. Few banks provided housing loans to non-salary earners. Banks charged higher interest rates on home loans than on other loans to salaried clients. Those clients were also more competitively targeted and priced in the market.

Table 4 summarises the use of collateral by PLIs. Most beneficiaries pledged more than one type of collateral, with personal guarantees being most common. MFIs tended to rely on mortgage collateral more often than banks, reflecting MFIs' tendency to serve non-salary earners, while banks can obtain sufficient security through loans against salarys. Since mid-2006 however, land registration and legal enforcement of property pledges has improved in both countries, paving the way for widespread use of mortgage collateral.

Table 4. Types of collateral for housing loans

			Country		**PLI**			**Purpose**	
	Total		BiH	Kosovo	MFIs	Small Banks	Large Banks	Improve-ment	Pur-chase
	N	%	%	%	%	%	%	%	%
Guarantor	270	82.7	93.7	70.2	79.7	76.5	95.3	80.6	90.2
Salary	192	57.3	44.6	70.9	61.6	60.7	46.8	60.6	44.9
Assets	112	34.4	10.3	61.8	55.3	34.6	9.4	39.3	17.0
Mortgage	108	32.8	15.4	52.5	34.5	45.1	12.5	36.3	20.3

Source: EFSE Impact Study 2006, IHS

From 2003 to 2005 the PLIs' total housing portfolios in the sample grew by 45%. Over the same period the PLIs' consumer finance portfolios grew by 91%. For MFIs, housing lending was a new business. EKI in BiH and Finca Kosovo initiated housing lending in both markets in 2004. At year-end 2005 EFSE financing comprised just under 40% of MFIs' total housing portfolios – though in the first few months of 2006, three new housing loans products were launched for MFIs. However, the proportion of housing portfolios in PLIs and subsequently EFSE declined, given the explosive growth of other financial market segments in the region.

The programmes' housing finance to PLI banks declined from 25% of housing portfolios to 17% by 2005, reflecting the initial catalysing effect on housing finance in these countries. Rising market sophistication made those incentives increasingly obsolete as banks and MFIs increasingly financed their housing portfolios through own funds and alternative sources.

Conclusion

This chapter has explored the strategic challenges faced by international donors supporting housing in the post-conflict Balkan region, and the approach followed by several major donors that led ultimately to the establishment of EFSE. The results of the impact study demonstrate the importance of a loan-based programme as a second phase in a post-conflict situation. Strong targeting of beneficiaries through low loan amount limits and target averages contributed to the programmes' success in providing access to housing finance to lower income groups.

A targeted, purely grant-based programme might have reached further down-market. But such an approach would not have supported the sustainable development of domestic financial markets. The European funds' loan-based programme and subsequently EFSE have the advantage of creating revolving credit lines, creating a sustainable option for refinancing housing loans in the region. This makes an even more efficient use of public funds, i. e., by leveraging private capital to achieve maximum impact.

The overall impacts of the housing programmes are difficult to measure. However, the impact study does identify substantial benefits that have accrued to households in BiH and Kosovo. Importantly, the programmes' success in housing finance lies not only in its strong portfolio growth and end-borrower outreach, but also in its demonstration effect on local financial institutions in the region.

References

Bosnia and Herzegovina. Ministry for Human Rights and Refugees, Department for Housing Policy and Analytical Planning. "Housing and Urban Profile of Bosnia and Herzegovina: An Outline of Devastations, Recovery and Development Perspectives," pages 5–6. Available online at http://www.mhrr.gov.ba/PDF/Housing&Urban%20Profile%20of%20BiH.pdf.

Dauskardt, R. and van der Windt, N. (2007), "Building sustainable housing finance systems: Impacts of the European Fund for Southeast Europe," EFSE Housing Impact Study 2006, IHS. Available online at www.efse.lu/publications/papers.hmtl.

European Agency for Reconstruction. "Kosovo 2000," summary of action programme. Available online at http://www.ear.eu.int/kosovo/main/kos-annual_programme_2000_part1_housing.htm

European Agency for Reconstruction. "Kosovo 2001 Action programme part II." September 2000. Available online at http://www.ear.europa.eu/kosovo/main/kos-annual_programme_2001_part2_housing.htm

IMG Assessment Kosovo: http://www.img-int.org/Central/Public08/Documents.aspx

International Management Group (IMG) of behalf of the European Commission (1999) “Emergency Assessment of Damaged Housing and Local/Village Infrastructure.” Available online at http://www.img-int.org/Central/Public08/Documents.aspx

Kosovo. The Statistical Office of Kosovo (2006), “Private income in Kosovo 2003–2005.” Available online at http://www.ks-gov.net/ESK/esk/pdf/english/social/living_cond_03_05/Private_income_kos.pdf.

Minister Mirsad Kebo, BiH Ministry for Human Rights and Refugees, presentation (without title), 12 January 2006, Sarajevo. Available online at http://www.mhrr.gov.ba/PDF/Presentation%20by%20Minister%20Mirsad%20Kebo.pdf.

RRTF Report (1997). Available online at http://www.ohr.int/ohr-dept/rrtf/key-docs/reports/default.asp?content_id=5565

CHAPTER 9

Approaches and Policies at KfW Entwicklungsbank

Mark Schwiete[1], Stefan W. Hirche[1], and Jana Hoessel[2]

[1] KfW, Development Bank
[2] Consultant and CFA

Introduction[1]

Housing or the provision of shelter is an essential element of German Development Cooperation. Not only is it a requirement for poverty alleviation; it also contributes significantly to a number of Millennium Development Goals by improving living conditions. Moreover, the creation and improvement of housing is a basic imperative for post-conflict reconstruction and for restoring civil society. In another dimension, smart housing construction and home improvements that reduce emissions and improve energy efficiency can also have a strong effect on environmental conservation.

Actual and potential demand for housing is enormous, especially for home improvement and certainly among the poor. While the public sector in many developing and transition countries has sought to meet this demand, efforts have often focussed on large, centrally-planned public works projects which take a top-down, one-size-fits-all approach to housing finance for the poor. Aggregate housing demand, however, is comprised of individuals or households who seek to improve their standard of living, whether to obtain adequate shelter for the first time, or to improve or expand their current shelter. This is where housing finance can help. Individuals and households are in the best position to identify the problem and design customised solutions for their housing, provided they have access to finance.

Nevertheless, the supply of housing finance remains severely constrained in developing and transition countries. Many poor families cannot obtain credit for shelter or home improvement. The reasons for this are manifold. On the one hand, poor clients may lack formal ownership, a common prerequisite to obtaining credit from banks. On the other hand, banks are often hesitant – or unable – to provide financial services to the poor. Many financial intermediaries in developing and transition countries lack adequate refinancing, especially longer-term financing,

[1] Our thanks to Luise Richter and Olaf Zymelka for their valuable comments and advice.

D. Köhn and J.D. von Pischke (eds.), *Housing Finance in Emerging Markets: Connecting Low-Income Groups to Markets*, DOI 10.1007/978-3-540-77857-8_9,

and the appropriate tools, processes and products to realise market potential and improve housing of the poor.

German Financial Cooperation and KfW tackle these challenges using a comprehensive approach to developing housing finance. Support can range from extending classic microfinance into home improvement by promoting primary and secondary housing finance markets and to establishing land registers and cadastres. KfW also helps develop the preconditions for sustainable housing finance by supporting its partners in the design and construction of municipal infrastructure. While these efforts are not as large or well known as KfW's microfinance initiatives, they demonstrate the spectrum of KfW's initiatives to promote sustainable development, following the same high standards in implementation.

KfW's approach is to mitigate financial sectors' supply side constraints. First, KfW provides long-term funding to individual institutions to help them close their refinancing gaps and match the maturities of their assets and liabilities. This is especially important in housing finance, where longer loan maturities increase the affordability of housing for end-borrowers. Moreover, longer-term refinancing helps to reduce the risk profile of financial institutions.

Second, in addition to financial support, KfW finances capacity building assistance on behalf of the German government. Assistance is targeted to the individual institution and may, for example, include the training of loan officers to better serve low-income clients, or introducing new credit technology to downscale a bank's business lines and implement new financial products/services. This two-pronged approach demonstrates KfW's dedication to building sustainable institutions which serve low-income clients – and attract new ones. And it helps to form the foundation of sound, inclusive financial systems.

KfW Housing Finance Activities

KfW's housing finance initiatives comprise part of an holistic effort to develop partner countries' financial systems. They cover a wide spectrum, ranging from housing microfinance to swift post-disaster housing finance assistance. KfW's success is innovative and iterative: it endeavours to position itself on the frontier of housing finance development, improving its earlier initiatives through lessons learned and new methods and technology.

Lack of Formal Ownership

> *'What the poor are missing are the legally integrated property systems that convert their work and savings into capital.'*
>
> Hernando de Soto, The Mystery of Capital

According to Hernando de Soto, the greatest hurdle in improving the housing situation of low-income groups is the lack of access to a legal property rights system. The challenges to improving the housing situation of the poor are manifold, and regardless of whether one agrees with de Soto's well-debated thesis, the importance of a clear, defined system of land titling is evident. The foundations of such a system, which are absent in many developing and transition countries today, are land registry and cadastre.

German Development Cooperation supports countries in building this foundation for inclusive housing finance systems. KfW supported Georgia, for example, in surveying economically active land plots to create a reliable land register and cadastre system. From 2003 to 2008, most of Georgia's land was surveyed – registering roughly three million parcels of land, buildings and owners. Across the country, IT-based land registers and cadastre have been established and modern procedures implemented. This has increased legal certainty and contributed to Georgia's second rank in IFC's Doing Business Index 2009 for ease of registering property.[2] The programme complements the development of a mortgage finance system. This has provided a sound basis for the strong growth in mortgage lending in Georgia, rising from USD 3.7 million in 2001 to USD 576.4 million in 2007.

Housing Microfinance

Support for housing microfinance is an important channel of KfW's systematic approach to building inclusive financial systems. The roots of housing microfinance stem from the approach and philosophy of "traditional" microfinance. Housing microfinance was first applied to housing improvement and later expanded to financing purchases of basic housing. KfW provided refinancing as well as technical assistance to ProCredit Serbia, for example, successfully expanding its business to include housing finance in its menu of services. ProCredit Serbia made over 2,500 housing improvement loans between June 2005 and June 2008. With an average loan size of about EUR 6,000, these loans clearly serve low-income groups, including the owners of micro and small enterprises, agricultural producers and salaried workers. These early initiatives were leveraged into a broader effort to mainstream housing microfinance in the Balkans, based on housing improvement loans refinanced by the European Fund for Southeast Europe (EFSE).[3]

KfW also extended housing microfinance to rural households in South Africa. Together with the South African government, KfW established the Rural Housing Loan Fund (RHLF), a specialist development finance wholesale vehicle. The

[2] From the Doing Business Reports 2005 to 2009, Georgia reduced the number of days to register property from 39 to 3, the number of procedures involved from 8 to 2 and the cost from 2.5% of property value to a nominal GEL 50 (EUR 25).

[3] (See the chapter by Nico van der Windt, Rolf Dauskardt, Martin Heimes and Jana Hoessel for more detail).

RHLF uses non-bank intermediary lenders to make small unsecured loans of less than USD 1,400 with maturities of up to 36 months. These loans are issued to rural low-income borrowers to support their incremental building activities. From its inception in 1996 through mid-2008, RHLF refinanced more than 150,000 home loans. These loans enabled households to undertake home improvements and expansions; some even financed construction of basic core units.

Primary/Secondary Market Development

The German-Armenian Fund's successful housing finance programme demonstrates KfW's pioneering approach. The Republic of Armenia has a strong interest in promoting a vibrant market for housing finance. The objective is to foster economic growth and social development by creating better access to adequate housing for lower-income families. With these goals in mind, the Armenian government approached KfW for assistance in coordinating the joint development of first the primary housing finance market and at a later stage, the secondary housing finance market. KfW assisted the implementation of a bottom-up, systemic approach to development of sustainable housing finance markets in Armenia, beginning with the foundation of a strong legal and regulatory system.

First, experts reviewed the existing legislation and regulatory environment to create a sound basis for the primary market. Second, the experts created a securitisation and covered bond law in preparation for the development of a secondary market. Third, to ensure that banks could originate and service mortgage loans professionally, the programme assisted the establishment of a sustainable housing finance training course. Fourth, KfW assisted the market participants in establishing and adhering to minimum quality standards for mortgage lending, which are continuously reviewed and updated according to market developments. These include:

- loan application requirements (minimum information to be collected on potential clients);
- standardised forms for loan and pledge/mortgage contracts;
- a standardised assessment of the creditworthiness of the potential client;
- requirements for the assessment and valuation of the real property to be pledged;
- requirements for insurance (of both the pledge and of the client (accident or life)); and
- standard procedures of arrears management as well as minimum reporting standards.

While these minimum quality standards are developed by the market, the Central Bank of Armenia supports the sector-wide adoption of these standards. To allow financial institutions to make long-term local currency loans, the German-Armenian Fund provides matching liquidity for long-term mortgage loans (the minimum loan term is ten years) to lower- and middle-income households as long as these loans meet the minimum quality standards.

Since the programme's inception in early 2007, it had financed more than 550 mortgage loans with an average size of less than EUR 13,000. Although not seasoned, portfolio quality was good as of mid-2008. While the number of disbursed loans might not seem impressive, the programme's minimum quality standards form the base of a deep primary market and lay an indispensable cornerstone for the introduction of either covered mortgage bonds or securitisation at a later stage.

The sub-prime crisis exposed many of the risks of securitisation. However, when used properly, securitisation remains an effective tool to promote development of housing finance markets that already benefit from a strong primary market. Less expensive longer-term funding and equity relief are two of the key advantages of securitisation. KfW Entwicklungsbank promotes the development of residential mortgage bond securitisations (RMBS) in selected developing and transition countries.

Examples of these transactions include Blue Granite International (Republic of South Africa), Red & Black (Russia) and Ukraine Mortgage Loan Finance No.1. KfW's successful securitisation transactions in the developing world adhere to the strict standards to which KfW selects the underlying products, the partners and the transaction. Selected products are well established within their respective asset class, and the required minimum asset quality threshold of the securitised portfolio is high. Partner selection focuses on a group of high-quality partners within each country-specific context. Finally, transaction selection is generally focussed on less complex transactions, which match the maturities of the securitised assets and the refinancing sources. Selected transactions focus on the securitisation of portfolios of private sector firms within developing and transition countries, which also include private sector investors.

Housing Finance and Energy Efficiency

An essential element for the success of housing finance is significantly increased outreach. The challenge is to bring housing finance to scale, to improve the quality of housing for as many poor households as possible. Recent global trends have turned the tide increasingly against the poor: the poor are inordinately affected by the tremendous increase in energy prices over the past few years as well as by rapidly increasing environmental pollution. Particularly in countries with harsh climatic conditions, such as Eastern Europe and Central Asia, a comprehensive approach to improve the living conditions of the poor should include measures to reduce energy consumption via housing improvements.

In Germany, KfW has made energy efficiency finance a priority within its housing finance activities. KfW's domestic programme seeks to unite the goals of economic growth and environmental protection within the sphere of affordable housing finance. This combination within a single initiative lies at the forefront of innovation in housing finance. The results are impressive. Since its successful launch in 2006, the programme has made more then 260,000 housing loans, facilitating more than EUR 30 billion in housing investments. It has helped to secure more then 400,000 jobs. The estimated carbon dioxide reduction is in the range of 2 million tonnes per year, which corresponds to annual energy savings of 2.5 billion kilowatt hours. In 2008, the households that benefitted from the programme saved almost EUR 200 million in heating costs.[4]

Such programmes and the lessons learned from them require adaptation to the particular circumstances of emerging markets. Their potential is enormous. In Eastern Europe, KfW launched an energy efficiency initiative in 2007. Under this initiative KfW supports interested partner banks – through both funding and tailored technical assistance – to expand their product range to include energy efficiency finance. In cooperation with IFC, KfW is developing an energy efficiency portfolio to create a deeper level of institutionalisation with a self-sustaining structure along the lines of EFSE.

In a pilot project KfW supported ProCredit Ukraine with long-term funding and TA-financing to introduce an energy efficient loan product. This product targets investments by small and medium enterprises that improve energy efficiency and energy saving home improvements. The target is to realise a 20% saving in energy consumption. KfW's efforts to integrate energy efficiency in its housing finance activities are off to a positive start.

Post-disaster Housing Finance Support

Recent natural disasters, particularly in developing countries, call for swift action to help millions of displaced people to return to their homes or to construct new ones. Immediate relief is the primary objective, but long-term financial sector development may play a supporting role in these urgent situations. The financial sector can perform its role as an intermediary in reaching the poor in a fast and efficient manner with appropriate products that can be integrated into respective projects. With funds from the German government, KfW enabled 4,500 households to rebuild and repair their homes in tsunami-affected regions of Sri Lanka. In Pakistan, KfW facilitated financing for the reconstruction of 4,500 private homes and related infrastructure. In India, KfW provided post-earthquake assistance in the state of Gujarat.

---

4 Calculated by KfW; 2008 heating cost figures are estimated, based on 2007 energy prices.

These programmes take a community-based, owner-driven approach to reconstruction. Using grants from the German government, disaster-affected households plan and organise their own home reconstruction or repair, demonstrating KfW's adherence to the principle of individualised solutions for housing finance for the poor – even in cases of urgent need. To ensure that homeowners build structurally sound and cost-efficient homes, KfW also funds complementary technical assistance through construction advisory services provided by international engineers and architects.

Guiding Principles

Whereas poverty alleviation is the overarching goal of all Financial Cooperation projects, financial sector development specifically aims at creating more stable, more inclusive and more responsible financial systems. For KfW Entwicklungsbank *responsible finance* can be summarised as practices that are designed to create a fair balance of interests among a financial institution and its customers, employees and business partners on the one hand, and with its shareholders and refinanciers on the other.

The principles of responsible finance guide all of KfW's financial sector operations. These principles are especially important in housing finance. Investing in housing is not a cash-flow generating activity. The ability to repay interest and principle on a housing loan is dependent on income – not the future cash flows of a micro entrepreneur, for example, whose future cash flows may themselves be enhanced by a micro loan. In contrast to classic microfinance, the boundary between housing finance and consumer lending is less well defined. Therefore, responsible practices must ensure end-borrower understanding and debt capacity.

KfW contributes to disseminating responsible practices in four dimensions:[5]

- Customers (financial literacy);
- Financial institutions (transparency, adequate environmental and social standards);
- Regulatory authorities (protection of consumers' interests); and
- Donors and investors (long-term commitment, promotion of good governance, no end-borrower conditionalities).

These principles are demonstrated in KfW's housing finance projects:

[5] For details see "Responsible Finance – a leitmotif for KfW financial sector promotion"; http://www.kfw-entwicklungsbank.de/DE_Home/Sektoren/Finanzsystementwicklung/Sachinformationen_1/Responsible_finance_Adler.pdf.

- **Systemic approach**. KfW's activities go beyond the support of individual financial institutions. Rather, it pursues a comprehensive and systemic approach to financial system development. To develop and apply best practices, KfW makes use of long-standing, close contacts with ministries, central banks, commercial banks and microfinance institutions in its partner countries. For example, KfW's assistance to the Armenian government to jumpstart the local housing finance market (see above) was developed through close, long lasting cooperation with the Central Bank of Armenia through the German-Armenian Fund.
- **Selecting the "right" partners**. KfW promotes the development of financial institutions that regard responsible banking practices as a fundamental element of their business model and have appropriate strategies in place to achieve this objective. Financial institutions that provide transparent lending terms and that are customer-friendly are the preferred partners of KfW Entwicklungsbank. The lending approaches of housing finance partner institutions are examined closely: KfW's partners should evaluate creditworthiness by analysing loan-to-value-ratios and reflecting on the development of real estate prices. They should also analyse the repayment capacity of potential clients as an essential part of their due diligence. The vetting of potential partners applies equally to every transaction, whether it be a direct investment in a microfinance institution or a more complex securitisation transaction.
- **Focusing on suitable products**. Financial sector projects centre on successful intermediaries whose business activity is not primarily geared to short-term financial returns, for example by focusing on consumer credit. Rather, they respond to the opportunities of relevant target groups for housing finance. Rural locations, which are generally underserved relative to urban areas, are a focal point. Innovation also plays an important role: new instruments, such as securitisation structures, may be established where existing instruments cannot fill the gaps. Much attention is given to the structure of these instruments.[6]
- **Contributing to international discussions**. By hosting and participating in international conferences and in intensive and continuous dialogue with relevant stakeholders, KfW helps to set standards for the development and trends in financial sector development.

[6] See the discussion of securitisation in the sub-section above titled Primary/Secondary Market Transactions.

Challenges Ahead

Looking ahead, increasingly scarce natural resources, rising energy prices, environmental degradation and volatile financial markets may coalesce to form rough seas. To navigate these difficult waters, improvements are necessary in five key areas:

1. Managing long-term currency risk;
2. Reducing transaction costs;
3. Increasing housing supply for the poor;
4. Enhancing energy efficiency of new and existing housing; and
5. Managing financial market crises.

Management of long-term currency risk is essential to reducing risk in developing financial markets. Many institutions and especially microfinance institutions finance a large portion of their portfolios with hard currency loans. They are faced with the choice of whether to bear the foreign exchange risk themselves or to pass it on to end-borrowers. Often, no option is optimal: financial institutions may be unable to hedge their exposure, or the cost of hedging may be prohibitively expensive. On the other hand, passing exposure on to clients increases 'hidden' credit risk, which is effectively carried by the institution.

Moreover, local deposits are generally not a suitable funding source for housing: first, deposit mobilisation is limited to institutions with deposit licences, and second, the vast majority of local deposits are short-term, leaving the institution with the challenge of handling maturity mismatches. KfW has recognised this challenge and has initiated efforts to provide foreign exchange risk coverage.[7] The promotion and development of local bond markets would be another vital step to engender domestic sources of longer-term funding.

High transaction costs continue to impede further outreach in housing finance, particularly in rural areas. Here, technology and innovation can help. Improved technology can help financial institutions better assess borrower risks, or help connect remote branches to the head office. Mobile banking may help clients make payments on loans without having to travel to the nearest branch.

Improving the supply of housing finance without improving the supply of affordable housing to low-income groups will only compound affordability problems and create housing bubbles. Governments – both central and local – and international financial institutions must work together to promote policy that makes sense for the large numbers of the poor in developing and transition countries. Close cooperation is also essential to find better, more efficient and more effective ways to promote housing finance to developers.

---

[7] As an example of its efforts to provide local currency funding, KfW invested in TCX, a fund created by FMO with a mandate to provide for currency and interest rate hedging in developing country currencies.

Increasing environmental degradation and rising energy prices have highlighted the importance of improving energy efficient housing, especially for the poor, who are least able to cope. It is a positive sign that increasing attention is being paid to this important aspect of housing finance. Within the development community, KfW undertook an effort to disseminate knowledge and promote innovation by hosting its seventh financial sector symposium entitled, *Greening the Financial Sector – How to Mainstream Environmental Finance in Developing Countries?*[8]

Finally, the international market for residential mortgage bond securities (RMBS) from emerging markets requires revitalisation, notwithstanding the fact that research to date has indicated that the US sub-prime crisis has had no direct contagion effect on banks in developing countries. The quality of emerging market housing loan portfolios has remained almost unchanged throughout the crisis and is driven by domestic factors. In countries with a strong and dominant local investor base as in India, markets demonstrated only a small reduction in demand for RMBS paper during the crisis. In sharp contrast stand those markets which relied to a significant extent on international investors, whose appetite for RMBS vanished.

The development finance community can and should play a role in revitalising these markets. Development finance institutions, as long-term, responsible investors, can keep funding lines open in times of distress when liquidity from private investors dries up. This can have a clear financial effect – maintaining liquidity during a time of crisis – and also an important demonstration effect.

The lessons of the sub-prime crisis are now emerging. These should be incorporated into government policies, the initiatives of international financial institutions and development financiers, and the practices of financial institutions around the globe. Predatory lending practices, poorly-informed housing buyers, and distorted incentive structures, which helped cause the sub-prime crisis in the US, highlight the importance of responsible financial practices as the bedrock of housing finance for the poor. The way forward is through innovation, guided by ethics and based on the principles of responsible finance.

None of these are easy tasks, and all of them require cooperation on the part of governments, international financial institutions (IFIs), policymakers, experts and academicians. In the context of the global crisis, KfW organised its eighth international symposium with its development partners in December 2009 entitled *Preserving Access to Finance during the Global Crisis.*[9]

In housing finance, the type of coordination needed is demonstrated by the Africa Housing Initiative. The challenges for housing finance are greatest across Sub-Saharan Africa and the needs are enormous. KfW is joining other IFIs in es-

---

8 See http://www.kfw-entwicklungsbank.de/EN_Home/Topics/Financial_Sector/Events/Symposium_2008/index.jsp.

9 For Agenda, Papers, Presentations and Summaries of debates see http://www.kfwentwicklungbank.de/EN_Home/Sectors/Financial_system_development/Events/Symposium_2009/index.jsp.

tablishing this initiative to address the shortage of housing and finance for housing in Africa. By pooling resources, the participating IFIs intend to contribute to structural improvements in the markets in which they will engage.

Index of Regions and Institutions

Africa

Americas

Asia and Oceania

D. Kohn and J.D. von Pischke (eds.), *Housing Finance in Emerging Markets: Connecting Low-Income Groups to Markets*, DOI 10.1007/978-3-540-77857-8,

Europe

Global

Index of Keywords

L

M

MIX
Papier aus verantwortungsvollen Quellen
Paper from responsible sources
FSC® C105338

If you have any concerns about our products,
you can contact us on
ProductSafety@springernature.com

In case Publisher is established outside the EU,
the EU authorized representative is:
Springer Nature Customer Service Center GmbH
Europaplatz 3, 69115 Heidelberg, Germany

Printed by Libri Plureos GmbH
in Hamburg, Germany